PROGRESS IN DRUG ABUSE

PROGRESS IN DRUG ABUSE

Proceedings of
the Third Annual
Western Institute
of Drug Problems
Summer School

Edited by

PAUL H. BLACHLY, M.D.

Professor of Psychiatry
University of Oregon Medical School
Portland, Oregon

CHARLES C THOMAS · PUBLISHER
Springfield · Illinois · U.S.A.

Published and Distributed Throughout the World by
CHARLES C THOMAS • PUBLISHER
BANNERSTONE HOUSE
301-327 East Lawrence Avenue, Springfield, Illinois, U.S.A.
NATCHEZ PLANTATION HOUSE
735 North Atlantic Boulevard, Fort Lauderdale, Florida, U.S.A.

© *1972, by* CHARLES C THOMAS • PUBLISHER
ISBN 0-398-02233-X
Library of Congress Catalog Card Number: 74-180803

With **THOMAS BOOKS** *careful attention is given to all details of
manufacturing and design. It is the Publisher's desire to present books
that are satisfactory as to their physical qualities and artistic possibilities
and appropriate for their particular use.* **THOMAS BOOKS** *will be true
to those laws of quality that assure a good name and good will.*

3/29/74
#15.50

Printed in the United States of America
HH-11

Contributors

Paul H. Blachly, M.D., *Professor of Psychiatry at the University of Oregon Medical School, Director of the Western Institute of Drug Problems Summer School, and Director of the Methadone Blockade Treatment Program for Heroin Addicts in Portland, Oregon*

Neil L. Chayet, Esq., *Counsellor at Law, Boston, Massachusetts*

Gurbakhash S. Chopra, M.D., *Director of the Drug Addiction Clinic, Calcutta, India, presently in Seattle, Washington*

Karl J. Deissler, M.D., *Medical Director, Synanon Foundation, Inc., Oakland, California*

Joel Fort, M.D., *Professor, School of Social Welfare, University of California, Berkeley, California*

H. F. Fraser, M.D., *Consultant, Medical Research Division, the Lilly Research Laboratories, Eli Lilly and Company, Indianapolis, Indiana*

Kenneth Gaver, M.D., *Administrator, Mental Health Division, State of Oregon, Salem, Oregon*

Robert E. Jones, *Circuit Court Judge, Portland, Oregon*

Arnold J. Mandell, M.D., *Professor and Chairman, Department of Psychiatry, University of California School of Medicine, La Jolla, California*

John Marks, Ph.D., *Associate Professor, Department of Psychiatry, University of Oregon Medical School, Portland, Oregon*

David W. Maurer, Ph.D., *Professor of Linguistics, Department of English, University of Louisville, Louisville, Kentucky*

John I. Maurer, M.D., *Cowell Student Health Center, Stanford University, Stanford, California*

Governor Tom McCall, *State of Oregon, Salem, Oregon*

Richard Phillipson, M.D., *Visiting Scientist from Great Britain and Wales, Health Services and Mental Health Administration, National Institute of Mental Health, Chevy Chase, Maryland*

Richard C. Pillard, M.D., *Psychopharmacology Laboratory Division of Psychiatry, Boston University School of Medicine, Boston, Massachusetts*

Reginald G. Smart, Ph.D., *Associate Research Director, Addiction Research Foundation, Toronto, Ontario, Canada*

Michael R. Sonnenreich, *Deputy Chief Counsel, Bureau of Narcotics and Dangerous Drugs, Washington, D. C.*

Charles Spray, M.D., *Director, Outside-In, Clinic, Portland, Oregon*

Robert L. Taylor, M.D., *Department of Psychiatry, Stanford University Medical School, Palo Alto, California*

Jared R. Tinklenberg, M.D., *Instructor, Department of Psychiatry, Stanford University Medical School, Palo Alto, California*

Preface

The papers herein represent the most advanced thinking on the problem of drug abuse. They were presented at the Third Annual Western Institute of Drug Problems Summer School held at Portland State University in August of 1970. They should be viewed as a follow-up on the papers published from the proceedings of the second institute entitled *DRUG ABUSE: Data and Debate* (Charles C Thomas, 1970). The table of contents of that volume is listed in the appendix for easy referral.

The Western Institute of Drug Problems Summer School is a joint activity of the Alcohol and Drug Section of the Mental Health Division, the Division of Continuing Education and the University of Oregon Medical School. Its activities are of interest to almost any discipline that comes into contact with drug abusers ranging from physicians and jurists to educators, pharmacists, clergymen and politicians. It has more recently expanded its activities to include a special workshop on methadon.

Public interest for these short authoritative courses regarding drug abuse, which incidentally grant academic and AAGP credit, has been such that we plan to repeat them in response to the felt need. The summer school coming in the second week of August works well for educators and the scenic location encourages many to bring their families to combine vacation with business.

Digestion of the proceedings of the meetings is stimulated by both disciplinary and cross-disciplinary small group discussions, permitting the participants to rub shoulders with those most knowledgeable in a particular field.

Each speaker is encouraged to point the way to additional research studies, new legislation, or educational techniques that will help us to improve the present unsatisfactory methods we have for dealing with problems of drug abuse.

Included in the appendix is an up-to-date review of the literature on marijuana by Dr. Richard C. Pillard and a practical medical article on "The Management of Bad Trips" by Dr. Robert L. Taylor.

The reader is urged to follow up the references, to correspond with the authors directly with regard to specific questions and with the administrator of the Western Institute of Drug Problems Summer School regarding future courses (Mr. George Dimas, Alcohol and Drug Section, Mental Health Division, 309 S.W. Fourth Avenue, Portland, Oregon).

Acknowledgments

We are particularly appreciative of the permission given by Richard C. Pillard, M.D., and the *New England Journal of Medicine* to reproduce the article on marijuana and to Robert L. Taylor, M.D., and the *Journal of the American Medical Association* to reproduce "The Management of Bad Trips and Evolving Drug Scenes." Victor Vogel, M.D., kindly gave us permission to utilize some information in his book with David Maurer, Ph.D., entitled *Narcotics and Narcotic Addiction* 3rd ed. (Charles C Thomas, 1971), which is used in Dr. Maurer's chapter dealing with crime and addiction.

Contents

PROGRESS IN DRUG ABUSE

1

The Community—Conditioning the Scene of Drug Education

Governor Tom McCall

Forty-three states are represented here, all the provinces of Canada and three other nations. We could say that the growth of this Drug Institute is one of the many constructive things that has happened. There have been projects that seem to offer sensible ideas and aids, there have been increasing numbers of those who care, and there has been a great expansion in this field. Yet I am still scared . . . scared of what this pernicious and sinister engulfment that comes under the heading of drug problems will do to us.

We meet with the best of intentions; we are concerned; we have paperproof of projects and proposals; we have clippings to show a widening spectrum of the community is getting into the situation and I think we do have an overwhelming endorsement from leadership in every social area. But what results in cold figures and human terms do we have? There have been many gatherings, talks, decisions and promises, but there has been a shortage of reaction and involvement by those most concerned —the victims. In some respects it has been like discussing the Irish potato famine in Tahiti, punctuating your concern by plucking another ripe mango to toy with and to savor, but how do we change this? How do we get something going that involves everyone?

It once was a Western custom to pool resources and muscles to do the job at hand—barn raising, threshing, shearing and branding. What is the West now willing to do together at this Western Institute besides forget?

With regard to drug education, Oregon has done quite a bit
in the way of alerting the community, involving the community
and working with the community. The distressing thing is that
until we started the Oregon Drug Alert Program, we had no idea
how far behind the problem we were. Of course, we are still
lagging and lagging dangerously, not only in Oregon but in every
state, and everywhere this problem rears its pernicious head. We
are late in recognizing the seriousness of the drug problem in this
country. We do not know its extent even now. We do not know
whether drug abuse among the young will peak out next month
or next decade—or ever. We know only that we must, in some
sensible way, act at once to prevent further abuse and help those
already affected.

We know that public officials and the schools must assume a
frighteningly great responsibility in this mess, even though studies
seem to indicate that our public institutions and our present
family structures are largely at fault. Our school program in the
State of Oregon features three different textbooks and guidelines
of how to teach students about drug abuse in fourteen grades.
This program is being taught to thousands of teachers in Oregon
and has excited interest in many other states. Yet, I think, no
matter how we document the problem and how well we prepare
our materials and how heavily we involve ourselves, all of us must
be prepared for the mirage, too—the shining citadel on the horizon
that seems to say, maybe we have achieved cure, normalcy, balance
and the old human rapport—for that mirage is often followed by
the tumble to drug depths not previously dreamed. How long
then can we live with failure while working and striving towards
success?

The generation most involved is composed of bright, sincere,
creative young people that are the sons and daughters of parents
from every segment of the population. They are the life of the
North American continent itself, and we have much to learn from
them about ourselves. It is imperative that we clarify our intentions and our alternatives in dealing with drug abuse among our
young.

There is little agreement, for example, as to the nature of
narcotic addiction—whether it is an emotional or physical illness

—or what the long-range effects of marijuana and hallucinogenic drugs are. Obviously more research is needed, but how long can you hold back waiting for the results of the research when you know that you cannot wait? We must explore ways to reclaim the kids who have experimented one too many times and have drifted away from us into that frightening twilight.

Our twin mission is to reclaim the disengaged and prevent the disattachment of those not yet hooked—an assignment that can be said in one sentence but which is a long, long way from that simplicity in achievement. What we must push for, I believe, are our preliminary goals! Parents and other concerned adults must equip themselves with an understanding of drugs and why they are abused, and youth must be encouraged to broaden its perspective about life experience and the placement of drugs in that context.

I might also add, personally, that we all tend to forget that alcohol is a drug. There is as much potential dynamite in a jug of gin as there is in most of the less readily available drugs.

With the launching of the Oregon Drug Alert, we made our statewide commitment to do something about this terrifying problem. We are continuing that project and I hope it is simply a beginning; we do not claim much more than that for it. We were amateurs in a sense tackling what was no problem for amateurs. Since the issue was crowded by contradictory evidence and doubtful research and very nearly strangled in emotionalism, we elected to formulate our own program.

We knew the program and the project and the challenge would require a fresh start (including new minds and otherwise uninvolved people), a flexible attitude toward what might be discovered en route and an absolute honesty in dealing with the problem that has often been obscured by falsehoods and misrepresentations.

We felt that marijuana, for instance, had become the unnecessary center of everyone's attention. While the detailed arguments about marijuana occupied everyone's foreground, other more serious problems were being shunted into the wings.

Working through the Alcohol and Drug Section of the Oregon State Mental Health Division, which Dr. Gaver heads, and cooperating with the excellent programs of the Kiwanis and the Junior Chamber of Commerce, we launched a new phase in our ongoing program with an event called Oregon Drug Alert.

Last November, we called together a group of experts and specialists from the state government staff and from outside the government into the Civic Auditorium in Portland. Many private citizens came. We wanted to discuss the overall drug problem existing in Oregon. During the proceedings, a nice young man, who wore a great sombrero and a beard that reached to his waist, got up and said that he thought the meeting was one of the most irrelevant proceedings he had ever witnessed. "Why don't you go up to the Courthouse where we are demonstrating and find out what life is," he said to me. Although he gave me great credit for compassion to conduct the meeting he said I was too much and too obviously pro-Establishment. I finally said to him, "I agree with you 100 percent." He was a fine person with a fine mind and his thoughts hit home with a great thud; however, I said, "But what would you do about it," and he said, "Governor, I would be darned if I know." With that, I replied, "I am Governor and I will be darned if I know either, but it is my responsibilitry to do something."

So we wanted our State of Oregon to look for the broad picture. We did not want to get bogged down with the old arguments. We wanted to take the widest kind of approach, looking at the issue from the legal standpoint, the health standpoint and its community effect.

Any comprehensive report, we felt, had to deal with the effective and proper use of drugs as well as examining the abuses involving drugs. We also felt that it would be folly to start a campaign aimed at giving all our attention and all our funds to the addict, for that segment is only a part of what we feel needs attention.

We gave high priority to the development of a program that might forecast the drug problem before addiction occurs. We wanted in essence an "early warning" system that would enable us to provide treatment and counsel before gross symptoms appeared.

Our intent was to (1) develop proper attitudes towards drugs, including proper use and proper abstinence; (2) develop a technique that would supply effective action before the symptoms become acute; and (3) continue expansion of an adequate treatment and rehabilitation program with three major thrusts: (a) self-help programs, (b) psychological-social-medical programs and (c) the maintenance programs. Certainly no state has approached Oregon's success for percentage of heroin addicts on methadone treatment, addicts whose numbers in the United States are estimated at 200,000 and whose annual drug bill is guessed to be five billion dollars.

Another helpful structural plan that we used to assist in sharpening these meetings was to establish ten areas of involvement, occupying five Oregon cities, to be discussed throughout the meetings. Each of these ten areas became a point of probe. They included youth, legalities, education, treatment and rehabilitation, voluntary community action groups, churches, parent representation, colleges and universities, adult civic organizations and the drug dependent. Progress we can say has been made. It is not the kind of progress that is absolute, but it is the kind of progress that goes crab-like—not fast enough but slowly weaving toward its goal. It is not enough progress to even corral a problem that has left many of us who are intimately involved with it gasping first with disbelief, then with fright and then exhaustion in a searing corner of our personal hell.

Since we had the first of these Drug Institutes in Oregon in 1969, many other states have followed our example and many areas of legislation have reflected what we have in these sessions so vehemently discussed. Our Oregon meetings have encouraged a crossing of the lines, the involvement of many levels of government. These sessions have helped encourage the adoption of the "illness" concepts—a humanitarian and absolutely intelligent decision that the drug addict is not a criminal to be punished but a sick man to be cured. I was most pleased to go to the White House conference on drug addiction and hear that policy enunciated by the President of the United States. Our legislature in Oregon has shared an enlightened attitude although none of us has anything but rancor for the professional pusher, who, believe me, is a problem-figure not only of local but of national and international magnitude.

Governor Claude Kirk of Florida calls the Oregon anti-drug abuse program the best of any states. I cannot say whether we deserve that laurel. Certainly we may be ahead of some but if we have those laurels deservedly, let me say in the same breath, for heaven's sake, never rest on them because we must keep encouraging each other in every possible way. If we lose this one, we lose it all. We are dealing with the most precious possession we have —our young people—and they must be saved.

Demonstration youth projects in Oregon are gaining ground. We arrived at these activities by letting the young people themselves be heavily involved in the planning and presenting of these particular projects, and these dialogue sessions have been tremendously effective. We not only have drug users and addicts involved, but we have people who are young and outside the problem as well. These segments have much to say to each other and much help to give to each other. They lead the way in their own direct, honest, cross-dialogue; they hear each other very well and attendance is 100 percent. So here is an area where we do have great expectations.

We are also developing new programs for borderline cases of other kinds of related problems. We are starting to experiment in outpatient treatment for young people with early drug dependency. Also we are not overlooking research, delving into the key areas of legislation, education, training and information, and treatment and rehabilitation. One of the most important hours I ever spent was in Washington, D. C., with Mary Sweitzer, head of the Children's Bureau of Health, Education and Welfare. This was the last day she had in that important office and I made my pitch for the construction of a project in experimentation that would give the youthful drug abuser a bridge leading from the enticement of his drug-abusing life to some comparable enticement that did not involve drug abuse across this bridge. She said to John Twiname, who was succeeding her that day, "John, I am going to be across town in that office," and she pointed to a magnificent building where she was going to be working for a foundation in her retirement, "I am going to call you every week and see how Governor McCall's project is coming."

I want you to know that we are going to have a project that will find more enlightened and more innovating ways to solve the problem than giving a guy a pick or throwing him in solitary confinement or putting him in the criminally insane ward when he is not insane or criminal. We are going to have more enlightened ways of taking care of the problem because we are going to set up a kind of life that is competitive and wholesome to wean them away from life that is terribly destructive and unwholesome. So it is our premise that the *problem* must be attacked, not just the symptoms. We know that there are no easy answers. We know that punishment has never in itself stopped crime, nor will regulations stop drug abuse, but we still must have regulations. There is much to be discovered and understood inside this issue.

We want to talk to and work with the drug users. We want to balance all the drug abuse talk with more comprehension of drug usage, and I am speaking of good usage that serves mankind well. So when we find the answers to the very root of this issue, we will have found answers that benefit every strata of society and every aspiration of man.

2

Why People Use Drugs and What Should Be Done About It

Joel Fort

There are many styles of public speaking or writing and among the most popular is to avoid challenging any accepted beliefs or biases of the listeners or readers. A second popular style is to promulgate myths, particularly used to aggrandize a particular bureaucracy or politician. Neither of those styles is mine and to illustrate that I would like to suggest that all of you stop using one of the most dangerous drugs in America, a drug that is killing 400,000 people a year—the nicotine (and arsenic, cyanide, coal tars, et cetera) in cigarettes—and that you become aware that this is part of the true context of drug abuse in the United States. No moral or rational person should ignore the dangers of cigarettes or alcohol while devoting all of his energies to the sensationalized horrors of marijuana, heroin or LSD. Had we not been taught as a society that it was somehow desirable and acceptable to put a dried plant leaf in our mouths in the case of tobacco, search for a match, put that plant on fire, then inhale the fumes to poison our tissues and then exhale in order to pollute everyone else's air space, we would not have the widespread marijuana smoking we have today. God did not give us chimneys in our heads. Having been taught one unnatural pattern of cigarette smoking, it is perfectly easy to take on a related pattern. Therefore, since there is great evidence of the dangers of tobacco smoking, a consistent and nonhypocritical person should seek to eliminate *all* forms of smoking rather than concentrating just on marijuana. We might then have a better and more effective society and more successful drug education programs.

Many things lead you to believe that we meet here only to deal with the drugs of the politician, whether he be an AMA politician or a governor, mayor, or President. The real context of drugs begins with those most widely used by young and old—alcohol and tobacco—which are also the most widely used illegal drugs if you remember the age prohibitions for those under 21 or 18. Parenthetically any of you who might be defining drug abuse as any illegal drug use have to include in your concern the widespread violations of law and order involved in the massive use of alcohol and tobacco by young people at rock festivals, in schools and elsewhere, even though in most statements about the drug problem this will be left out.

Now, of course, "honorable men" are never wrong, as we see evidence of every day in the mass media, so they certainly would not tell us that drugs mean only marijuana, LSD and narcotics. The true context of drugs, however, goes beyond alcohol and tobacco to sedatives, stimulants and tranquilizers, which are used by about 30 million Americans, not quite the 70 to 80 million each using alcohol or tobacco, but still a very large number and again with very massive abuses. Only after recognizing this fact does an honest person give full attention to a discussion of drugs. The *viewer with alarm* (who predominates in our society) will always call marijuana and the LSD-type drugs "hallucinogenics," falsely implying that everyone under all circumstances will become psychotic under their influence; and the *pointer with pride,* (equally vocal but in a smaller minority) will always call them "psychedelic," incorrectly implying that everyone under all circumstances will have their consciousness expanded under their influence.

Then we have the narcotics and there are only narcotics, not "hard narcotics" and "soft narcotics." A drug is either a narcotic or it is in some other category, and it makes no more sense to talk about a soft narcotic than it does to talk about soft pregnancy. It should certainly be easy and noncontroversial for you to call drugs by their precise name. So you would refer to marijuana as "marijuana" and not as a soft narcotic or mild hallucinogenic, and you would call alcohol, "alcohol," instead of demon rum, thereby avoiding biasing whatever you said by very emotional words. Obviously there are a lot of emotional words in this field. If, for example, I were to hold up a clear colorless substance, alcohol, in a glass and call that substance a beverage, you would have quite a different reaction than if I referred to it as a medication and still a different reaction if I called it a narcotic, as it was called up to about thirty years ago if you look up old magazine and newspaper articles. The word, "narcotic," of course is the keystone of the language of the drug specialists because it brings in the hard-on-drugs concept and the term, "hard drug." Both of them are meaningless, but we have been conditioned or brainwashed to fall out of our chairs with a knee-jerk reaction of horror ready to march on our state capitols if someone totally without experience in pharmacology, psychology, sociology and education drops the words, "hard drug," out of the side of his mouth. We do not know what it means, but we know it is bad and that we must do something about it, usually passing a criminal law against it.

We go on to call the user of a drug that we disapprove of by such endearing terms as "dopefiend," "addict," "pothead," "speed freak," "acid head" or "drug abuser," obviously terms that are designed to move that person into the mainstream of society rather than ever deeper into a drug culture. The whole thing is institutionalized in the society, so that without any pangs of conscience a professional person can exclude from help a drunk or a "fiend" and see them in a completely different dehumanized way than all other kinds of social and health problems in American society. We also fail to distinguish use of a drug from abuse or addiction or habituation. Any drug, whether pot, booze or something else, can be used occasionally without becoming dependent. Only some use is regular and only some of that involves abuse, meaning excessive use that damages health or social or vocational adjustment.

As a subcategory of drug abuse, we have addiction, which only occurs with alcohol, barbiturates and other sedatives, and narcotics (meaning morphine, opium, heroin, methadone, Demerol®, etcetera). As it became clear, due to the aggressive informal research of millions of young people, that drugs, such as marijuana, which have been called narcotics and addictives, really were not in that category, we had to invent the new term of "psychological dependence" as part of the moral corruption. Such altruistic and philanthropic organizations as the American Medical Association tell us that because marijuana produces psychological dependence, all users of marijuana should continue to go to prison. It sounds very impressive when you use the term, "psychological dependence," because any person who wants to impress others with his status, importance and technical knowledge just has to use polysyllabic language, bringing in the pathological frame of reference and the one-dimensional viewing with alarm out of context that is guaranteed to get you national headlines, put you on the chicken-and-green-pea banquet circuit, and obtain government grants. It is also guaranteed to perpetuate the problems of our society, which is what is done every day when pot, acid or junk are talked about. I believe that the hippy phenomenon and the drug scene have rescued more people from well-deserved obscurity than any other phenomenon in American society.

If you just talk about psychological dependency as *habituation*, it sounds much more acceptable because the layman knows that this means getting so used to something psychologically over a period of years that when that something is no longer available to you, you become restless, irritable, out of sorts and do not know what to do with yourself. It is true that marijuana, like caffeine, nicotine, alcohol, sleeping pills and all other mind-altering drugs, can produce habituation or psychological dependence. It is not unique with any one drug. It does not happen with everybody who uses the drug. You must use the objective definition of drug abuse to determine the degree of problem involved. To put it into its fullest context, there are millions of Americans who for years have spent five to six hours a day in front of their television sets, so that when a tube suddenly burns out they become restless, irritable, out of sorts and do not know what to do with themselves. Those people are habituated to TV, and you may feel as I do that this can be as detrimental to their self-actualization and the society's welfare as habituation to pot, alcohol or any other drug *can* be. Some people are psychologically dependent on their husbands or wives (or on a variety of other things that are not necessarily detrimental to their welfare) and, despite the high divorce rate, may be beneficial to them.

Next we come to the most crucial concept of all, the mind-altering drug effect. This is the core of the demonology or mythology that has been developed about many drugs in our society. The right-wingers would tell us that within seconds of exposure to certain drugs everyone becomes a murderer, rapist, heroin addict and lifelong inmate of a mental hospital, while the left-wingers would tell us that within seconds of such exposure everyone would become a fully developed creative genius and live happily ever after. The drug scene is one of the most polarized, most emotional issues in American society and there is probably no field, with the possible exception of foreign policy, that is as pervaded by ignorance and fear. The true mind-altering drug effect is best illustrated by the most common group drug experience in our society—the cocktail party. Contrary to the popular image of the effect of drugs, not everyone at such a social event centered around this drug behaves in the same manner after consuming comparable quantities. Some become passive, withdrawn or sleepy; some become loud or aggressive; some amorous or even lascivious. This illustrates what is true of all potent mind-altering drugs; the basic ingredient in the drug effect is the personality, mood and character of the user, which interacts with the pharmacology of the drug whether it be a depressant or stimulant and interacts with the setting or environment in which it is taken. I know of incidents where people have *believed* that they were consuming rum or other alcoholic ingredients in a certain "harmless" punch or at pot parties where the people *believed* they were consuming marijuana when they were actually consuming an inert substance. Strangely enough, 90 percent of people at such events behaved exactly as if they had consumed the actual drug. They got "contact highs" from each other and they did what was expected at a cocktail party. The most important lesson to learn from these incidents is that people can have a good time without consuming a mind-altering drug. We should begin to communicate that in our behavior as well as in our statements.

To understand this mind-altering drug effect concept in specific terms, I will give just one example about sexual behavior that you can also apply to crime or to other deviant behavior said to result from certain drugs. There is a lot of talk about certain drugs producing "sexual excesses." I have never been sure what that meant, but it appears to be a very successful concept before the American Legion, the PTA, the Elks, et cetera, in stimulating, with perhaps a touch of envy, imagery of orgies that young people supposedly engage in. In any case, if you want to understand the interrelationship of a drug to sexual behavior or any other human complex behavior, you might think of it this way. Take the average American esconced in his armchair watching his favorite television program such as the Beverly Hillbillies, Bonanza, Julia . . . or Mission Impossible perhaps hoping that the whole program will self-destruct or that Phelps will turn down the mission this time. In any case, as that person watches his favorite program, assume that some "drug pusher," or maybe his wife interested in some sex, approaches suggesting that they take a drink or pill or smoke pot. There is no drug that will move him away from his favorite program to engage in sexual inter-actions whether that be kissing or more elaborate forms of such interaction. On the other hand, if for biological and psychological reasons he has some interest in sex, as a great many Americans do, he can certainly use a mind-altering drug in association with that already existing interest, perhaps remembering what Shakespeare wisely pointed out in *Macbeth* about alcohol, that it may stimulate interest but diminish performance. What comes out of the drug experience sexually, intellectually or otherwise is mainly what you are as a person.

Why do people use drugs? Most often that question would be phrased, Why do young people use marijuana, LSD and narcotics? As Gertrude Stein lay dying in Paris, it is said that her long-time companion, Alice B. Toklas, subsequently immortalized by Peter Sellers, asked, "Gertrude, what is the answer?" and her dying words were supposed to have been, "What is the question?" That is a very profound statement because we get the kinds of answers we want by the way we phrase our questions. Any one drug can only be understood in the total context of all mind-altering drugs from alcohol to heroin and nutmeg and most of all in the context of the society in which that drug is used. Drug usage is a baro-

meter or symptom of an often pathological and deeply alienating
society. When you look at it in that context and ask the question,
why do people use drugs, the first level answer is that we live in
the most drug-ridden, drug-saturated, drug-obsessed society in the
history of mankind—a society where from infancy onward we have
institutionalized the industrial slogan of "Better living through
chemistry," meaning specifically that every time we have a pain,
problem or trouble we are taught to pop a pill, take a drink or
smoke a cigarette, particularly one that is one inch longer than
another and therefore will kill you two years sooner. This age
of chemistry is massively fostered by the two million dollars a day
spent by the alcoholic beverage and tobacco industries for TV,
radio, magazine, newspaper and billboard ads that stress (and
particularly aim at programs watched by young people) the earliest
possible use of these drugs and, by implication, other mind-altering
drugs in the greatest possible quantities. If, for example, you
watched two recent Super Bowl games, you must realize that if
Len Dawson, Joe Namath and their teammates had consumed
even a fraction of the beer and tobacco it was implied they regularly used, they would not have even been able to stagger onto
the fields, let alone win those championships. Yet that is the way
we push drugs in American society. The imagery that is stressed
by these companies, these "drug pushers," are the sexual pleasure,
eternal youth and happiness that you will somehow magically get
from these and other chemicals. Added to this is the message of
the over-the-counter pseudosedative industry including that little
gentle blue pill, Compoz®, that has made women presidents of
their clubs; men successful business executives; students straight
A geniuses; and more recently has been found to be necessary to
take every morning to tolerate the bad news in the newspaper.
Then we have that other pill, Sominex®, that tells us that if we
have not fallen asleep within fifteen minutes, we are some kind
of deviate or nut and must rush down to the drugstore and pick
up some pills in order to sleep. All of this together combines with
the role model example of parents, teachers and other adults that
communicates to children almost from birth that whenever you
relate to other human beings, whether at a wedding or funeral,

whenever you seem to be happy, you apparently must depend upon one or more mind-altering drugs.

The role model example cannot be overemphasized including the hypocrisy of a teacher or a doctor talking about the risks of tobacco smoking, while he himself is smoking or is seen to rush off to turn on with nicotine and add to environmental pollution the moment the talk is over. The average American child spends 22,000 hours in front of a television set between age 0—that is, the moment they pop out of the birth canal and are put in front of the tube in the maternity room—and age 18. This represents more hours than they spend in classrooms and consequently more exposure to and inculcation of pro-drug attitudes of all kinds, as well as attitudes of violence, consumerish and desirable female secondary sexual characteristics.

Then we have the massive overavailability of all these drugs as a causative factor. Certainly, alcohol, tobacco, pharmaceuticals and the over-the-counter preparations are massively overavailable; marijuana, relatively so; and in decreasing proportion but still overavailable, all the other mind-altering drugs. No drugs are harmless. All have some risks. Aspirin alone kills or disables several thousand young people each year and produces birth defects in lower animals; yet we do not know how it works, despite being massively used by hundreds of millions of people. These out-of-context statements could be used to criminalize all users of the drug in order to save them (and also prevent others from using it for any beneficial purposes). The naivety of the so-called hard-line approach is almost beyond belief and has to be directly confronted if we are to move the society ahead and solve the real drug problem. An Ohio legislator once introduced a bill to make it a felony to possess catnip after *The Wall Street Journal* published an article about ten young people turning on with catnip. As the construction industry in that state geared up to build more jails and prisons and as the drug police agencies looked forward to even greater power over human lives, fortunately the bill died in committee. There is another example in the airplane hijacking field. Nobody would be more opposed to airplane hijacking than I am because I travel extensively to lecture and consult around the country and I do not care to make any unscheduled visits to

Russia, Spain, Israel, Egypt or Cuba. The problem is, how do you stop complex human behavior such as airplane hijacking? Congressmen have been reelected for being hard on hijacking because they introduced bills calling for stiffer penalities as the answer. What their constituents have not been told is that the death penalty is already provided for. So it is very hard to understand how you can provide a harder punishment than the death penalty. Yet there are millions of people who would probably respond to a clarion call for the death penalty for the first offense of marijuana possession and castration for the second offense.

There are, of course, psychological reasons why people use drugs and I do not mean by that, psychopathological. If you ask the ordinary person why they use alcohol, nicotine, marijuana or sleeping pills, the following would be among the most common reasons given: to relax, to escape, to feel good (which we call with some drugs turning on and with other drugs just good for business behavior) or to socialize with one's friends. All of this together can be put under the rubric of pleasure-seeking behavior, which is why I titled my book that way.* About pleasure-seeking we have a very mixed attitude in American society. There are those among us who, after carefully dichotomizing their own pleasure-seeking behavior, aggressively dedicate themselves to eliminating such behavior in other people and in fact calling it un-American. As with many of the things that we talk about in this field, it is good to go back to basic definitions. Although it is true that many of our current leaders would no longer pass or support the Bill of Rights or Declaration of Independence, these remain basic American documents by which we should guide our lives, and among other things the Declaration of Independence guarantees us life, liberty and the pursuit of happiness. Thus, by definition the pursuit of happiness is totally American and the opposition to it is totally un-American. What is reflected is a streak of puritanism which was best defined by H. L. Mencken as the haunting fear that someone somewhere may be happy. Many

---

The Pleasure Seekers, the Drug Crisis, Youth and Society. Indianapolis, Bobbs-Merrill Company, 1969.

are indeed haunted by that fear and "turn on" through seeking to eliminate such sources of happiness.

The real point is that drugs at best are one of many possible sources of pleasure. It may be possible to develop a society in which millions of young people, instead of finding school boring, monotonous or a form of slavery and instead of preferring to be under the influence of pot, beer, nicotine, reds — not Communists but Seconal® capsules — or other mindaltering drugs, would enjoy learning, knowledge and the whole educational process. The alternative sources of pleasure or happiness are one of the keys to changing the drug-ridden society.

One other aspect of causation is the criminogenic effect of our present policies. Spinoza wisely pointed to this some three hundred years ago when he said, "He who determines everything by law foments crime rather than lessens it." What he was talking about is what sociologists commonly refer to as "crime without victims," for example, private sexual behavior most of which is illegal in America, private drug use, gambling, and so forth — things that in other contexts we call vices or immoralities when engaged in by others. With this private behavior, as opposed to crimes against the person such as murder, rape and manslaughter or crimes against property like burglary, embezzlement, auto theft, et cetera, paradoxically when you define it as forbidden, deviant or illegal, you make it far more interesting and attractive to a large segment of the society than it otherwise would be. This is particularly true among those who see themselves as disaffiliated from, or in revolt against, the broader society, as do an ever-increasing number of youths. This is so true that once when I was speaking in San Antonio, a local commune leader came up to me after a speech and said semi-jokingly, he would like to carry out a book denunciation party of my book in order to make it a national best seller. If you can get a congressman to attack your book or if you can get a piece of "obscene" literature seized by some vice police, you can have it sold out almost over night.

At another level the criminogenic effect means that we label as criminals millions of otherwise normal people and arrest hundreds of thousands of them for their private drug use. I do not confine my concern to the effect of this on the marijuana user. I am talking about all drug use, whether it be alcohol, tobacco, heroin, LSD or marijuana. But with marijuana alone we are arresting hundreds of thousands each year. By our present definitions an arrest record or imprisonment is beneficial for one's life. It obviously opens up job opportunities for you and sees that you complete your schooling.

Of that number some tens of thousands are sent to reform schools, juvenile halls, jails and prisons. But that is all right because of another aspect of American society, the substitution of euphemisms and images for reality. We all "know," because honorable men have told us so, that if you build a multimillion dollar institution, staff it with very expensive administrators and guards and call it a rehabilitation center, that rehabilitation takes place there because certainly honorable men would not lie to us. What in fact does take place in that facility is that the drug user is given a postdoctoral course in real crime, an aggressive introduction to homosexuality and an actual lesson on how to fix heroin and where to obtain it; and he is in general, dehumanized. After release, they are sent out as ex-convicts and ex-dope fiends to look unsuccessfully for jobs, schooling, et cetera. This is all part of the present American system of indiscriminate criminalization as the supposed answer to drug problems.

Bearing that in mind, let us turn to what to do. The first thing to do is to reject the person who tells you all you have to do is pass another law or elect him to office. There is no form of complicated behavior that can ever be solved or handled by any oversimplified pseudosolution. The politician or other demagogues who pander to the American craving for oversimplification have to be seen as irrelevant to this particular problem. As part of this, one of our social problems is the fact that two-thirds to three-quarters of all our legislators are lawyers and they think only in legalistic expediency-oriented terms and are very incapable of dealing with behavior in alternative or more successful ways — not to mention the fact that every law that is passed adds to the business of the lawyer-legislators who carry on a private practice while they are serving in the legislature.

We must learn to think through what the real problems are objectively and not accept someone else's definition of "problems." The first route is the definition of *drug abuse* above. The second would be the concept of *hard drug* that I have evolved over the years. We should take up the language of the street, the "narc" and the politician and precisely define it so we know what the *real problems* are. There are at least three dimensions of hard effects of drugs: death and disability; psychosis or insanity; physical dependence and addiction. After assessing these three dimensions we must balance them against the hard effects of our social policies which I have briefly summarized. We then can do a kind of cost benefit analysis hopefully not just in financial terms but in human terms, balancing the price of the present system against the price of the real drug problems.

I think both the John Birch Society and the weathermen would have to agree that *death* is a hard phenomenon. Any drug that is significantly involved in producing death would by my definition be "hard." Alcohol and tobacco together kill and disable about one million people a year in the United States alone. Objectively, they are our hardest drugs. Barbiturates and other sedatives are involved in the deaths of more than 20,000 people a year accidentally or by suicide. LSD-type drugs have been involved in perhaps some fifty deaths over the years, and other drugs can, of course, be involved in this dimension. I am not making this list exhaustive but rather illustrative to help you think.

To quote our President, "let me make one thing perfectly clear at this point." When I talk about drugs in context, it in no way implies a lack of concern about any other drug because I am emphasizing the hardness of one drug. It has long been my position, and this is one of my more controversial views in an immoral society, that a moral and rational person should seek to reduce and eliminate all unnecessary death or disability and psychosis or addiction whether the substance or phenomenon involved is defined as good for business or bad for business, is legal or illegal, or whether it be something that you yourself use or do not use. None of these problems can properly be defined in terms of newspaper or magazine publicity. It is unlikely that in our lifetime we will see the same kind of sensationalistic attention given to the 1200 people who die each year in New York City alone from overdoses of alcohol as compared to the 600 people who die from overdoses of heroin. My goal would be to eliminate problems from heroin, alcohol, tobacco, et cetera, since they all devastate ghettos, suburbia and the central city. They are all problems of black and white, young and old, rich and poor. It is utterly hypocritical and inhumane to pick one of them out of context to aggrandize your own career or your own agency.

The second dimension of hardness, *psychosis,* also involves many drugs. Alcohol is again most prominent with acute psychosis such as delirium tremens and chronic psychosis accounting for a very large proportion of emergency drug treatment as well as admissions to state mental hospitals. Chronic stimulant abuse such as Methedrine,® speed, Dexedrine® and Benzedrine® produces acute psychotic reactions. There are the acute and chronic psychoses that occur with LSD-type drugs, a list of which reads very much like the federal bureaucracy — STP, DMT, MDA, one named in honor of the FDA, and many others. Marijuana has also been involved in this dimension of hardness. A small number of people, quite small in proportion to the 20 million users and the number of times that they use it, have acute psychotic reactions after taking marijuana. An honest person would never talk about that out of context nor would he leave it out of the discussion of possible hard effects from drugs. He should, however, always get across that the personality and character of the user are still the most essential ingredients and doubly emphasize that if you have some instability or underlying mental illness you are much more likely to have an adverse experience from any potent mind-altering drug and particularly from the most potent ones such as LSD.

As for the *addiction,* alcohol, sedatives and narcotics are all capable of producing it with daily heavy use of increasing amounts for six to eight weeks. Thus, we have many drug problems involving many different drugs and to solve them we have to do many different things. The American drug program should begin with a total ban on all advertising of alcohol and tobacco. We should then prominently label all bottles, packages and containers that have these substances in them; not the vague inconspicuous, ambiguous message now hidden on the side of cigarette packages, but a very explicit message educating people about the relationship between the use of these drugs and blood-alcohol levels (drunk driving), cancer, heart disease, high blood pressure, emphysema, bronchitis and so forth. We should stop subsidizing tobacco farmers to grow more tobacco in order to kill more people each year, including our friends abroad to whom we export it presumably to reduce their overpopulation problem. Massive educational programs are needed in the public schools, beginning in elementary school and extending to adult education. If you doubt whether it is necessary to start around ages 6 to 9 remember the 22,000 hours of television viewing and also remember that some big city students in the second and third grades today are jumping rope to the rhyme: "ABC, LSD, marijuana is good for me." That is inculcating, along with the television, the idea of the importance and acceptability of drug usage as a normal part of life. The school educator can no longer be the temperance worker who goes into the school, drops a worm in a glass of pure alcohol and as it shrivels up says, this is what happens to your brain. The drug educator can no longer be the expert in fingerprinting, booking, surveillance and the use of informers—that is, the drug policeman, who goes into schools masquerading as an expert on pharmacology, sociology and education by saying because you use drug X or Y your brain will rot away. This is one of the prominent causes of the massive use of drugs today. Because young people found that they were being lied to, and had been lied to for so many years, particularly since it is in no way unusual for government officials to lie to people, They next concluded that what they were told by an even more responsible person was also false; and they equated, in the sense of minimizing, the effects of heroin, LSD and speed with marijuana and alcohol. What I am talking about as drug education has, with very token exceptions, never been tried. We can tell how ineffective and destructive our present approach has been, so we must begin in bureaucracy in general to make people accountable for their actions if we are ever going to improve the system. We must not just go on to do more of the same. Education has to be objective and factual. It has to demythologize drugs and it has to deal with drugs in context from alcohol on to glue and gasoline.

By demythologizing, what I mean is that you must get across correctly that whatever happens from a drug depends more on the person than the drug. Just as some of the dangers about some of the drugs are greatly exaggerated, so are many of the benefits. There is no drug that is necessary or inherently beneficial for mankind; there is no drug that will make an ignoramus into a creative genius; and there is no drug that will solve family or school problems or rebuild a neighborhood while you are on a trip with that drug, whether it be alcohol, pot, speed or anything else. That can be gotten across, and most importantly we must get across positive alternatives to drug use in school and in the rest of the society. The more we make going to school a mind-expanding experience for young people, the less likely they are to turn to a chemical for its alleged properties of mind expansion. This should go on each year and over a period of time during that year, and it certainly should involve student participation along with a specially trained teacher.

Treatment and rehabilitation are an important part of the solution and should mostly focus on long-term outpatient comprehensive programs such as the ones I have developed in San Francisco that blend nonprofessionals and professionals in one setting. They should not stress one approach as the answer because there is no panacea in terms of treatment, whether it be methadone maintenance, Synanon or Daytop, or any other, certainly including psychiatry or psychotherapy. A good clinic would accept alcoholic, tobacco smokers, narcotic addicts, LSD bad trippers, speed "freaks" and so forth. They all have serious forms of drug abuse and they all need specialized services which they usually cannot get. They should all be accepted as individual human beings who, among other things, have a particular drug problem for which they are going to be offered the most effective and innovative services humanly possible.

Finally, all of these things should be done together. I am not saying that any one of them is the answer. I am saying just the opposite. For we must do as many of those things as we possibly can along with major reforms in our laws. Most people concentrate just on the laws. I have left that for the last because I wanted to convey that all of those other things have greater significance and yet have been totally overlooked. Within the law the most important reform is to separate out the private user from the major trafficker. It is totally inhumane and barbaric to criminalize a person for the private use of alcohol, marijuana or heroin, and parenthetically it is hypocritical for us now to be concerned about the impact of our drug laws simply because white middle-class kids are experimenting with marijuana or heroin. The drug problems are not new; they have been here while I and Paul Blachly and many other people were working on them more than fifteen years ago, because they involved people that we were concerned about even then. Drug problems have evolved to include larger groups and other segments of the society, but they are in no way new problems. We have to deal with all of them and with all the kinds of users rather than one or two. The drug users should not be criminalized. Drug use is a public health matter, meaning education and prevention as the answer. Criminal law should be reserved only for the major trafficker in a drug we consider unacceptable and most of all reserved for clearly antisocial behavior, such as drunk driving or any other criminal act involving a drug. Most criminal acts involve drugs only secondarily and far more involve alcohol than all the other mind-altering drugs put together.

While doing all these things together, the most important single thing we should do is attack the roots of alienation in our society. We cannot deal with this any longer out of context. We have to face up to the fact that millions of Americans, perfectly respectable older Americans, do not find their lives meaningful and are already concentrating on retirement at age 65 and along the road to that on coffee breaks, vacations, parking spaces, keys to the washroom or prestigious titles on their doors or desks. As a symptom of that, they are using more and more drugs and more and more different ones. We have to attack the roots of alienation, particularly the dehumanizing effects of the bureaucratic-political process. The fact that so many of us feel increasingly hopeless and despairing about our ability to effect the course of our lives is directly related to drug usage of all kinds. So I would say that the way to deal with that is not to choke off unpopular ideas or kill the messenger bringing bad news (as they used to in the Middle Ages) but rather to compete in the market place of new ideas by presenting alternative ethics and by helping people to live those ethics. Instead of the psychedelic ethic which tells us to turn on, tune in and drop out, we should be able as individual human beings—as Americans and as professionals—to live a life which communicates that we should turn on to the world around us and to people, tune in to knowledge and feeling, and drop in to changing and improving the quality of life.

3

Today's Drug Problem
What's Happening in 1970

Kenneth D. Gaver

Today there is more discussion and more literature about drug abuse and greater acceptance of the reality of this social problem. There is also more discussion regarding what government ought to do than there is actual action to achieve results.

More people know more kids who have been in trouble. There are more parents worrying over a son or daughter who has been "busted." There are the Kennedys and the Shrivers. A well-known television star is saying that his daughter's death was due to acid. There is some citizen concern (although we do not think there is enough). Occasional groups of citizens band together to help, while equally as many band together to discuss drug use over a couple of martinis. Some have helpful ideas, but most have words of regret or condemnation. More adults are more concerned about youthful misbehavior——whether it is delinquency, antiwar protests (which are thought not to be in good taste), campus violence or drug abuse—than about reasons for the behavior (how things got this way) and what needs to be changed.

There is some serious talk in this country about legalizing the use of marijuana, but nobody seriously talks about legalizing the use of heroin. Anybody can legally buy alcohol. There is a real medical concern over the spreading use of hard drugs, especially heroin, and the increasing use of amphetamines. Because of this concern, there is an increased demand for facilities and programs for users and ex-users of drugs of all types. The medical men— the psychologists and the rehabilitation specialists—all scratch their heads and ponder and wish they knew what to do about the drug disease.

Let's look at the scene in a little more detail for a moment and from several vantage points—the incidence of drug abuse, governmental action, therapeutic innovations and public attitudes.

INCIDENCE OF DRUG ABUSE

No systematic survey reports a decline in the use of the principal drugs of abuse. No survey reports a decline in the use of marijuana, lysergic acid, similar types of hallucinatory drugs, barbiturates, amphetamines or hard narcotic drugs. We all wish that a survey would show such a decline, and we all predicted it; but we have yet to demonstrate it. Also no survey shows any sound evidence of any significant decline in the use of the drug abused most of all—alcohol—and that is not a drug of youth.

Surveys, on the other hand, are not as popular as they used to be. About a year or eighteen months ago, the newspapers carried stories about a survey conducted by students at this high school or that high school or this college or that college. One could get a survey from the local police department as to the extent of drug usage at the local high school. One could get a countersurvey done by the students at the high school as to their estimate of the extent of drug use. A professional group in the community could start a project to survey drug abuse in the community. One could get surveys of colleges done by such eminent scientific journals as *Playboy*. Today, however, surveys do not seem to be as popular as they once were. One national survey of drug abuse, a careful scientific study initiated some time ago, has yet to tell us of the patterns and the extent of drug use among the population generally.

There are, however, some alarming reports of drug abuse on the production line. Increasingly, we see newspaper stories and quotations from industrial leaders and labor leaders who are concerned that the use of drugs is spreading from the disengaged youth to the very much engaged production line worker. Industrial firms which two years ago stated they had no drug problem now are beginning to realize that perhaps within the plant and on the assembly line there are indeed persons who are under the influence of one or another type drug. So we now will shift from high school surveys, I suppose, to industrial plant surveys.

Today, I think it is fair to say that most Americans will admit that American troops in Vietnam often really do smoke pot. Two years ago, one would get an argument. Of course, there were those who brought back secretive comments about the use of marijuana by troops in Vietnam, and one could get official surveys which said that its use was extremely limited among very few soldiers. Yet now most people recognize the fact that probably a fair number of the troops have, at one time or another, smoked or still smoke marijuana.

Today, there is also documented evidence of the spread of heroin use, not only among the traditional groups who were socio-economically susceptible to using heroin, but also among the middle-class youth, even to a few college students and certainly to many communities where the use of heroin had heretofore never been dreamed of or suspected. This, incidentally, was accurately predicted about two years ago by eminent colleagues in one of the provinces of our neighboring country to the north. In fact, today there is the use of heroin among groups which three years ago might never have considered it. I am not trying to frighten you with that statement; it is a fact.

We know also that heroin addiction, total drug deaths and juvenile drug deaths continue to rise in the major metropolitan areas, such as New York City. Our own Oregon surveys show a gradually continuing rise of admissions to clinics and hospitals because of problems relating to drug abuse.

GOVERNMENTAL ACTION

In my comments, I do not purport to reflect exactly the status of governmental action, particularly at the federal level; but I think that federal action bears some comment. I apologize that my comments cannot be more favorable.

First, the President proposes; Congress argues; and the professionals battle for territory over the Controlled Dangerous Substances Act. How many months has this argument gone on? But, in fact, it is a control act; it is a law-and-order act; it is an act incorporating the "no-knock" features. It is not a prevention program; it is not a treatment program; it is not a rehabilitation program. The main thrust of the Federal Government's concern with the drug problem today is not with an act incorporating corrective social action.

Second, congressmen propose federal grants for treatment and rehabilitation programs. Senator Harold Hughes has held hearings throughout the nation. From the evidence of his hearings, it is clear that there are far more people in desperate difficulty as the result of drug abuse than we would ever heretofore have suspected. So, a bill is proposed providing 90 percent federally funded grants to the states or to local communities to operate treatment and rehabilitation programs. But, as yet, little happens. A pittance is made available through the Mental Health Centers Act—a pittance lodged in an administratively awkward and clumsy package difficult for small states to utilize.

Third, United States authorities try to find economic sanctions to eliminate the production of opium in Turkey. Turkish farmers say, however, that opium is the bread-and-butter crop, so they are not interested in stopping the growth of opium. As a matter of fact, they would like to keep "poppy" down on the farm.

Next, the Food and Drug Administration proposes new and restrictive regulations on methadone maintenance programs, one of the few encouraging programs in this country which show promise for the seriously addicted heroin addict. Yet, we see the proposal for restrictive regulations, which immediately impose an excessively high cost of care as a result of demanding medical studies and treatments for conditions other than the addiction per se.

Finally, the National Institute of Mental Health started a belated program of public education. I say it is belated because the kind of material that is being put out by the National Institute of Mental Health was produced by a small state like Oregon first—perhaps not with the advantage of the financial resources of the Federal Government, but certainly with the advantage of having been available two years earlier. That is true not only for Oregon but for many private, nonprofit foundations which produced this information before the National Institute of Mental Health was even authorized to get into the business. Fortunately, accompanying the federal program of public education and information is some support for teacher training and drug education which will take effect this fall—four or five years after the identification of the burgeoning problem of drug abuse.

At the state level, such popular programs called Oregon Drug Alert, Tennessee Drug Alert or the Governor's Drug Alert have been developed. As usual, Oregon was first in this field. As usual, state after state emulated this program. Oregon's Governor has spoken of the Oregon Drug Alert as a great central organizing force in an effort to reach the uninvolved citizenry. I shall not elaborate upon Oregon Drug Alert except to say that there is going to be a follow-up citizens' involvement conference soon. Drug alert programs are hard to evaluate; but, at the very least, they represent an official and very important recognition by the heads of state government of the need for public concern, public involvement and public participation in the whole area of drug use, drug abuse and drug addiction.

Also, at the state level, governor's budget requests call for not only more narcotics agents, more controls on drugs, but, simultaneously, more clinics and more rehabilitation centers. We have had the opportunity to review communications from governor after governor across this country who have indicated that their requests to the legislatures of the states will include enhanced capabilities for control, treatment and rehabilitation.

In Oregon, the Mental Health Division, at the Governor's specific request, developed a proposal for a drug-dependency treatment program for young drug users. We had already developed detoxification capabilities in a number of hospitals, public and private. We had established a methadone maintenance program. We had encouraged the community clinics to develop innovative programs for dealing with youthful users. However, at the Governor's request, we developed a proposal for a specialized treatment program for young drug-dependent persons, and it was presented to the Oregon State Emergency Board which, in its best wisdom, deferred action on granting the funds. That deferral specifically led to the Governor's visit with Miss Mary Switzer in Washington, D. C., where he personally delivered a request to the Federal Government for a grant to the State of Oregon to develop this drug-dependency treatment program. We are pleased to report that this grant was approved and that this program is now under development. We hope to gain from it experience and knowledge about how best to help these persons.

In Oregon and in other states, the methadone replacement programs, whatever particular form they take, grow by leaps and bounds. In Oregon, the methadone replacement program, intsead of reaching 150 patients in two years, found itself with 250 patients in one year. That same pattern has been repeated in similar programs in the East and Middle West.

THERAPEUTIC INNOVATIONS

I am no expert in treatment rehabilitation programs for the drug user. Later in these proceedings, you will, however, hear from experts who will explain a variety of approaches and discuss their pros and cons. You will hear about storefront and first contact clinics and hear the representatives of these clinics assess their results. You will hear discussion of Outside-In, a clinic in Portland which was the result of one man's concern but now has finally received the sanction not only of the government of the City of Portland, but also the sanction of the State of Oregon in financial assistance. The White Bird Clinic in Eugene and the Open Door Clinic in Seattle will also be discussed. These are unique and special programs located out of the community, away from the Establishment, because of the special chance to reach the otherwise unreachable. You will also hear about nonmedical residental treatment programs such as Synanon.

Such treatment innovations as exist will be discussed by experts. You will hear of the methadone replacement program, one of the few programs which offer a controlled chance to the hard user. There will be discussion of outpatient treatment and rehabilitation programs, experiments, trials and hopes. If I could second-guess the discussants, I would predict that they will tell you there is nothing very specific or predictable about how to approach the user of non-narcotic drugs. I would guess that you will hear that treatment is highly individualized and that at this stage of our knowledge, treatment has to deal more with the person than with effects of his drug abuse.

There will be comment about hospital programs and their limitations. It has been generally conceded to date that the most useful hospital role is one of detoxification or that the hospital may be a place to start methadone replacement. However nobody gives much credit anymore to California's program at Corona, nor does anybody give much credit anymore to federal programs at Lexington and Fort Worth. They are very necessary programs, but they do not hold the kind of promise that we had hoped for. Overall, it appears that the hospital or institutional programs can make their offerings in the areas of detoxification or the initiation of intensive replacement programs.

Last of the unique treatment innovations are the voluntary citizens' efforts—the citizens' hot lines, the citizens' referral services. At the least, these voluntary programs help to identify professionals who are willing to help. They steer the user who is in trouble; they provide solace to a family; or they form the nucleus for a future community-based counseling and rehabilitation program.

PUBLIC ATTITUDES

If I could predict public attitudes, I would go around wearing three feathers in my cap. The public attitude about drug use and drug abuse today is very hard to grasp. We know that the public generally deplores the use of pot, acid or "H" just as much as ever. But, in spite of deploring it, more people try it than ever before. The public and the police profess dismay at how to behave toward the drug abuse which so often flagrantly accompanies the crowds to that newest and greatest of all spectator sports —the outdoor rock festival. Recently, we have read that police just stand by. It is too big; there is too much all in one place. What are you supposed to do about it anyway?

The public has its concerns. Campus violence is a hotter issue than drug abuse. Maybe that is because it is more tangible and more directed to the public institutions. Drug use and drug abuse are more personal. They are less obviously threatening to the public, to the public's buildings, to the public's grounds and to the public's institutions. Some citizens do, however, as an expression of their public attitude and interest, aid the unfortunate. Without them, we would not have an Outside-In; we would not have a White Bird Clinic; we would not have mayors' councils; we would not have budding community-based clinics. But, as I see it, there is no great wave of public direction. It is hard to know what the public wants in this area. It is easy to hear the concern and the worry, but it is hard to know what the public is inclined to do or how much it is willing to pay for the price of relieving the pain of the ones in trouble over drugs. It is hard to know how far the public will go toward forgiving the thousands of others who use drugs for kicks or experiments or even out of a wish to express a sentiment of protest.

CONCLUSION

What's happening in 1970? Well, there are more people using more drugs more openly, more getting bad trips, more getting hooked on "H" more often, and more winding up in clinics and hospitals. There are more kids with police records, more kids in crash pads in schools, more parents worried, and more predictions of woe and trouble.

Despite all the statistics, all the patients in clinics, all the arrests, all the king's men, all the stories and all the tragedies do not scare anybody. In spite of them, more people use more drugs more openly and more often than in 1969. That's what's happening in 1970! How come?

4

The American and British Drug Problems—Some Comparisons

Richard Phillipson

When I first thought of writing this paper, I told Dr. Stanley F. Yolles, Director of the National Institute of Mental Health, that I wished to present a summary of existing knowledge of drug problems in the two nations and I would endeavor to avoid straying into controversial matters. In the play *Don Quixote*, it was said, "Every comparison is odious," and in *Much Ado About Nothing*, Shakespeare said, "Comparison makes men happy or miserable." I trust I will not have the latter effect on any one. It could be, however, that some of the facts that I will present to you may arouse some doubts in your minds as to whether one *can* compare the drug problems in our two nations, impartially and without bias.

To begin, I would like to quote from Dr. Yolles' article entitled "The Current Drug Scene":

> I am sure that the year 1969 will be remembered in the United States as 'the year of the drug debate.' As recently as last summer, in respect to penalties and other control procedures, proposals introduced in the Congress to control drug abuse varied widely, and their proponents expressed fundamentally opposing views. In recent months, however, attitudes have become less polarized as the facts about drug abuse have become more widely known. These changes in attitude were

Note: The author is indebted to many colleagues both in the United States and Britain, in the National Institute of Mental Health in Washington, in the Home Office, in the Department of Health and Social Security, and in the Addiction Research Unit of the Maudsley Hospital, London. Without their ever generous assistance this paper could never have been presented.

clearly expressed by President Nixon at a recent Governors' Conference when he stated that, although he had once assumed that increasing penalties would solve the drug abuse problem among our youth, he now believes that it is through education and understanding that a solution will be found.

In 1970, we are rapidly moving into an area of understanding of brain function. The synthesis of protein, the breaking of the genetic code, increased experiments in RNA and memory functions, increased understanding of chemical functions within the brain, and the effects of drugs on brain and body functions, the understanding of learning behavior which has progressed in animal studies to the point where animals can be conditioned to control body functions—all of these lead towards the *artificial* alteration of human behavior.

Our technology provides us with highly potent synthetic materials and, through the mass media, the means to inform any person who can read, listen or look at these dangerous substances. In this situation, it is all too easy for anyone of any age who does not like the way he lives to try a drug 'high,' in search of mystique of esoteric meaning, of euphoria, or of oblivion. I can only regard the psychedelic drug movement as a new brand of anti-intellectualism.

Fear of reality, known or unknown, has always been the major impetus for seeking escape through drugs. The prophets of the new drug cults are convinced that modern man needs to think less and feel more. Drug-taking is a sensual, not an intellectual, experience. Indeed, the titles of a recent psychedelic happening starring the cult's leader was appropriately titled, *The Death of the Mind.*

As scientists involved in drug phenomena, we are in somewhat the same dilemma which faced the nuclear physicists who split the atom. We have their example before us, and we should profit by it. No amount of breast-beating and cries of mea culpa will put the stopper back on the pill bottle, any more than it can put the old-fashioned atom together again.

.   .   .   .

The drug dilemma facing this country has become a national concern. However, as the general alarm over drug abuse increases, so does the illicit use of drugs. Scientists, physicians, law enforcement officers and the judiciary, as well as the public, have become trapped in a debate noteworthy more for its emotional content than for its reason. This is very evident in attitudes toward the use of marijuana.

In the British drug scene, Sir Denis Hill of The Institute of Psychiatry, London, in a Foreword to a volume entitled *Modern Trends in Drug Dependence and Alcoholism*[2] said the following:

> As modern societies become more complex culturally and economically, the use and also the misuse of drugs increases. The number of chemical substances upon which physical or psychological dependence becomes possible also increases, as does their availability. While drug dependence has been recognized for centuries, its epidemic manifestations in highly developed societies, such as the United States, Britain or Japan, is a comparatively new problem. Heroin addiction had a different background in the United States from that in Britain, and public attitudes to it have been different. Although, on both sides of the Atlantic, there is now official recognition that the drug addict, no less than the chronic alcoholic, is a sick person requiring treatment and care. In the United States, as a result of deeply ingrained attitudes, the idea that a narcotic addict is more sick than sinful is indeed experimental.

As Dr. Yolles writes, "American puritanism goes deep and those who set the pattern of moral attitudes to disorders of behavior derived their opinions more from Cromwell than from Charles."

In Britain, with a welfare state and a permissive society, the idea that the victims of drug abuse should be subjected to compulsory detention or compulsory treatment was never acceptable.

The contemporary British experiment to contain, reduce and ameliorate the epidemic of hard-drug addiction without compulsory powers to detain the patient himself is based on an act of faith, but it is not without its logic and is supported by experiments conducted earlier in the United States. It has two major objectives. One is to prevent the criminal consequences of addiction for the patient himself. The second is to prevent the development of a criminally organized black market in herion. The development of finance and manpower suggested in Britain is as nothing compared with that which the Americans propose and a fraction of that which the Japanese used to reduce the prevalence of amphetamine addiction in their country from over a million sufferers to a mere handful.

Professor Hill concluded his Foreword with the following thoughts:

> The next three years should demonstrate how successful the 'British system' has been. But whatever the outcome, it is evident that the basic problems of addiction—whether to drugs or alcohol—have still to be identified, and tackled. There is an enormous unmet need for research both of a biological and of a sociological nature.

Today I hope to deal, albeit briefly, with the size of the problem, as well as with some legal, medical and epidemiological aspects of the problem. The population of Britain is one-fourth that of the United States of America and the narcotic addict population, still under 3000 strong, is almost entirely confined to Metropolitan London, whereas in America, conservatives estimates put the number of narcotic addicts at 120,000 or forty times greater than the British problem; originally confined almost solely to New York City, the narcotic addict population has now spread to many of the states and territories of the Union.

For example the figures of known active narcotic addicts recorded by the Bureau of Narcotics and Dangerous Drugs (BNDD), as of December 1969, showed a total of 68,088 addicts with 33,341 in New York State, 5,729 in Illinois (mainly in Chicago) and 7,516 in California. Also Table 4-1 shows new narcotic addicts reported to BNDD during the years 1965–1969.

TABLE 4-1

NEW NARCOTIC ADDICTS REPORTED TO U. S. BUREAU OF NARCOTICS
AND DANGEROUS DRUGS DURING THE YEARS 1965–1969

State	1965	1966	1967	1968	1969	Total
California	1032	566	644	745	973	3960
District of Columbia	150	120	79	188	531	1068
Illinois	504	386	448	374	514	2226
Maryland	332	277	289	413	358	1669
New Jersey	378	406	655	601	1262	3302
New York	2662	3113	2743	2966	7385	18869
Pennsylvania	130	171	251	216	380	1148
Texas	129	154	302	226	229	1041

Total (7 states & District of Columbia for five years)   33,289
Total United States, 1969   68,088
Total Addicted to Heroin, 1969   64,915

Again the Community Council on Housing in New York City recently surveyed tenement buildings in a 40-block area and determined, through door-to-door visits, that approximately 22,000 adults and 30,000 children and adolescents lived in these buildings. Another 6,000 people are living on the streets, in alleyways and in abandoned buildings in the same area.

The survey data shows that of these 58,000 persons, approximately *10,000 adults* are addicted to narcotics; *6,000 adolescents* (aged 16 to 21 years) are addicted; *2,000 children* (aged 7 to 15 years) are addicted; and this figure does not include users of non-narcotic drugs of abuse. Within this population, 2 percent of the addicted adults support themselves and their habit by maintaining regular employment; 90 percent receive public assistance; 98 percent engaged in criminal activity.

Sixty percent of the addicted adolescent females support themselves through prostitution. Ninety-three percent of the addicted adolescent males support themselves through criminal activity.

Of the 2,000 children (aged 7 to 15 years) addicted, approximately 90 percent live by themselves with no adult supervision and no means of support other than prostitution and criminal activity. In 1969, 230 addicted female children under 16 years of age have become pregnant; about 23, including one addicted child of 11 years of age, are presently pregnant.

Turning now to legal aspects of drug abuse in the two nations, in the United States in August 1969, the Chief of the Legislative Services Branch of the National Institute of Mental Health compared the most significant provisions of five bills relating to drug use and abuse introduced during the first session of the Ninety-first Congress; since that date two more bills have been introduced by Senator Hughes of Iowa. Time does not permit detailed discussion of any of these seven bills here, but I would like to quote briefly from a statement by Dr. Morton G. Miller, of the National Institute of Mental Health, expressed before the Special Subcommittee on Alcoholism and Narcotics of the Committee on Labor and Public Welfare, United States Senate, with regard to one of these seven bills, S.3562.3. This is a bill to provide a comprehensive federal program for the prevention and treatment of drug abuse and drug dependence.

Speaking in March 1970, Dr. Miller said the following:

I appreciate this opportunity to appear before you today to describe the current efforts of the National Institute of Mental Health and our plans for the future in the area of narcotic addiction and drug abuse. The Institute, as the focal point of narcotic addiction and drug abuse activities within the Department of Health, Education and Welfare, administers a variety of programs under the broad authorities granted in the Public Health Service Act, Amendments to the Community Mental Health Centers Act, and the Narcotic Addict Rehabilitation Act of 1966. These activities are focused within the Institute in the Division of Narcotic Addiction and Drug Abuse. For fiscal year 1971, the Department is requesting over $56 million for our total narcotic addiction and drug abuse effort; an increase of $8 million over 1970.

As we understand it, S.3562 would duplicate our existing authorities to conduct and support research, training, services, and public information and education activities. I believe that this would result in wasteful and unnecessary overlap and duplication. Further, I would question the establishment in Title VIII of the Bill of an Advisory Committee on Drug Abuse and Drug Dependence. The functions of this Advisory Committee are rather nebulous. It is to 'evaluate the program of the Administration.' I must point out that the Secretary already has available to him the services of the National Advisory Mental Health Council, which is authorized to and has been for a number of years reviewing and recommending all research and trainnig grants in the area of drug abuse as well as other mental health problems. The bill ignores this valuable source of expertise or at least makes no reference to the necessity to submit research and training grants to this body for consideration.

Drug abuse is a difficult problem systematically to analyze and quantify. The first area of concern is how many individuals are abusing drugs nationally. By drug class, the following statistics are useful. We estimate that there are approximately 120,-000 narcotics addicts in this country. The actual number is unknown. If there is error, it is probably on the conservative side. As we develop better data from local sources, we frequently find more narcotic addicts than were previously estimated for that community. For example, New York City has now a register, partially supported by an Institute grant that now identifies over 60,000 persons as addicts, in an unduplicated count. Traditional estimates usually attributed an addict population of 30,000 to New York City.

When we consider amphetamines and barbiturates we have no scientifically respectable national incidence and prevalence data. The great amounts of these substances which disappear out of legitimate channels of distribution certainly cause me to conclude that the abuse patterns merit the public level of concern which is now present.

. . . .

Though no firm data is available, we estimate that between 12 to 20 million Americans have at least experimented with marijuana. Several million of our citizens have probably taken LSD and other potent hallucinogens.

In Britain, just before Parliament was dissolved last month, the Misuse of Drugs Bill had reached the Committee stage after a second reading in the House of Lords. This Bill would replace the Dangerous Drugs Acts 1965 and 1967 and the Drugs (Prevention of Misuse Act) 1964 with new and more extensive provision for controlling drugs. A note on the Misuse of Drugs Bill, supplied to me by the Home Office, London, had the following to say on major provisions and objectives of the Bill: "Total, flexible and speedy control over all drugs of misuse is conferred upon the Home Secretary by the 'Misuse of Drugs Bill' published today (Wednesday) March 25, 1970. It repeals three previous Acts and takes wide new powers."

For the first time in British drugs legislation, the Bill

1. Distinguishes sharply between unlawful possession on the one hand and trafficking on the other. Several additional trafficking offenses—to take account of the widening range of trafficking activities—are created and penalties are increased to massive proportions; this is in line with British thinking the drug traffickers merit the severest punishment. Nevertheless possession remains a serious criminal offense.

2. Gives the Home Secretary powers to counter, without international consultation, any misuse situation that arises; in particular he may at any time by Order in Council bring new substances under control and make any regulations he considers necessary for control of production, supply and possession (Clauses 2, 7 and 10).

3. Takes powers to stamp out overprescribing by banning practitioners from prescribing specific controlled drugs if it is

established that they have been prescribing "irresponsibly (Clause 13).

4. Gives the Home Secretary power to demand information about supply of controlled drugs from any pharmacist or practitioner in any area, if it appears to him that in that area there are special social problems caused by extensive misuse of controlled drugs (Clause 17).

5. Provides for the establishment of an Advisory Council and Expert Committee on Misuse of Drugs to assist in the preparation of controls and other countermeasures. If, for example, a new substance of misuse emerges, the Home Secretary will be so advised and may, by Order in Council, place it on the control schedule.

With regard to penalties, the Bill distinguishes between those penalties appropriate to trafficking cases and those appropriate to simple possession. It separates the drugs of misuse into three classes related to their harmfulness.

1. *Class A*—includes opium, herion, morphine, Pethidine® and other narcotic drugs recommended for strictest control by United Nations Single Convention on Narcotic Drugs 1961. It also includes cannabinol and certain other hallucinogens including LSD regarded by the World Health Organization as particularly dangerous. It also includes injectable amphetamines, notably Methedrine about which the Advisory Committee on Drug Dependence has expressed concern. This is the first time that injectable amphetamines and LSD have been subjected to the same regime of control as heroin. This class also includes certain drugs, not used in medicine before controlled and not generally referred to as STP, DMT and DET.

2. *Class B*—contains six narcotic drugs, including codeine and pholcodeine, recommended for lesser control by the Single Convention; cannabis, cannabis resin; also five stimulant drugs of the amphetamine type, such as amphetamines (for example, Benzedrine); dexamphetamines (for example Dexedrine); and Drinamyl (sometimes called "purple hearts").

3. *Class C*—contains other amphetamine-like drugs which, on the basis of present experience, are considered to present lesser dangers (Clauses 2 and 25 and Schedule 4).

Penalties are related both to the class of drugs and to the type of offense. The penalties for *unlawful possession* of Class A drugs (including heroin) and Class B drugs have been revised (some up and some down). Under previous legislation it was necessary to provide a wide margin in the penalty for possession to deal with traffickers who could rarely be caught by the other main offense—that is, supply. The new penalties for possession no longer need to provide such a wide margin, but they are very substantial and in some cases increased because of new knowledge of the dangers of certain drugs and the need to provide weighty reinforcement of the sanctions against large-scale traffickers. In their new role, the penalties distinguish between, and take account of, the relative harmfulness of drugs and preeminently the harmfulness of heroin.

Next I shall discuss medical aspects.

In America, a memorandum from Dr. Stanley F. Yolles, Director of the National Institute of Mental Health, dated May 1970, gave details of the concentrated attack on drug abuse recently announced by the White House.

The following was the statement made by President Nixon:

> In recent months, there have been stories about two herion addicts that starkly illustrated the ominous nature of the narcotics problems. Like many addicts, one of them not only used the drug, but sold it. Their stories were, in fact, different from those of other drug addicts in only one major aspect: each was only twelve years old.
>
> One boy is now being treated for addiction at a clinic. The other died from an overdose of heroin.
>
> Drug addiction among school age youth is increasing at an alarming rate. Although funds for drug education and training have grown sixfold between fiscal 1969 and fiscal 1971, the situation calls for much greater effort. Today, I announce a greatly expanded federal program to fight this growing problem.
>
> The major points of the new effort are
> - A $3.5 million program operated by the Office of Education to train school personnel, particularly teachers, in the fundamentals of drug abuse education.
> - Creation of a National Clearinghouse for Drug Abuse Information and Education, giving the public one central office to contact.
> - Publication of a book in which, for the first time, all of the concerned federal departments and agencies have pooled their knowledge of the national drug problem.

- Modification of a program of the Law Enforcement Assistance Administration to allow large cities to apply for funds to be used for drug education, as well as for law enforcement programs.
- Development by the Advertising Council of an expanded public service campaign on drug abuse in cooperation with the media and the Federal Government.
- Close cooperation of the Administration with concerned citizens' organizations.

Closely related to these projects is this Administration's decision to more than double the amount of money that will be spent this fiscal year on research into the effects of marijuana on man.

.   .   .   .

One of the great tragedies of the past decade has been that our schools, where our children should learn about the wonder of life, have often been the places where they learn the living— and sometimes actual death of drug abuse. There is no priority higher in this Administration than to see that children—and the public—learn the facts about drugs in the right way and for the right purpose through education.

In Britain, in March 1970, Mr. James Callaghan, the Secretary of State for the Home Department, moving the Second Reading of the Misuse of Drugs Bill,[4] in the House of Commons, expressed the following:

Drug-taking is a scourge. We know far too little of its causes or consequences. The law has a part to play—hence the Bill— but it is by no means the only agency, because law enforcement which attempts to control personal consumption, is difficult. I emphasize at the outset that there is a need for a concerted effort in the legal, social and medical fields. The Bill on its own, although it would serve a useful purpose, would by no means deal with the problem, which is growing so fast today.

Compared with even three years ago, the pattern of misuse of drugs is much more complicated and more serious. Then, the main problem was a sharply increasing growth of heroin addiction coupled with a widened use of pep pills, cannabis and LSD. Drug users, even that short while ago, tended to go for a single drug of their choice. Today, the increase in heroin addiction has tapered off, almost certainly because control by the treatment centers of supplies to addicts has reduced the amount available to potential new addicts in the black market. But there is a more sinister side. Some would say that because of this very control many addicts have resorted to substitute drugs.

Indeed, two years ago, in 1968, there was an epidemic of 'fixing' by amphetamines which was largely fed by the activities and over-prescribing of no more than two doctors in London. It could be stopped only by a voluntary scheme for restricting supplies to hospital pharmacies. Many of the needle-users, a term to which I shall return later, then turned to methadone, a narcotic used by some treatment centres to wean addicts off heroin and made available for general practitioners to prescribe. They are free to prescribe it.

I want to give an indication of the measure of the problem, and the speed with which addiction can come upon us. There are now just over 2,000 registered addicts of heroin. Of these, 700 are under the age of 20. But as a result of the increase in the overprescription of methadone in 1969 alone, 337 cases of addiction to methadone first came to the notice of the Home Office. Methadone ampoules now command much the same black market price as heroin did before the 1968 restrictions. More recently—within the past 12 months—some addicts have taken to the highly dangerous and destructive practice of injecting themselves with barbiturates.

It therefore comes to this. We can draw comfort from the fact that heroin addiction appears to be less of a threat and that convictions for drug offenses in the first half of 1969 were no more than 10 percent higher than in the same period in 1968. Nevertheless, the possibilities of much more serious and new trouble are very real; first, because it is difficult to predict what the pattern of misuse will next be and those exposed to it have become much more vulnerable.

Second, there are evil men who see a profit in exploiting misuse, and have greater resources and greater opportunities for doing so, whether by manufacturing new drugs for this market or by smuggling and trafficking. Third is the speed of change in fashion for drugs, which is so depressing; and fashions can be spread by such a handful of irresponsible medical practitioners.

This has meant that our defenses are far too inflexible against these evils. The legislative scene is static, but the drug scene is constantly changing. And the Home Secretary concluded, 'There is a need for different treatment of different groups. The addicts of the hard drugs—those who are on heroin or have been weaned from it and are on methodone or are injecting barbiturates—are very sick people, unable to face the

problems of life, unable to come to terms with life or with their
fellows. These people need help and understanding and treatment. At the other end of the scale are the youngsters who experiment for kicks. Most of them escape the worst consequences,
but some are caught in the web at regular intervals.'

Before I close this brief reference to medical aspects of the
drug problem in Britain, I would like to refer to a statement in
the *Annual Report of the Chief Medical Officer of the Department of Health and Social Security, 1968,*[5] in which Sir George
Godber said the following:

> There is now evidence to suggest that medical services are
> beginning to contain the problem of heroin addiction. For
> example, it is known that the total amounts of heroin prescribed
> to addicts throughout the country are being gradually reduced
> and the number of new outpatients reported by the clinics fell
> from 398 in April 1968 to 67 in December 1968.
>   Moreover, of these patients attending the special clinics,
> many are no longer receiving heroin. For example, a sample
> of 702 outpatients in 1968 showed the following figures:
>
> | | |
> |---|---|
> | Receiving heroin on a nonreducing basis | 214 |
> | Receiving heroin on a reducing basis | 217 |
> | Withdrawn from heroin | 271 |
>
> Of those withdrawn from heroin, 111, or 40 percent, had been
> withdrawn from all narcotics.

I do hope these 111 patients, Britain's first "cures" since the
implementation of the recommendations of the Second Brain
Committee, are being followed up in a scientific way in the community.

Before I close, may I refer, albeit briefly, to epidemiological
aspects of the drug problem in our two nations. I am indebted
to Professor John C. Ball of Temple University, Philadelphia,
Pennsylvania for permission to quote the following:

> Although opiate addicts live throughout the United States,
> there is a marked concentration in three states—New York,
> Illinois and California. In these states are found 77 percent of
> the active addicts known to the Bureau of Narcotics (BNDD)
> and 50 percent of the patients admitted to the Lexington and
> Fort Worth Hospitals. Both the concentration of addicts in the
> more urbanized states and the absence of opiate users in the
> rural states is striking. Thus, New York, New Jersey, Michigan

and Illinois are high addiction states, while Maine, New Hampshire, Iowa and the Dakotas have extremely few addicts. It is important in this regard to compare rates of addiction as well as the absolute numbers of drug users.

An analysis of geographic distribution by states somewhat obscures the fact that opiate addiction has become a metropolitan phenomenon. Most addicts live in cities. Furthermore, they tend to be disproportionately concentrated in our largest cities. New York, Chicago and Los Angeles are the focal points of metropolitan addiction—well over half of the nation's addicts live in these three cities. The remainder of the addict population resides mostly in other large cities; 92 percent of Lexington-Fort Worth patients came from standard metropolitan statistical areas—that is, cities of at least 50,000 population. Still, some opiate addicts live in small towns, especially in the Southern States.

Not only are the users of heroin and other 'hard' narcotics concentrated in our metropolitan centers, but they reside in certain sections of these cities. The areas of high rates of drug abuse tend to be deteriorating neighborhoods and slum ghettos. The reason for this ecological concentration is that the onset and continuation of opiate addiction is commonly a group process which requires the existence of a drug subculture, and most addicts now live in these slum areas. Conversely, addiction rates are low in stable working-class and middle-class areas. Perhaps contrary to expectations, drug use is not prevalent in skid row sections of large cities.

In Britain, a summary of a paper by Stimson and Ogborne of the Addiction Research Unit, the Institute of Psychiatry, London, entitled "A Survey of Addicts Prescribed Heroin at London Clinics"[6] reads as follows:

A representative sample of heroin addicts being prescribed heroin was selected from London clinics. One hundred and eleven (86.7%) of the sample selected were interviewed between March and November 1969.

Eighty-four (76%) were male and twenty-seven (24%) were female. The mean age was 25.0 years, with 69 percent being age 25 and under. Thirty-nine percent were currently in full-time employment, and current employment status was significantly related to previous work pattern. Eighty-four percent reported that in the month prior to interview they used drugs other than those prescribed for them by the clinic and 89 percent regularly used unsterile injection techniques. Thirty-four percent reported criminal activities other than those covered by the Drugs Acts during the three months prior to interview. Fifty-one percent had at some time been given inpatient treatment for withdrawal from drugs; 36 percent had at some time been given hospital treatment for physical complications associated with drug use; the most frequent complication reported was abscesses (46%).

. . . .

Current employment status and the degree of involvement with other addicts was significantly related to other areas of behavior. It appears that there are some addicts who are 'stable,' but these are a small proportion of the total population investigated here. Evidence concerning the validity of the interview data is presented.

REFERENCES

1. Yolles, Stanley F.: The Current Drug Scene. Paper read before Communicable Disease Center, Department of Health, Education, and Welfare, U. S. Public Health Service, Atlanta, Georgia, February 13, 1970.
2. Phillipson, Richard V. (Ed.): *Modern Trends in Drug Dependence and Alcoholism. New York,* Appleton-Century-Croft, 1970.
3. Statement by Morton G. Miller, M.D., Acting Associate Director for Special and Collaborative Programs, National Institute of Mental Health, before the Special Subcommittee on Alcoholism and Narcotics of the Committee on Labor and Public Welfare, United States Senate on S.3562 (a bill to provide a comprehensive federal program for the prevention and treatment of drug abuse and drug dependence) March 24, 1970.
4. Parliamentary Debates (HANSARD) *House of Commons Official Report, 798 (No. 87):* 1445-1560, March 1970.
5. *Annual Report of the Chief Medical Officer of the Department of Health and Social Security, 1968.* London, Her Majesty's Stationery Office.
6. Stimson, G. V., and Ogborne, A. C.: Survey of addicts prescribed heroin at London clinics. *Lancet,* May 30, 1970.

5

Synanon: How It Works, Why It Works

Karl J. Deissler

Though I represent Synanon, my remarks are my personal opinion or conviction and do not necessarily represent any official policy of Synanon. Compared to the other presentations and considering where I come from, I see the problem of drugs less optimistically than I thought some of the other speeches implied. I am pretty much like the receiving surgeon who is inclined to judge traffic by the number of accident victims which are delivered to the receiving station. I feel, and this is not meant to be a scientifically backed statement nor is it meant to be polemic, I feel today that the war against addiction in this country has been lost. The individual battles have been lost and it will be very, very difficult to win the war. I base this judgment on the following facts.

There seem to be the following six possible approaches to the problem of addiction. The first approach is the one which copies the techniques and attitudes of *prohibition*. It represents the efforts of the police and the Bureau of Narcotics, and I do not know another approach that would possibly have made the problem worse. Drugs have become totally ubiquitous. If I took one of my best ex-addicts and gave him $100, I doubt very much that there is a community today, short of the small hamlets, where within a reasonable period of time he would not be able to produce any drug he desired. The prohibitive approach has to be accepted as a total failure, and I think any hope that the approach in the near future will be more productive is very doubtful.

I have the gravest concern about the effectiveness of the second approach of *information and education*. Synanon Foundation supplies in Oakland alone, monthly, speakers at such a rate that they speak to between 4,500 and 5,000 high school students, grade school students, junior colleges and colleges. However, I am beginning to be concerned about this activity. The present part of information and education seems to be such that I have a suspicion that rather than it being corrective, helpful or preventive, it has the opposite effect. I have particularly grave misgivings lately about the utilization of so-called ex-addicts as speakers. I believe in our particular area there are more ex-addicts active in the information and education program than the combined units of Lexington, Fort Worth and Corona claim to have cured. I know of specific instances where high school students who have no relations to addiction whatsoever find it convenient to pose as ex-addicts at $50 a crack, and I also am aware of ex-addicts who work as counselors and at the same time maintain a lucrative business as pushers.

The third approach of course is the *punitive* one, and I hope that this audience, with its influence, sophistication and the ear of the eminent Governor, will combine all the efforts to join Chief Justice Berger in putting an end to the fruitless, cruel, sadistic and fantastically expensive procedure and attempt to cure addicts by punishment and incarceration. There is no such thing. At times, in court appearances and in other connections with the punitive system of our society, I wonder whether the society as a whole is not acting out some psychopathology in the persistence of a procedure which has been proven to be totally destructive, totally wasteful and immensely expensive.

The next approach, of course, is the one which gives me the greatest concern. In the article in *Time* magazine, which reported the historical, momentous and significant speech Chief Justice Berger made on the issue, he was quoted as saying that he felt the problem of addiction had to be taken away from the punitive organs of society and turned over to *medicine*. I happen to be a physician. I hope you will assume that I make the following statement with modesty and humility, but I am convinced there is no greater mistake you can make than to go that route. Medicine as such in relation to addiction, including psychiatry and psychology, to the very best of my knowledge has no tool, no structured approach, which gives the least hope whatsoever to cure an addict. As a matter of fact, it implies the severe danger that if you call an addict, a patient, he will respond within the pattern of his extraordinary dependency craving and will say, "Great, Doc. If I am the patient, you are the physician." He will lie down forever. I can claim, I think (and I hope it does not strike you as arrogant, but I think it is factual), that I know more ex-addicts namely several thousand better, longer medically and socially, for I have lived among them longer than almost anybody I ever met. I have yet to meet one where I feel or he felt, or we together felt, that his problem of addiction was approachable either medically or psychiatrically or through counseling, irrespective of the fact that 75 percent of all counties in the United States of America have neither a psychiatrist nor a psychologist available for such services. I am afraid that there is little improvement in taking the problems away from the punitive system and handing it to the medical system. I see very little promise in this procedure and I would like to caution before this particular trend goes too far. Furthermore what hope is there, considering the number of addicts, to bring together a sufficient number of addicts requiring treatment and psychiatrists and psychologists. The total number of addicts is larger than the possible resources that could meet their demand even in group therapy in psychiatry and psychology. The experience in Corona, Lexington and Fort Worth is not particularly encouraging along that line.

The next approach I shall go over very lightly because this is an issue about which I would likely to be too controversial, and that is, I was sorry to hear the government call for the *methadone treatment*. I do not believe that methodone administration can ever be the treatment for the problem of addiction. I think it is an immensely valuable tool. I think it deserves testing and the widest application, but methadone alone will leave the addict where he was before—addicted, except to methadone, but free of crime. Some of us aim a little further. Many of the methadone problems imply, as does the one in my neighborhood in the Bay Area, that the program, of course, is going to be combined with psychiatric and group therapy and psychological and social counseling. If that should occur, its cost will become astronomical. There is one very curious thing. I have the quotation from the man who is in charge of the program and his department has a statistic of the probable numbers of heroin addicts in his community. The same department has published a notice which shows that the number of applicants for the methadone program are three times the number of estimated heroin users, which I think is some kind of a curious thing.

Finally, all these programs, of course, are characterized among other things by their alleged goals or stated goals, and I think I owe you a definition of the goal Synanon has. There are some very curious goals. To my chagrin I found for instance the Narcotic Prevention Act apparently has the goal of producing human beings with drug-free urine, which I do not think is quite the answer to the problem. While trying to find a definition, I happened to be in New York and walked into the World Health Organization Center, where I found a magnificent slab or marble with the following inscription: Health is a state of complete physical, mental and social well-being and not merely the absence of disease or infirmity. I think it is fair to say that *Synanon's goal is to offer the addict an opportunity for health as a state of complete physical, mental and social well-being and not merely the absence of drug use or drug abuse or addiction.* It is no less than that and you are invited to measure our failures and our successes on the yardstick of this goal. At the present time Synanon is twelve years old. It originated as you know through the initiative of Mr. Charles Dederich. On the day I left we had 1561 people in residence in Synanon. During these twelve years, an extraordinary thing has happened. In the last five years alone the median age has dropped progressively from 35 to 32 years of age and precipitously last year to 21 years of age, fully half of the population is less than 21 years of age. The youngest is 14 years of age, and we regret that the peculiar laws of the State of California, requiring court orders and guardianships, make it impossible to take the applicants we have between the ages of 8 and 14. In the last six months something has happened, in our area at least, which made me purposely make the rather extreme statement that since we have lost the battles, I think we are in danger of losing the war. I have never in my wildest fears anticipated the increase of heroin abuse that we have seen in the last six months. Members from the

Haight-Ashbury Clinic have mentioned increases from five to ten fold, and all of these increases have occurred in the youngest age group. What has happened there I do not know, but what we receive now as applicants promise us that our problem has acquired a new and immensely omnious dimension.

The Synanon program relies entirely on free participation. The doors into and out of Synanon are open 24-hours a day; hence, the only people who are there want to be there. Anybody can leave anytime. Now what is the premise under which the Synanon process takes place? In my mind, and these premises are subject to at least daily if not weekly discussions, is this: I think that addiction today, maybe not ten years ago, maybe not twenty years ago, I do not know, has escalated from a fad into an epidemic and today is a pandemic. If Sidney Cohen's figures are correct—that under certain conditions like the period following the Civil War, 4 percent of the people given the availability of addictive drugs will become abusers—you realize we might be looking forward to the possibility that we would have to deal with 8 million people who are prone to be drug abusers to the extent to which the 4 percent of the total population participated in the great epidemic after the Civil War. Maybe there is some hope in the fact that this is an epidemic, because epidemics come, epidemics stay, and for some mysterious reason, epidemics disappear. However during an epidemic, it makes relatively little sense to ask the individual victim of cholera, "By the way, why did you get cholera?" I am beginning to wonder whether with the population material we are working with at Synanon, whether it is altogether too meaningful to ask the individual, as if he could answer, Why did you become an addict? The addictive drugs are all available. The restrictive forces have failed. The punitive forces have not deterred. Information and education has accompanied fantastic escalation. So what could be the other factor? I personally believe that the present epidemic of addiction is the manifestation of or the symptom of extreme social pathology. I think this nation is as sick as the known addiction suggests, and I am afraid that it will get immeasurably worse before it gets better.

So we have then three factors: (a) the ubiquitous cholera-epidemic-like availability of the agent—namely the drug; (b) the susceptibility of a certain part of the population which will not stand stress; and (c) the stress arising from all pervasive social pathology. This is the premise from which Synanon approaches the problem of dealing with those who entrust themselves to us. Synanon then believes that the first challenge is to create an *environment* which reduces as much as possible this social pathology, this societal illness, and replaces it with an environment in which people can recover from the consequences of this social pathology or acquire a new life style, a new mode of living or join a social movement which makes them able to deal with themselves and their relation to others in a way other than through drug abuse, addiction and alcoholism, and for that matter, violence.

Consequently Synanon is organized in communities of people who live together. For the population we are dealing with, and I suspect that this is true for the largest percentage of all real addicts (I do not mean the occasional marijuana smoker), any program but a residential program will go the route of all the nonresidential programs of the past. I believe that the first necessity is to take the addict out of the background in which his addiction grew. I think there is no greater folly, and I particularly regret that this folly is incorporated in the NARA Act concepts, than to try to treat the addict in his own community, in his home surrounding, and an even greater folly is to do what is so dear to the religion of the social service workers—namely, to reunite him with his family, his background and his community. This is where he became ill and by returning him there the relapse is practically guaranteed from the experience we have. To make this a little bit graphic, the criminal felonious ex-addict who comes to us after he has hit bottom, so to speak, a human being who is in danger of drowning in the social sewer in which he found himself, is it really a reasonable, rational goal to teach him to swim so he then can swim in the sewer? I believe any program that follows this fallacy of treating the addict in his home community and his home setting is doomed, whether he is there or whether he returns. The only community that accepts him is the addiction connected, the drug-connected community, and this is the truer, the smaller the community is. He will associate and be known by the former users, co-users, by the former pushers, by the former peddlers, the former pimps, the former prostitutes. I think it is asking a little bit too much that he show the magnificence of our therapeutic efforts by surviving in this surrounding.

Synanon believes that the addict should be removed from the traumatic pathogenic environment at the earliest possible time. We go to great extent in order to do that. Any addict from the Oakland area who applies to Synanon is immediately rotated to one of the distant facilities such as San Diego or Santa Monica.

It is very difficult to do any thing for an addict because he has in his very gut a hostile alienation from the square world. Facitiously sometimes, I am inclined to say that it is as impossible to teach an addict as it is to treat him. If you want to punish him, he will outlast any jailer. If you want to treat him, he will extend his dependency craving beyond any numbers of years of treatment. If you want to teach him, he will experience a hostile, dichotomy or alienation to the teacher. The fortunate thing is that his capacity of *learning from his peers* is almost unequalled. All the work at Synanon is done by ex-addicts, and this might be as good a place as any. All the plumbing, the carpentry, the electrical work, and so forth, with the exception of the elevators which the State of California forbids us to touch, is done by ex-addict residents. They do exceedingly well provided we shield them against teachers. All we do is kind of casually assign them to a work crew of their peers and through the process monkey-see, monkey-do, they learn faster than I have ever seen anyone do who was taught. I have gained a great deal of respect for this particular requirement without which, I am sure Synanon, with its more than 1500 people, would not work.

I think it is impossible to treat or even successfully approach an addict group which is homogeneous in itself. This is the reason why Synanon facilities are located in downtown areas, in large cities, as close to schools and colleges and universities as possible. To isolate the addict with addicts dooms him from the moment you do that. He learns that he cannot be taught anyway, and he learns from *interaction* with those people who have acquired the technique of living with themselves and/or others. Now we take extraordinary pains to produce the largest amount of interaction between our ex-population and the general population, which goes so far that within two weeks it is entirely possible that a felonious ex-addict will sit in the dining room next to Doctor Blachly or a judge (maybe the very same judge who convicted him), or an attorney, or other outside people. I believe that this interaction, this learning process in a natural setting within a living community to be one of the most contributing and effective factors there is in Synanon.

Synanon is by necessity and on the basis of experience (no longer by necessity only, but equally by choice) approximately 85 to 90 percent self-supporting. Any addict in Synanon knows that if he does not see to it, himself, that the dishes get washed, there will be no clean dishes to eat from. If somebody does not tend the heat, there will be no heat. If somebody does not run the elevator, no elevators will run. If somebody does not hustle food, there will be nothing to eat. This peculiar fact of this tremendous interdependence teaches the addicts something from which we have learned a great deal—that it is immeasurably easier to live in a residential communal setting by *cooperation* than by competition. How far this can be pushed, you can see from the fact that there exists something called Synanon Industries, which is an attempt to raise money to be sure, but like all work in Synanon, the end-product of the work is not nearly as important as the fact that human beings who have been addicts are able to cooperate in working. At any rate Synanon Industries today is the largest distributer of advertising material west of Chicago with approximately 125 people combined in crews of six, spreading out all over the United States of America and last year selling more than $2,500,000 of this advertising material. Of course the money is not the point. The point is that something works in Synanon which makes it possible for an ex-felon criminal addict to be entrusted with a job of taking a car and five of his peers and go anywhere from Hawaii to Puerto Rico, enter an office usually on a fairly high level of a fairly high corporation and sell them anywhere from $500 to $50,000 worth of advertising material; and you know it is no less of a miracle that he comes back with the sample, with the orders and, by God, even with the car. I think that this alone is an achievement. Now many times we are asked, what proof do we have for the validity of our program? Well, we have one extraordinarily simple one. You know, I understand that the methadone program is so dear to the hearts of our politicians. If you do not believe me, read the statement of the Mayor of the City of San Francisco, because, the Lord bless him, it is so cheap, the cheapest solution he probably ever heard of. I wrote him a letter pointing out to him that if it is true that an addict costs the community through theft and other expenses $100 a day, which I am sure most knowledgeable people will acknowledge to be an extraordinarily conservative figure, the mere fact that Synanon exists and has 1500-plus ex-addicts in its confines free of drugs because they have no money (pushers come to us only once, because we don't have that green stuff they are interested in) saves the community $54,000,000 a year, and in addition to that we are 85 percent self-supporting. Those who question the economic validity argument I feel should consider this particular argument as a relatively valid report.

Synanon does not believe that it has the wisdom, the know-how or the experience because it considers itself model builders. Of course I do not believe any of the statistics which claim that there are about 200,000 heroin addicts in the United States. I think this is self-delusion. I would not be surprised if there were that many addicts in the State of New York, but neither can I prove the opposite. However, Synanon does not believe that any of us at this point is capable of setting an end-point for the rehabilitative approach, neither in time nor in objective. The best way to look at Synanon's work is like this: We do not intend to reach a specific point in a specific period of time. We lack the technique. We lack the wisdom. We lack the arrogance. All we do is give the person who comes to Synanon an opportunity to utilize the setting, the life style, the social movement, the environment, the climate—I do not care what you call it—to rehabilitate himself if he can. How long it takes him is his problem. We are not prepared to either hasten the process or slow it down. The door is open 24-hours a day any time he feels ready. He is perfectly welcome to leave. Any time he has left and fails, we will make it a little harder for him to come back, but he can come back. The second modality occurs when the addict says, "Well, I have been here 1-2-3 years——. Incidentally we like to discourage people who cannot commit themselves to a minimum of three years, because essentially Synanon is the recapitulation of a lifetime of misdevelopment. If it has taken eighteen to twenty years to become a criminal addict, it is not too unreasonable to offer three years to recapitulate in a saner environment the misfire process of growth. However after three years, he might say he would like to leave. The practice and tradition is that his peer group, his extended family, will counsel with him; and they might counsel him to go and they might counsel him to stay, they might counsel him to try, but the decision of what he does remains his. The number of those who have left and have succeeded spectacularly is relatively small but not insignificant. For instance, the Director of Metromedia, and I say this with his permission, in Santa Monica is an ex-addict. One of the senior editors of Doubleday went this route and became very successful. An accountant in San Francisco is one of our graduates. Still there are many failures.

The third modality occurs when the man says, "You know, I'm tired of doing the thing in Synanon. I would like to see what I can do on the outside." I believe that this, what we call life-styling, is the most promising approach in the immediate future. These are people who have become experts in Synanon gasoline stations or Synanon Industry or Synanon Sales or any other of the innumerable activities the people engage in, and they find or need to get acquainted with somebody who wishes to hire them. However they wish to remain in Synanon with the support which they have experienced in the past. This number of so-called life-stylists is increasing very heavily and through a curious misunderstanding it had another secondary effect. We have a number of applicants who are not addicts but became acquainted with Synanon through the so-called square units of Synanon game players, and they are now beginning to move into Synanon in increasing numbers retaining their jobs on the outside. This is an extremely welcomed development because it increases the interaction on a very direct level between our ex-addict population and these so-called life-stylists, and I think the benefit to both will be very considerable and what we have learned from it has been a very important lesson.

Finally Synanon is prepared to be confronted with the fact that a certain percentage of those who enter Synanon simply will not be able to leave. They survive drug-free, violent-free and relatively at peace with themselves and society in the lifestyle of Synanon, but they either know or accept the counsel that they will never make it on the outside. Now fortunately Synanon is capable of accommodating these people. The total number of Synanon residents is increasing so rapidly that we have so far had no trouble, and no foreseeable trouble, to absorb those whose ego strength, personality impairment or character defect, call it what you wish, is such that there is no hope that they can ever graduate out of the Synanon setting. I think this is a willingness on the part of Synanon which, I believe despite the fact of course that I am directly involved in the participant field, has a certain claim of humanity and nobility in attitude.

The last group are those whom we call Synanon employees. These are simply people who have been in Synanon long enough and have been so valuable to us that we simply hire them. We do this no differently than the way General Motors might hire somebody who has gone through a training program successfully and has become someone they want to keep, for not only are these people carpenters and electricians, but anybody who has been at Synanon a significant number of times has a type of training which so far is not available anywhere else. Now as far as the direct tools are concerned, of course the best known, the most criticized, the least understood, the most difficult to handle is the Synanon game. It is so frequently described in magazines and in books, for instance, *Synanon: Tunnel Back* by Doctor Lewis Yablonski and *Synanon* by Guy Endore, that I will make this description relatively short. The Synanon game is a confrontation of anywhere from eight to twenty people with the idea that the encounter and the human situation as a matter of fact entitles nobody to be anybody else's judge as to his being, but conversely that society collectively and its components individually are well entitled to criticize and condemn not the being but the doing of the individuals that impairs society or inflicts undesirable effects on its members. Now I believe it is a very interesting characteristic of our society, and might be well worth considerable thought, that if you structure a situation similar to a Synanon game where people are encouraged, allowed and helped to express emotion (and the Synanon game is essentially a sport-type or a sport-like exercise which encourages, enables and teaches verbalization of emotions), if you let this take place in our Western Society with its Judao-Christian tradition, the first reservoir you tap is an unbelievable reservoir of infantile rage, aggression, hate and resentment. One must have experienced it to believe it. Sometimes I have trouble believing it even now. Incidentally it does not seem to make much difference whether you take fifteen addicts or fifteen squares and put them in this particular situation, the first thing you get is an overwhelming impression of wordless rage and somehow I believe the first service the Synanon game renders, other than finding modes of expression, is to ventilate this self-destructive hate and rage. It takes an awfully long time because there is so much emotion to drain off. It is very characteristic for the addictive population, as well as for the general population, that our culture apparently does not teach us any graduated expression of rage or hostility. Either it is repressed or if it comes out, it has the flavor of kill or get killed. The attack is always all-or-none and maximal, and the essence of the attack has the flavor as if life were being defended. The first things the Synanon game teaches and the Synanon participant learns is that not every criticism is meant to be a killer and not every defense is predicated on killing the opponent. After a certain period of time, something very extraordinary happens. I am very reluctant to use four-letter words in this mixed audience, but in this case it is unavoidable, because after the hostility and rage is turned off, something which I usually prefer to call negative hostility evolves—the four-letter word, of course, is L-O-V-E. This emotion is even more difficult for our society to handle. If it is difficult to project the wish to kill, the readiness to love has no preformed form of expression, no gradation and no appropriateness. It comes out in a manifestation which has been given new dimension, very astute interpretation, and very intelligent presentation by the chairman of this meeting, Doctor Blachly, because this positive feeling is perceived as seduction or as being seduced with the additional monumental threat and great possibility that it may be misinterpreted as either heterosexual or homosexual seduction and the necessary defenses in our society. It might interest you that so far Synanon has not had one single successful encounter with those people outside the Jewish or Christian, white tradition. We have had products of shame cultures—namely, Chinese and Japanese. We do not know how to handle them and they cannot handle the game because they are not able to deal in the framework of guilt and we are not able to deal in the framework of shame.

Finally, the problem of the future of Synanon and its commensurate meaning to the magnitude of the drug problem as a whole is a very difficult subject matter to touch. However, foreseeing the growth of the problem and being confronted with an ever-increasing number of life-stylists and people who have to, or wish to, remain in Synanon, we have begun to enlarge this model on a rather ambitious scale. We are in the process of developing a city of a minimum of 5,000 people in Marshall Tamalas Bay where we hope to put the concepts which I have discussed here to an experiment significantly massive in size so it will become statistically valid, valuable and productive.

6

Drug Use Among High School Students and Their Parents in Lincoln and Welland Counties

Reginald G. Smart, Dianne Fejer and Eileen Alexander

R ecently a number of surveys have been conducted among elementary and high school students in large Canadian cities. In particular, surveys in Toronto,[5] Montreal[3] and Halifax[7] have provided detailed incidence data for the use of tobacco, alcohol, marijuana, LSD, glue, opiates, other hallucinogens and psychoactive drugs (tranquilizers, stimulants and barbiturates). These studies all used large, representative samples of the student population: the samples ranged in size from 1,606 students in Halifax to 6,447 students in Toronto. With only minor modifications the same questionnaire was administered in all three cities, and thus, drug use rates could be easily compared.

Despite wide geographical separation and cultural differences, the frequency of use of many drugs was similar across the three cities. For example, the percentage of students having used marijuana in the six months prior to testing was 6.63 for Halifax, 6.7 for Toronto and 8.45 for Montreal. Prevalence rates were also very close for LSD; while there was more variation for glue use.

Several surveys have been done in smaller urban areas, for example London, Ontario[6]; Fort William, Ontario[1]; and Port Arthur, Ontario.[2] The survey conducted in London, Ontario, involved all of the high school students in the city attending school on the day of testing (11,454 students). Prevalence rates for the illicit drugs such as marijuana and LSD were slightly lower in London than in Toronto, Halifax or Montreal. However, in Fort William and Port Arthur rates of use for marijuana were higher than the above-mentioned cities but lower rates were found for LSD. These last two studies both involved small samples. In particular, the study in Port Arthur can not be taken as representative of high school students in the area since those surveyed were summer school students who had failed their previous year at school.

What is lacking so far in these studies is data from areas outside of cities. No large-scale study with adequate sampling procedures has been made in regions with persons living on farms, in rural-nonfarm houses, small villages or towns. One major value of the present study is that it was made in counties which include all of these living arrangements. Welland and Lincoln counties include large cities (that is Niagara Falls, population 57,490, and St. Catharines, population 105,906 in 1969) as well as small towns, villages and, of course, purely rural areas. Drug use in such areas has never been adequately studied in Ontario, but there are good reasons to believe that drug use in them might be less than in large cities. Alcohol and tobacco have been shown to be less frequently used in less densely populated areas and drug use could well present a similar picture. Also, there is the problem of distributing illicit drugs such as marijuana from large centers over thinly populated areas—possibly an uneconomical practice for drug sellers.

A second major lack in drug use studies is a consideration of how parents' psychoactive drug use relates to drug use among their children. The Toronto study[5] demonstrated that more drug users than expected had parents who used both alcohol and tobacco. There is a need now to see whether parents of drug users are more likely to be heavy users of various psychoactive drugs such as tranquilizers, barbiturates and stimulants. It should be remembered that this generation of parents which is having the first trouble with adolescent drug use is also the first generation to have tranquilizers and antidepressant drugs available. It could be argued that the psychopharmacological revolution of the 1950's has created a general tendency to like and value perceptual and mood modification for its own sake. At present, much of this modification takes place amongst adolescents using illicit drugs such as marijuana and LSD. If this general proposition has any value then, children of parents who are heavy pill users should be users of various psychoactive and hallucinogenic drugs. Accordingly, much of the present study is concerned with the association between parental and adolescent drug use.

Another general aim of this study is to contribute to the epidemiology of drug use. Questions were asked about various demographic and social characteristics. The association of these with drug use will contribute to our knowledge of its basic correlates. The association of drug use with age, sex, grade, social class and so forth has been explored elsewhere,[3,5,7] and this study is an opportunity to confirm or deny the earlier findings.

METHOD

Sample Selection

The survey was planned to include a 25 percent sample of grades 9, 10, 11, 12 and 13 students in all board of education schools, Roman Catholic separate schools and private schools in Welland and Lincoln counties. All school boards wished to participate in the survey. However, seven individual schools refused to take part. These included four board of education schools, two in each of the counties and three private schools. The remaining twenty-five board of education schools, three Roman Catholic schools and one private school constituted the population from which the sample was drawn.

The 25 percent sample was selected by grade and class within each school separately. Lists giving the classes in each grade, usually designated A, B or C, et cetera, and the number of students per class were obtained from each of the principals who wished their school to take part in the survey. Since class lists and particularly the letter designation of the class often followed a pattern based on the course of study, classes were chosen randomly for each grade.

When the number of classes per grade was not divisible by 4, classes were not split into fractions. Taking parts of classes would be disruptive to the school routine and would further complicate the sampling procedure by requiring a random sample of the students in these classes. In these cases one class less than the quota for the 25 percent sample was chosen for a particular grade in one school and in the second or third school (depending on the number of classes in question) having the same number of students in the same grade, one class more than the number required for the 25 percent sample was chosen. In schools with very small numbers of students and therefore few classes per grade a larger than 25 percent sample was selected in order to ensure that the school would be represented in the survey. The total sample included 5900 students.

It was possible to follow the sample selection plan with little difficulty in most of the schools. Only two deviations were necessitated. In one school the principal wished an additional class to be included in the survey. This request was followed. The principal of a second school removed about fifty technical students from the testing room prior to the administration of the questionnaire for disorderly conduct. Since the number of students involved in these two situations was small, it was felt that these deviations would not seriously bias the sample.

The Questionnaire

The questionnaire included forty-five multiple choice items. Students were requested not to write their names on the questionnaire booklet or answer card and were instructed that their cooperation in answering was voluntary and not compulsory. Only eighteen students refused to complete the questionnaire.

The questions covered the following areas:

1. *Demographic and Social Characteristics:* such as age, sex, area of residence, religion, ethnic origin, social class, family stability and scholastic performance.

2. *Drug Use of the Student:* inquiring about the use in the last six months of twelve drugs—tobacco, alcohol, marijuana, hashish, solvents, barbiturates, opiates, speed, stimulants, LSD, tranquilizers and other hallucinogens (other than marijuana, hashish and LSD); also about procurement of drugs; initial time and place of use; and parental attitudes toward student drug use.

3. *Use of Drugs by Parents and Siblings:* including questions on the use of alcohol, tobacco, tranquilizers, stimulants and barbiturates by mother and father and the use of marijuana and glue by siblings.

The questionnaires were administered by specially selected students from Niagara College. Testing took place on the same day in all schools with one exception, and all students in a school were tested at the same time. Administering the questionnaires on the same day minimized discussion among the students. One school could not be given the test on the day set and was tested a day earlier. Since this school was in a rural area at some distance from other schools, it was felt that little contact would be made with students who had not yet taken the test. Students had no prior knowledge of the test before its administration. In order to further ensure the confidentiality of the questionnaire, principals and teachers were not present in the testing room.

The students answers were then computer analyzed. Their answers on each of the twelve drug use questions were cross-tabulated with each of the questions on demographic and social characteristics, parental and sibling drug use and other variables inquired about. Chi-square tests of independence were performed on each cross-tabulation.

RESULTS

Drug Use by the Students

Table 6-1 shows the frequency of use of various drugs found in this study. Tobacco and alcohol were the most commonly used drugs among the students in Welland and Lincoln counties. About 40 percent of the students in grades 9 to 13 had smoked tobacco in the last six months and almost half of these smoked more than twenty cigarettes each week or considered themselves regular users. The majority of students (70.3 percent) drank alcoholic beverages. More than 25 percent of those who drank did so regularly, four or more times a month.

While the illicit drugs—marijuana, hashish, LSD, speed, glue, other hallucinogens (other than marijuana, hashish and LSD) and opiates—were not nearly as popular as alcohol and tobacco, a substantial number of students have tried them. In particular, marijuana was the most prevalent of the illicit drugs used. Of all the students 12.4 percent had smoked marijuana in the six months prior to the survey. Slightly fewer (10.8 percent) had smoked hashish, while 8 percent had taken LSD. Considering the frequency with which the above drugs were used, the pattern was almost identical. About a third of each group of users had taken the drug seven or more times (the maximum category). Slightly more than a third could be considered experimenters, having used them only one or two times. The remainder were moderate users, taking them three to six times. Glue and solvents were the next most commonly used of the illicit drugs: 7.6 percent of the students had used them. Speed and other hallucinogens were taken by between 5 and 6 percent of the students. Opiates were the least popular of the illicit drugs (3.6 percent users). A smaller proportion (about 25 percent) of the users of these last four drugs (solvents, speed, other hallucinogens and opiates) had used them seven or more times. Almost half of each group of users were only one or two time users.

The psychoactive drugs—tranquilizers, stimulants and barbiturates—varied in their popularity (Table 6-1). Tranquilizers were the most commonly used (10.1 percent) by the students. Stimulants were taken by 9 percent and barbiturates by about 6 percent of the students. Amongst users these drugs were less frequently taken than were the illicit drugs. Only about 20 percent of each group using a particular psychoactive drug did so as many as seven times in the six-month period: while almost 60 percent had used them only one or two times. These psychoactive drugs may be acquired by a physician's prescription or may be bought

TABLE 6-1

STUDENTS' RATES OF DRUG USE

Drug	Percentage of Users
Alcohol	70.3
Tobacco	40.6
Marijuana	12.4
Hashish	10.8
LSD	8.0
Glue	7.6
Opiates	3.6
Speed	5.6
Other hallucinogens	5.6
Tranquilizers	10.1
Barbiturates	5.8
Stimulants	9.0

illicitly. The differentiation in the source of the drug could, however, not be made from the data at hand.

Social and Demographic Characteristics of Drug Users and Nonusers

Grade and Sex

The prevalence of drug use varied with the grade the student was in and, thus, also his age. For most drugs including alcohol, tobacco, marijuana, hashish, LSD, other hallucinogens, stimulants and barbiturates the proportion of users increased from grade 9 to grade 12 and then declined at grade 13. For all of these drugs differences among the grades were statistically significant. No significant differences in the percentage of users by grade were found for opiates and speed. Glue and solvent use was greatest in grade 9, declined to grade 12 and increased considerably in grade 13. Tranquilizer use increased sharply from grade 9 to 11 but then leveled off: there was less than a percent difference between grades 11, 12 and 13 (Table 6-2).

The variation from grade to grade was small for tobacco (36.7 percent users in grade 13 and 45.5 percent users in grade 12) but large for other drugs with the exceptions of opiates and speed. Only 57.4 percent drank alcoholic beverages in the last six months at the grade 9 level, but this increased to 83.9 percent in grade 12. For marijuana, hashish, LSD, other hallucinogens and barbiturates there were twice as many users in grade 12 as in grade 9.

For many drugs, boys were more often users than girls. The extent of the difference in use between the sexes varied with the social acceptability of the drug. For alcohol, tobacco and the psychoactive drugs (tranquilizers, stimulants and barbiturates) sex differences were very small. The ratio of females to males for tobacco was 1:1.25 and for alcohol, 1:1.15. There was no significant differences between males and females in the use of barbiturates and stimulants. Female users outnumbered male users only in the use of tranquilizers but the difference was not large (male: female, 1:1.4).

For the illicit drugs, sex differences were greater. Again, however, differences seemed to depend on both the degree of pop-

TABLE 6-2

RATE OF DRUG USE BY GRADE

Grade	Al-cohol	To-bacco	Mari-juana	Hash-ish	Glue	LSD	Opiates	Speed	Other Hallu-cinogens	Tran-quilizers	Barbi-turates	Stim-ulants
						Percentage of Users						
9	57.4	38.3	8.0	6.5	10.2	5.2	2.9	4.8	3.8	6.3	3.7	7.2
10	67.5	38.7	11.4	9.6	8.5	6.8	3.6	5.3	4.8	9.2	5.4	8.3
11	73.6	41.4	13.4	12.3	6.0	9.8	3.8	5.8	6.6	12.8	6.3	8.9
12	83.9	45.5	17.5	16.2	4.0	11.5	3.7	5.7	7.2	12.4	8.0	11.6
13	80.7	36.7	15.7	12.8	6.6	7.7	5.2	7.7	6.3	12.4	7.8	9.3

TABLE 6-3

DRUG USE RATES BY SEX OF STUDENTS

Sex	Alcohol	Tobacco	Marijuana	Hahish	Glue	LSD	Opiates	Speed	Other Hallu-cinogens	Tran-quilizers	Barbi-turates	Stim-ulants
						Percentage of Users						
Boys	75.4	44.7	15.1	13.2	7.8	10.1	4.4	7.5	6.9	8.2	5.7	9.2
Girls	65.1	36.2	9.4	8.0	7.0	5.5	2.6	3.4	3.7	11.8	5.6	8.5

ularity and the amount of danger associated with the drug. For the milder hallucinogens, marijuana and hashish, the ratio of females to males was about 1:1.5. However for the less commonly used substances generally viewed as more dangerous—LSD, speed, opiates and other hallucinogens—the ratio of females to males was 1:2. Of all illicit drugs only solvent use showed no sex differences (Table 6-3).

Area of Residence

As noted earlier, this is one of the few surveys in which students were drawn from both urban and rural areas. There were five categories for area of residence: (1) farm, (2) country not farm, (3) small village (fewer than 200 people), (4) village or town (200 to 5,000 people) and (5) city (more than 5,000 people). The majority (71 percent) of the students lived in cities.

However, place of residence made little difference in drug use rates. Only for alcohol, marijuana, hashish and glue was place of residence a significant factor. The highest proportions of users of alcohol and marijuana were found in cities. For alcohol, those who lived on farms had the smallest percent of users but for marijuana this occurred in small villages. Hashish was most often used in small villages (11.8 percent users) and in cities (11.7 percent users). The proportion of glue users was largest in the small villages, followed by the farms, but smallest in the cities. As can be seen, there was no general tendency for drug use to vary with population density.

Ethnic Origin and Religion

Parental country of birth was, for some drugs, related to the proportion of students using that drug. This was much more apparent when father's birthplace was considered than for the birthplace of mothers. However, no significant differences were found in birthplace of either parent for hashish, glue, stimulants and LSD.

While over 70 percent of the students had parents born in North America, only for tobacco use did this group have the largest proportion of users and this was only statistically significant (p<.001) for birthplace of father. Drinking alcoholic beverages and taking tranquilizers was most prevalent among students with parents born in Eastern Europe (Poland, Czechoslovakia, Hungary and Russia). Curiously, for barbiturates, opiates, speed, other hallucinogens and marijuana (mother's birthplace only) the highest percent of users had parents born in countries other than North America, the British Isles and Eastern and Western Europe. There was, though, a consistent tendency for students with parents born in Europe (France, Germany, Italy, Austria, Scandinavia and others) to be least often users of drugs.

All but a very small minority of the students were either Protestant or Catholic. For all drugs use was less common among Protestants than Catholics, but except for alcohol, these differences were very small. Use of all drugs was most prevalent among Jewish students and students who stated that they had no known religion. In particular, for tobacco and marijuana those stating that they had no known religion were most often users followed closely by Jewish students. For all the other drugs, Jewish students were most often users. Also, for all drugs except barbiturates the proportion of Jewish students using them was over 20 percent. This was found even for drugs such as opiates and other hallucinogens which were rarely used by the total student population.

Family Stability

Family stability is often viewed as an important factor in deviant behavior or emotional disturbances among adolescents. In the use of drugs it also appears to play some part; only for alcohol use were differences in the living arrangements of the students not statistically significant. Family stability was viewed in terms of whether the student lived with (1) both parents, (2) mother only, (3) father only or (4) in other arrangements (other relatives, alone, et cetera).

Invariably the highest proportion of users was found among those students living in "other arrangements." For all drugs, with the exception of tobacco, the proportion of drug users in this group was almost twice as high as for any other category of living arrangements. Drug use was notably higher when the student was living with only his mother compared to those living with both parents or only with the father. Except for tobacco, glue, opiates and other hallucinogens, where use was least common among students living with both parents, the proportion of drug users was smallest when the students lived with their fathers. The most important exception here was regarding glue and solvent sniffing: use was highest among those students living with their fathers, when compared to those living with mothers or both parents. Since glue and solvent sniffers are by far the youngest group of drug users, the age of the child is probably important in relation to family living arrangements and drug use.

Social Class

Occupation of father was used as an index of social class. There were significant differences for only three of the twelve drugs in the occupation of father and the student's use of that drug. Marijuana (p<.01), hashish (p<.001) and tranquilizers (p<.01) were used most often by students whose fathers were employed in professional positions. In other words, use of these drugs was most often associated with students from upper middle class families. In general, though, there was little relation between occupation of father, or more broadly social class, and drug use by the student.

Grade Average and Course of Study

Since this survey involves only students, it is important to see if any relationship exists between scholastic performance and drug use. It should be noted, however, that assumptions about this relationship must be made cautiously. Scholastic performance depends on a wide variety of variables including intellectual ability, interest and motivation.

For all types of drug use on which the students were questioned those with failing grades, averages either below 40 (the lowest category) or 40 to 50 had the greatest proportion of drug users (Table 6-4). Of those with grade averages below 40 over 20 percent were users of each drug included in the survey. The proportion of users in the lowest grade average group was as high as 31 percent for marijuana and glue. It cannot be assumed, however, from this data, that drug users are of lower intelligence; rather for some reason, possibly their drug use, their school performance is very low.

TABLE 6-4

GRADE AVERAGE OF STUDENTS AND RATES OF DRUG USE

Grade Average	Alcohol	Tobacco	Marijuana	Hashish	Glue	LSD	Opiates	Speed	Other Hallu- cinogens	Tran- quilizers	Barbi- turates	Stim- ulants
						Percentage of Users						
Under 40	70.7	51.7	31.0	29.3	31.0	26.3	20.7	27.6	20.7	24.1	20.7	26.3
40–45	78.1	61.9	20.1	15.5	12.2	13.4	7.9	11.2	6.1	13.6	8.3	14.1
50–65	74.6	49.3	13.7	12.1	7.6	8.5	3.2	5.1	5.7	9.5	6.0	9.1
65–75	67.7	33.8	9.8	8.3	5.9	6.3	2.3	4.3	4.6	9.6	4.7	7.4
Over 75	62.4	23.5	10.6	9.7	7.5	7.3	5.0	6.5	5.6	10.3	5.7	8.9

Overall, there was a general tendency for the proportion of drug users to decrease with increasing grade averages up to the category of 65 to 75. At the highest performance level (over 75), there was a slight increase, for most drugs, in the percentage of users (Table 6-4).

Students were also asked about the course of study they were taking in high school. These courses vary in their focus, number of years for completion and the opportunities for higher education left open. For example the five-year arts and science program provides the classical type of general education and is also a preparation for university, while any two-year programs are directed toward training for a special skill and not intended as preperation for higher education.

The ratio of drug users to nonusers was lowest, for most drugs, among arts and science students, slightly higher among business and commerce and science, technology and trade students, and highest among students in two-year programs or special programs not specified on the questionnaire. Since drug use is highest among those students in programs which involve the fewest years to complete and also are not aimed at university preparation, perhaps achievement motivation is associated with drug use.

Drug Use by Parents in Relation to Students' Drug Use

An earlier drug use study in Toronto[5] demonstrated that illicit drug use was especially common among students whose parents were users of both alcohol and tobacco. The present study attempted to extend this observation by asking about a variety of drugs other than alcohol and tobacco. Questions were asked about parents' use of alcohol, tobacco, tranquilizers, pep pills and barbiturates.

The results of these questions, of course, represent the students' perceptions of what drugs their parents used rather than an actual account of that use. We wondered whether some under reporting or over reporting of parental drug use would occur. However, a "don't know" category was inserted as a possible answer for each question. The data on mothers' and fathers' reported drug use is shown in Table 6-5. It can be seen that 15.3 percent of the parents were reported to be tranquilizer users, 14.8 percent barbi-

TABLE 6-5

REPORTED RATE OF PARENTAL DRUG USE

Drug	Mother's Use %	Fathers' Use %	Both Parents (Combined) %	U.S. Adults (30–49)* %
Tranquilizers	20.6	9.9	15.3	16.0
Barbiturates	19.7	9.9	14.8	11.5
Stimulants	10.2	6.0	8.1	8.0
Alcohol	40.6	62.3	51.5	—
Tobacco	35.1	58.5	46.8	—

*Data from Parry (1968).

turate users and 8.1 percent users of stimulants. These figures are remarkably close to those reported by Parry[4] for a national sample of the United States in 1968.* Certainly, the reported parental drug use is of the magnitude expected and probably serious overestimations or underestimations have not occurred.

The questions required parental drug use to be described as daily, weekly, monthly or less, none, with "don't know" as a residual category. Each of the four reported parental drug questions were cross-tabulated with each of the twelve student drug use questions for mother and father separately. The results were remarkably consistent, in that *for every table* there was a significant association between parental and student drug use. For every drug examined, where parents were frequent drug users their children were as well. Where parents were infrequent drug users or non-users their children were likely to be nondrug users. It is important to note that this relationship for psychoactive drugs holds for illicit drugs, such as marijuana and LSD and to a much lesser extent for alcohol and tobacco. The conclusion is inescapable that parents who are users of tranquilizers, barbiturates and stimulants are likely to have children who are users of drugs such as marijuana, LSD, solvents and speed as well as the prescription drugs and alcohol and tobacco.

These relationships may be more clearly presented by considering only parental tranquilizer use and student drug use (Table 6-6). Mothers who use tranquilizers at all are more likely to have

---

*Unfortunately a study comparable to Parry's[4] is not available for Canada.

TABLE 6-6

THE FREQUENCY OF MOTHERS' TRANQUILIZER USE AND THE PROPORTION OF THEIR CHILDREN USING DRUGS AT EACH FREQUENCY LEVEL

Mothers' Tranquilizer Use	Percentage of Children Using Drugs											
	Alcohol	Tobacco	Marijuana	Hashish	Glue	Barbiturates	Stimulants	Tranquilizers	Opiates	Speed	LSD	Other Hallucinogens
Never	67.4	36.9	9.7	8.3	6.1	3.6	6.3	5.6	2.4	3.8	5.9	3.8
Less than Once a month	78.6	43.0	15.0	13.7	9.5	7.8	12.0	21.5	3.8	7.0	9.0	6.7
Every week	79.7	60.3	22.4	21.5	13.0	15.9	21.5	30.5	8.1	12.1	15.9	12.3
Nearly every Day	82.0	61.2	35.9	32.5	21.4	27.3	31.7	40.0	21.4	25.6	28.8	24.0

their children use drugs such as marijuana, opiates, stimulants, speed, tranquilizers, LSD, other hallucinogens, glue and barbiturates. The heavier the mother's use of tranquilizers the more likely the child is to use the above drugs.

Mothers who are daily tranquilizer users are three and a half times as likely to have children who are marijuana smokers, than mothers who do not use tranquilizers. Their children are ten times as likely to use opiates; five times as likely to use stimulants other than speed and LSD; seven times as likely to use tranquilizers, other hallucinogens and speed; four times as likely to use hashish; three times as likely to use glue; and seven times as likely to use barbiturates. However, their children are only one and a half times as likely to smoke tobacco and only 15 percent more likely to drink alcohol. It should be remembered that a similar picture could be drawn for mothers and fathers who are users of stimulants and barbiturates.

The extent of drug use among children of mothers who are daily tranquilizer users is perhaps most striking. About 36 percent of their children have used marijuana; 21 percent have used opiates; 26 percent, speed; 32 percent, other stimulants; 40 percent, tranquilizers; 29 percent, LSD; 24 percent, other hallucinogens; 33 percent, hashish; 21 percent, solvents; and 27 percent, barbiturates. These relationships can also be seen for parents who are users of stimulants. Both mothers and fathers who are stimulant users are more likely to have children who are users of psychoactive and hallucinogenic drugs. The more frequent the stimulant use of the parents, the more likely the drug use of the children. Compared to the nonstimulant-using mothers, children of mothers who are daily users of stimulants are four times as likely to use marijuana, hashish or tranquilizers, five times as likely to use LSD, seven times for solvents, stimulants and other hallucinogens, eight times for barbiturates, nine times for speed, and thirteen times for opiates. However, there use of alcohol and tobacco seems not much greater than that for children whose parents do not use stimulants.

It is possible to look at the data in another way. Suppose one compares marijuana users and nonmarijuana users with regard to the drug use of their parents. It can be seen that 33 percent of the marijuana users have mothers who are barbiturate users, about 20 percent of the mothers use stimulants, and 36.4 percent are users of tranquilizers. Fathers of marijuana users are also more often psychoactive drug users but less often than the mothers. About 20 percent of fathers of marijuana users take tranquilizers, 12.3 percent take stimulants, and 17.8 percent take barbiturates. All of these percentages are, of course, much higher than found for parents of nonmarijuana users (Table 6-7).

Users of speed even more often have parents who are psychoactive drug users (Table 6-7). Forty-six percent of the mothers of speed users are using tranquilizers, 32.6 percent of them are using stimulants, and 42.7 percent are using barbiturates. Of course, this is very frequent drug use compared to mothers whose children are not speed users. Fathers of speed users are also frequent pill users but much less so than the mothers. About 30 percent of them use tranquilizers, 19.4 percent use stimulants and 26.8 percent use barbiturates. Speed users, then, live in families in which parents are very likely to be pill users, especially stimulant users. The differences for all kinds of parental drug use are

TABLE 6-7

DRUG USE BY THE STUDENTS AND THEIR PARENTS' USE OF TRANQUILIZERS, BARBITURATES AND STIMULANTS

Drug Used by Students	Percentage of Parents Using Drugs					
	Mothers Using Tranquilizers	Fathers Using Tranquilizers	Mothers Using Stimulants	Fathers Using Stimulants	Mothers Using Barbiturates	Fathers Using Barbiturates
Marijuana	36.4	20.7	20.4	12.3	33.0	17.8
Hashish	38.4	22.0	21.0	12.7	34.5	20.0
Glue	35.4	19.4	30.4	15.2	35.6	18.2
Opiates	48.0	35.5	36.5	23.7	41.9	29.1
Barbiturates	50.0	32.3	33.2	20.4	52.3	28.5
Stimulants	43.4	24.0	37.8	20.8	43.9	22.8
Tranquilizers	56.4	33.0	26.2	14.2	46.5	26.1
Speed	46.0	29.0	32.6	19.4	42.7	26.8
Other Hallucinogens	44.7	28.0	28.8	19.4	37.5	24.2
LSD	39.4	24.0	25.8	14.6	35.4	20.8
Alcohol	23.6	12.0	12.0	6.1	22.8	11.7
Tobacco	26.7	13.4	14.3	7.3	25.6	13.2

very substantial when compared with parents whose children are not speed users.

Siblings' Use of Drugs

It is clear from the preceding section that drug use by the student is associated with their parents' use of drugs. Since the siblings of the students are from the same family, it would be expected that their drug use would be related to the students' drug use. In the inquiry about sibling drug use only marijuana and glue were included. Students were asked whether their brothers or sisters used (1) marijuana only, (2) glue only, (8) both marijuana and glue, (4) neither or (5) they don't know. Again it must be noted that data on sibling drug use represent the students' perceptions of that use and not the siblings' own account.

Of all students surveyed 13.1 percent had siblings who had used either marijuana or glue or both. By far the majority of the siblings using these drugs had used only marijuana. Removing those siblings who had used only glue (1.3 percent) the percentage of siblings having used marijuana was 11.8 percent. This is almost a mirror image of the students' account of their own marijuana use: 12.4 percent had used marijuana.

On all of the twelve drugs students who were users had siblings who had used either marijuana or glue or both much more often than did nondrug using students. This relationship was as striking for siblings as it was for parents and students. In particular, when the student used marijuana 51 percent had siblings who used either marijuana or glue or both. But only 8 percent of the non-marijuana using students had siblings who had used either of these drugs. Of the students using glue or solvents 38 percent had siblings who used marijuana and/or glue, compared to 11.3 percent of the nonglue using students. The relationship was almost this great for all of the illicit and psychoatcive drugs. Only for alcohol and tobacco was the relationship less striking.

Drug use then appears to "run in families." Children who use drugs have parents who use drugs and also brothers and sisters who use drugs.

Other Factors Associated with Drug Use by Students

When the Student Began to Use Illicit Drugs

Most of the students (76.8 percent) using illicit drugs (marijuana, and/or hashish, and/or glue, and/or LSD, and/or speed, and/or other hallucinogens) began to take them in the high school years, though a substantial proportion had begun to use them at the elementary level (grades 6 to 8). More specifically students started most often (41.9 percent) in grades 9 or 10, while 30.9 percent started in grades 11 or 12 and only 4 percent began in grade 13. It seems that initiation to illicit drug use begins most often in the early years of high school.

In order to determine whether drug use began while the students were in school or on their summer vacations they were asked at what time of the year (summer, winter, fall or spring) they started to use illicit drugs. Over half (54.9 percent) of the students began to use drugs in the summer, presumably when they were removed from the educational system.

Where Students Began to Use Illicit Drugs

The students were asked whether they began to use these illicit drugs, (1) at home, (2) at a friend's house or at school, (3) at the beach or a summer cottage, (4) across the border in the United States and (5) other or have not used drugs. As can be seen, one of the choices, "across the border," is based on the peculiar geographical situation of these counties, along the Canadian-United States border. The most popular (chosen by 49.4 percent of the students using drugs) place was at a friend's house or at school. Unfortunately because of the format of the question, these two places could not be separated. Following from the finding that drug use began most often in the summer months when the student was not in school, it would seem that at a friend's house would be the most common place. The second most popular place (28.2 percent) was at home, followed by at the beach or a summer cottage (17.8 percent). Very few students (4.5 percent) had begun to use illicit drugs across the border in the United States.

Availability of Drugs

To ascertain the availability of drugs the students were asked how many people they knew would give or sell them marijuana. It was assumed that with the exception of glue, marijuana would be the most easily available of the illicit drugs. Of all the students 57.8 percent knew at least one person who would supply them with marijuana and 33 percent knew four or more people. It seems clear, then, that marijuana is easily obtainable for more than half of the student population, if they want it.

Parents' Knowledge of Their Child's Use of Alcohol, Marijuana and Glue

Looking first at alcohol, it is clear that most (61 percent) parents of students who drink are aware that their child is using alcohol. As well, they usually not only know about it but condone it. This illustrates the wide acceptability of drinking even though for almost all of these students it is an illegal activity in Canada.

However the reverse is the case of marijuana and glue. Most of the parents (77.8 percent) of marijuana users were unaware that their children were using it. While most of the parents (61.5 percent) also did not know that their children were using glue the proportion was smaller than for marijuana. For 12.5 percent of the glue users, their parents knew about their glue use and said it was okay. It is difficult to determine why parents are more informed on their child's use of glue as compared to marijuana. Possibly it is related to the fact that glue users are younger and under more parental control than are marijuana users. Also, glue or solvent sniffing holds rather an ambiguous legal position in Canada as opposed to marijuana smoking which is clearly an illegal activity. Under these conditions children may feel more free to tell their parents about their glue use and also parents may feel that it is less deviant than taking marijuana.

DISCUSSION

The gross rates of drug use for this survey can be compared with rates found in other large Canadian cities (Toronto, Halifax, Montreal and London). Lincoln and Welland Counties had a considerably larger proportion of high school drug users than did these other areas. For Halifax[7] marijuana was used by 6.63 percent of the students and LSD by 2.37 percent. In Montreal 8.54 percent of the students had smoked marijuana and 3.02 percent had taken LSD.[3] However, these rates for Halifax and Montreal include grade 7 or 8 rates which were much lower than for the high school grades. For the Toronto survey[5] rates are available omitting grade 7. Only high school students (grades 9 to 13) were surveyed in London, Ontario.[6] The rates of use of marijuana and LSD in Lincoln and Welland Counties were 12.4 percent and 8.0 percent respectively. These figures are higher than the 9.1 percent in Toronto and 5.9 percent in London for marijuana. They are also higher than the 2.8 percent and 1.0 percent LSD use in Toronto and London.

There are two possible ways of viewing this high rate of drug use in Lincoln and Welland Counties. First, for some reason peculiar to these counties, drug use may simply be more prevalent there. However, there is a distinct possibility that drug use may have increased over the one to two years since the studies in Halifax, Montreal, Toronto and London were conducted. Only repeating these earlier surveys will establish which is most likely the case.

Sex differences in rates of drug use in this study followed a pattern similar to the earlier studies; that is, males continued to be more often drug users than females. However, for the illicit drugs in particular, the sex differences were smaller than found in Halifax, Montreal and Toronto. Smart *et al.*[5] reported that in all three of these surveys there were twice as many male marijuana and glue users as female users. However for Welland and Lincoln Counties the ratio of females to males for marijuana and hashish was only 1:1.5 and no sex differences were found for glue. Similarly, in these three surveys about three times as many males had used LSD while in Welland and Lincon Counties males only outnumber females by two to one for LSD.

Again, the extent of current drug use in all of these areas would be needed to interpret these sex differences. There are good reasons to expect that with increasing prevalence of drug use sex differences should diminish. In activities such as drug use where considerable danger exists females appear to be more cautious than males. But as drug use becomes more popular such dangers would be less often perceived and more females would find drug use acceptable.

The most common grade pattern in this survey was an increase in drug use from grades 9 to 12 with a slight decline at grade 13. This does not resemble the pattern found in any of the other three major surveys, all of which were somewhat different from each other. However, 40 percent of the students in this survey reported that they had started to use the illicit drugs in grades 9 and 10. Possibly, then, two or three years ago when the grade 12 students, presently the heaviest drug users, were in grades 9 or 10 this grade level would have had the peak usage. If such were the case the pattern would be similar to the Toronto survey conducted in 1968, which found peak usage in grade 9. However, such possibilities must be viewed only as conjecture at the present time.

At the initiation of this project, it was felt that drug use would probably be lower in rural or sparsely populated areas than in cities. This was based on the assumption that drugs would be more difficult to obtain in these areas. This was not the case. Of the twelve drugs investigated only marijuana was more often used in cities. Hashish and LSD were not significantly more often used in cities than in less densely populated areas. It would seem then, that drug use cannot be viewed as a large city phenomenon: rather, it is an activity which has diffused evenly into many types of communities.

Most of the other social and demographic characteristics investigated in this survey produced results similar to those found in the Toronto survey.[5] For example, drug use was most prevalent among Jewish students or those of no known religion and least prevalent among Protestants and Catholics. There were few differences in social class background between users and nonusers. There was some indication that drug use was more common among children from broken homes, and use was especially high when the student lived with a relative other than a parent or alone. Drug users also tended to perform very poorly in school, many having failing grades.

One unique aspect of this survey involved the investigation of parents' drug use. No other survey has collected data on the use of psychoactive drugs by parents. While the parental drug use reported here is based on the perceptions of the students and not on the parents' own reports, the rates of use of tranquilizers, barbiturates and stimulants closely approximate those given by Parry[4] for a national sample of American adults (age 30 to 49). Thus, some confidence can be placed in the students' reports as reasonable estimates of actual use by the parents.

There was a close association between drug use by the parents, especially the mother, and the use of drugs by their children. Parents who used tranquilizers, barbiturates or stimulants were much more likely to have children who used drugs than were parents who did not use these drugs. Also, as the frequency of parental drug use increased so did the likelihood that their children would use drugs.

An important question here relates to the meaning of the association between parental and adolescent drug use. In other words, do the students use drugs because their parents use drugs or is the reverse the case? It seems logical that parents would become distraught if they thought that their child was using drugs and so may take pills to overcome their anxiety. However, from the data available, it seems more probable that students take drugs after their parents do.

There are several indications that this last explanation is most likely. One important consideration relates to the parents' knowledge of their child's use of marijuana and glue. It will be recalled that about 78 percent of the students using marijuana and about 62 percent of those using glue said that their parents did not know they were taking these drugs. It would seem then that few parents have sufficient knowledge of the use of drugs by their children to become anxious enough to turn to pills. Also, if parents were to use drugs to overcome this sort of tension, tranquilizers would be the logical choice. However, the connection between the parents' use of stimulants and the child's use of drugs does not fit the tension reduction argument.

Finally, it is clear that the relationship between the students' use of drugs and use by parents is greatest when both parents and child are taking the same drugs, namely tranquilizers, barbiturates or stimulants. For example, 56 percent of the students using tranquilizers had mothers using tranquilizers and 52 percent of the students using barbiturates had mothers also using them. The relationshrip is much closer for these drugs than for marijuana (36 percent of the marijuana users had mothers using tranquilizers and 33 percent had mothers taking barbiturates), the preferred drug among the students. It seems likely, then, that students were first modeling their drug use after their parents' pattern of use. In some cases this drug-taking tendency generalizes to a broader acceptance of a variety of drugs, including marijuana, LSD, glue, other hallucinogens and others. In any case, it is clear that many adolescent drug users live in families where parental drug use is common.

The rates of marijuana and glue use among the siblings of the students also indicated that drug use involved the entire family. Fifty-one percent of the students who had used marijuana had siblings who had used marijuana and/or glue. Drug use among parents and their adolescents are not isolated but interconnected activities. Possibly, they are interconnected in such a way that a decrease in parental drug use may lead to a decrease in the child's drug use, although at present this must be viewed only as a supposition.

The association between the use of drugs by the parents and adolescents is an area which needs much future research. Propositions raised here, such as children modeling their drug use habits after the patterns of their parents are, as yet, partly assumptions. Detailed data obtained directly from parents on their drug use, child-rearing practices, their relationship with their child and their attitudes toward his or her drug use would be valuable additions to future surveys.

It seems evident that the target for drug education should not be just the student in school but the entire family. Parents need to consider whether their own drug use has a direct bearing on their children's drug use. Evidence presented here indicated that much student drug use cannot be decreased without a concomitant decrease in parental drug use. There are indications from this study that drug education should not be confined to the school system but should become more of a total community program. It should be remembered that over half (55 percent) of the students began to use illicit drugs in the summer, when they were out of school. Possibly then, the community does not provide enough activities to interest and involve them during the summer vacation. While in school much of their time is taken up in class or in completing assignments. During the summer many students probably are unemployed and understimulated in some unknown ways. Perhaps there is a need for communities to develop summer programs which counterbalance students' tendencies to experiment with drugs.

This study has further indicated that a substantial number of high school students are using drugs and that these high rates of use are not confined to the large cities. There is also ample evidence that any student who desires to take drugs will have little difficulty in obtaining them: 58 percent of the students know at least one supplier of marijuana. Further research into parental drug use and family relationships would aid in determining what may be the causative factors in drug use among adolescents. In the meantime it appears that drug education programs involving only adolescents are in poor social perspective. Unless the present results are misread, any substantial reduction in adolescent drug use or abuse will occur only after a reduction in parental drug use.

TABLE 6-8

INCIDENCE OF TOBACCO USE

	Frequency of Tobacco Use in Last 6 Months					
	0	*1–5/wk*	*6–10/wk*	*11–20/wk*	*20+/wk*	*Total*
	%	%	%	%	%	%
Lincoln and Welland Counties	59.4	11.6	3.6	4.8	20.6	100

GRADE AND FREQUENCY OF TOBACCO USE

Grade	*Frequency of Tobacco Use in Last 6 Months*					
	0	*1–5/wk*	*6–10/wk*	*11–20/wk*	*20+/wk*	*Total*
	%	%	%	%	%	%
9	61.7	13.4	4.7	5.0	15.2	100
10	61.4	11.7	3.1	4.6	19.2	100
11	58.6	10.9	3.1	5.4	22.0	100
12	54.5	10.1	4.0	4.8	26.6	100
13	63.3	9.0	2.0	2.5	23.2	100

SEX AND FREQUENCY OF TOBACCO USE

Sex	*Frequency of Tobacco Use in Last 6 Months*					
	0	*1–5/wk*	*6–10/wk*	*11–20/wk*	*20+/wk*	*Total*
	%	%	%	%	%	%
Boys	55.3	9.5	3.6	5.1	26.5	100
Girls	63.8	13.7	3.6	4.4	14.5	100

Progress in Drug Abuse

TABLE 6-9

INCIDENCE OF ALCOHOL USE

	Frequency of Alcohol Use in Last 6 Months					
	0 %	*—1/month* %	*~2/month* %	*~3/month* %	*~4/month* %	*Total* %
Lincoln and Welland Counties	29.7	29.2	13.9	8.6	18.6	100

GRADE AND FREQUENCY OF ALCOHOL USE

	Frequency of Alcohol Use in Last 6 Months					
Grade	*0* %	*—1/month* %	*~2/month* %	*~3/month* %	*~4+/month* %	*Total* %
9	42.6	26.8	11.7	6.3	12.6	100
10	32.5	28.6	13.8	8.5	16.6	100
11	26.4	29.0	15.1	10.3	19.1	100
12	16.1	33.4	15.7	10.6	24.2	100
13	19.3	28.6	14.7	8.3	29.0	100

SEX AND FREQUENCY OF ALCOHOL USE

Frequency of Alcohol Use in Last 6 Months

Sex	*0* %	*—1/month* %	*~2/month* %	*~3/month* %	*~4+/month* %	*Total* %
Boys	24.6	26.0	14.7	9.2	25.5	100
Girls	34.9	32.4	13.2	8.1	11.5	100

TABLE 6-10
INCIDENCE OF MARIJUANA USE

	Frequency of Marijuana Use in Last 6 Months					
	0 %	1–2 %	3–4 %	5–6 %	7+ %	Total %
Lincoln and Welland Counties	87.6	4.9	1.8	1.4	4.3	100.0

GRADE AND FREQUENCY OF MARIJUANA USE

Grade	Frequency of Marijuana Use in Last 6 Months					
	0 %	1–2 %	3–4 %	5–6 %	7+ %	Total %
9	92.1	3.7	1.4	0.6	2.2	100
10	88.7	4.4	1.6	1.3	4.1	100
11	86.6	4.6	2.0	1.8	5.0	100
12	82.6	7.2	2.4	2.3	5.5	100
13	84.3	5.4	1.9	1.9	6.4	100

SEX AND FREQUENCY OF MARIJUANA USE

Sex	Frequency of Marijuana Use in Last 6 Months					
	0 %	1–2 %	3–4 %	5–6 %	7+ %	Total %
Boys	85.0	5.6	2.1	1.7	5.7	100
Girls	90.6	4.2	1.6	1.2	2.4	100

Progress in Drug Abuse

TABLE 6-11

INCIDENCE OF HASHISH USE

	Frequency of Hashish Use in Last 6 Months					
	0 %	*1–2* %	*3–4* %	*5–6* %	*7+* %	*Total* %
Lincoln and Welland Counties	89.2	4.7	1.7	1.1	3.2	100

GRADE AND FREQUENCY OF HASHISH USE

Grade	*Frequency of Hashish Use in Last 6 Months*					
	0 %	*1–2* %	*3–4* %	*5–6* %	*7+* %	*Total* %
9	93.5	3.5	1.0	0.8	1.2	100
10	90.4	3.9	1.9	1.1	2.7	100
11	87.8	5.1	1.7	0.7	4.7	100
12	83.8	7.1	2.2	2.2	4.7	100
13	87.2	4.8	2.3	1.2	4.5	100

SEX AND FREQUENCY OF HASHISH USE

Sex	*Frequency of Hashish Use in Last 6 Months*					
	0 %	*1–2* %	*3–4* %	*5–6* %	*7+* %	*Total* %
Boys	86.8	5.5	2.3	1.1	4.3	100
Girls	92.0	4.0	1.0	1.2	1.9	100

TABLE 6-12

INCIDENCE OF GLUE AND SOLVENT USE

	Frequency of Glue and Solvent Use in Last 6 Months					
	0 %	*1–2* %	*3–4* %	*5–6* %	*7+* %	*Total* %
Lincoln and Welland Counties	92.4	4.6	1.0	0.4	1.6	100

GRADE AND FREQUENCY OF GLUE AND SOLVENT USE

Grade	*Frequency of Glue and Solvent Use in Last 6 Months*					
	0 %	*1–2* %	*3–4* %	*5–6* %	*7+* %	*Total* %
9	89.8	6.9	1.5	0.5	1.4	100
10	91.5	5.1	1.1	0.5	1.8	100
11	94.0	3.9	0.5	0.4	1.3	100
12	96.0	2.3	0.5	0.3	0.8	100
13	93.4	2.5	1.0	0.0	3.1	100

SEX AND FREQUENCY OF GLUE AND SOLVENT USE

Sex	*Frequency of Glue and Solvent Use in Last 6 Months*					
	0 %	*1–2* %	*3–4* %	*5–6* %	*7+* %	*Total* %
Boys	92.2	4.3	1.0	0.4	2.1	100
Girls	93.0	4.9	0.8	0.4	0.9	100

TABLE 6-13

INCIDENCE OF BARBITURATE USE

	Frequency of Barbiturate Use in Last 6 Months					
	0	*1–2*	*3–4*	*5–6*	*7+*	*Total*
	%	%	%	%	%	%
Lincoln and Welland Counties	94.2	3.2	1.0	0.5	1.1	100

GRADE AND FREQUENCY OF BARBITURATE USE

Grade	*Frequency of Barbiturate Use in Last 6 Months*					
	0	*1–2*	*3–4*	*5–6*	*7+*	*Total*
	%	%	%	%	%	%
9	96.3	2.3	0.4	0.4	0.6	100
10	94.6	2.8	1.1	0.7	0.8	100
11	93.7	3.4	1.0	0.5	1.5	100
12	92.0	4.7	1.5	0.3	1.5	100
13	92.3	3.9	1.2	0.2	2.5	100

SEX AND FREQUENCY OF BARBITURATE USE

Sex	*Frequency of Barbiturate Use in Last 6 Months*					
	0	*1–2*	*3–4*	*5–6*	*7+*	*Total*
	%	%	%	%	%	%
Boys	94.3	3.0	1.1	0.5	1.2	100
Girls	94.4	3.4	0.7	0.5	1.0	100

TABLE 6-14

INCIDENCE OF OPIATE USE

	Frequency of Opiate Use in Last 6 Months					
	0 %	*1–2* %	*3–4* %	*5–6* %	*7+* %	*Total* %
Lincoln and Welland Counties	96.4	1.9	0.6	0.2	0.9	100

GRADE AND FREQUENCY OF OPIATE USE

Grade	Frequency of Opiate Use in Last 6 Months					
	0 %	*1–2* %	*3–4* %	*5–6* %	*7+* %	*Total* %
9	97.1	1.7	0.5	0.0	0.7	100
10	96.5	2.0	0.7	0.1	0.7	100
11	96.2	1.6	0.5	0.4	1.4	100
12	96.4	2.2	0.6	0.1	0.7	100
13	94.8	1.9	1.0	0.4	1.9	100

SEX AND FREQUENCY OF OPIATE USE

Sex	Frequency of Opiate Use in Last 6 Months					
	0 %	*1–2* %	*3–4* %	*5–6* %	*7+* %	*Total* %
Boys	95.6	2.2	0.7	0.2	1.4	100
Girls	97.5	1.6	0.4	0.1	0.4	100

TABLE 6-15

INCIDENCE OF STIMULANT USE

| | *Frequency of Stimulant Use in Last 6 Months* | | | | | |
	0 %	*1–2* %	*3–4* %	*5–6* %	*7+* %	*Total* %
Lincoln and Welland Counties	91.1	5.0	1.6	0.6	1.7	100

GRADE AND FREQUENCY OF STIMULANT USE

| *Grade* | *Frequency of Stimulant Use in Last 6 Months* | | | | | |
	0 %	*1–2* %	*3–4* %	*5–6* %	*7+* %	*Total* %
9	92.8	4.4	1.1	0.4	1.3	100
10	91.7	4.4	1.9	0.4	1.6	100
11	91.1	5.3	1.5	0.7	1.4	100
12	88.4	6.5	1.7	1.2	2.2	100
13	90.7	4.1	2.5	0.4	2.3	100

SEX AND FREQUENCY OF STIMULANT USE

| *Sex* | *Frequency of Stimulant Use in Last 6 Months* | | | | | |
	0 %	*1–2* %	*3–4* %	*5–6* %	*7+* %	*Total* %
Boys	90.8	4.8	1.8	0.7	1.9	100
Girls	91.5	5.2	1.4	0.5	1.4	100

TABLE 6-16

INCIDENCE OF SPEED USE

	Frequency of Speed Use in Last 6 Months					
	0 %	*1–2* %	*3–4* %	*5–6* %	*7+* %	*Total* %
Lincoln and Welland	94.3	2.9	1.0	0.5	1.3	100

GRADE AND SPEED USE IN LAST 6 MONTHS

Grade	*Frequency of Speed Use in Last 6 Months*					
	0 %	*1–2* %	*3–4* %	*5–6* %	*7+* %	*Total* %
9	95.2	2.4	0.8	0.4	1.2	100
10	94.7	2.7	1.6	0.5	0.5	100
11	94.2	2.8	0.9	0.5	1.6	100
12	94.3	3.1	0.6	0.7	1.3	100
13	92.2	3.5	1.2	0.6	2.5	100

SEX AND FREQUENCY OF SPEED USE

Sex	*Frequency of Speed Use in Last 6 Months*					
	0 %	*1–2* %	*3–4* %	*5–6* %	*7+* %	*Total* %
Boys	92.5	3.6	1.5	0.6	1.8	100
Girls	96.6	2.0	0.4	0.3	0.7	100

TABLE 6-17

INCIDENCE OF TRANQUILIZER USE

	Frequency of Tranquilizer Use in Last 6 Months					
	0 %	*1–2* %	*3–4* %	*5–6* %	*7+* %	*Total* %
Lincoln and Welland Counties	89.9	5.6	1.5	0.9	2.1	100

GRADE AND FREQUENCY OF TRANQUILIZER USE

Grade	*Frequency of Tranquilizer Use in Last 6 Months*					
	0 %	*1–2* %	*3–4* %	*5–6* %	*7+* %	*Total* %
9	93.7	3.6	0.6	0.6	1.5	100
10	90.8	5.3	1.5	0.6	1.8	100
11	87.2	7.7	2.2	0.9	2.0	100
12	87.5	6.3	1.9	1.4	2.9	100
13	87.6	6.4	1.9	1.4	2.7	100

SEX AND FREQUENCY OF TRANQUILIZER USE

Sex	*Frequency of Tranquilizer Use in Last 6 Months*					
	0 %	*1–2* %	*3–4* %	*5–6* %	*7+* %	*Total* %
Boys	91.8	4.4	1.3	0.6	1.9	100
Girls	88.2	6.7	1.6	1.1	2.4	100

TABLE 6-18

INCIDENCE OF LSD USE

	Frequency of LSD Use in Last 6 Months					
	0 %	1–2 %	3–4 %	5–6 %	7+ %	Total %
Lincoln and Welland Counties	92.0	3.2	1.4	0.9	2.5	100

GRADE AND FREQUENCY OF LSD USE

Grade	Frequency of LSD Use in Last 6 Months					
	0 %	1–2 %	3–4 %	5–6 %	7+ %	Total %
9	94.8	2.6	0.5	0.8	1.3	100
10	93.2	2.7	0.8	1.6	1.7	100
11	90.2	3.8	2.6	0.4	3.0	100
12	88.5	4.6	2.2	0.7	4.0	100
13	92.2	1.9	1.4	0.8	3.7	100

SEX AND FREQUENCY OF LSD USE

Sex	Frequency of LSD Use in Last 6 Months					
	0 %	1–2 %	3–4 %	5–6 %	7+ %	Total %
Boys	89.9	3.7	1.5	1.2	3.7	100
Girls	94.5	2.6	1.2	0.6	1.1	100

TABLE 6-19

INCIDENCE OF OTHER HALLUCINOGEN USE

	Frequency of Other Hallucinogen Use in *Last* 6 *Months*					
	0	1–2	3–4	5–6	7+	Total
	%	%	%	%	%	%
Lincoln and Welland Counties	94.4	3.2	0.9	0.4	1.1	100

GRADE AND FREQUENCY OF OTHER HALLUCINOGEN USE

Grade	Frequency of Other Hallucinogen Use in Last 6 Months					
	0	1–2	3–4	5–6	7+	Total
	%	%	%	%	%	%
9	96.1	2.0	0.6	0.3	1.0	100
10	95.2	2.5	1.0	0.7	0.6	100
11	93.4	4.6	0.8	0.2	1.0	100
12	92.7	4.1	1.2	0.5	1.5	100
13	93.7	3.1	1.0	0.6	1.6	100

SEX AND FREQUENCY OF OTHER HALLUCINOGEN USE

Sex	Frequency of Other Hallucinogen Use in Last 6 Months					
	0	1–2	3–4	5–6	7+	Total
	%	%	%	%	%	%
Boys	93.1	4.0	1.1	0.5	1.4	100
Girls	96.3	2.2	0.6	0.3	0.6	100

TABLE 6-20

THE FREQUENCY OF FATHERS' TRANQUILIZER USE AND THE PROPORTION OF THEIR CHILDREN USING DRUGS AT EACH FREQUENCY LEVEL

Fathers' Use of Tranquilizers						Percentage of Children Using Drugs						
	Alcohol	Tobacco	Mari-juana	Hashish	Glue	Barbiturates	Stimulants	Tranquilizers	Opiates	Speed	LSD	Other Hallucinogens
Never	68.4	38.1	10.4	9.1	6.5	4.3	7.3	7.4	2.6	4.3	6.5	4.1
Less than once a month	80.4	46.3	20.6	18.1	10.1	12.9	16.4	26.1	7.7	11.1	14.6	9.1
Every week	81.4	56.7	20.4	18.4	13.3	19.4	18.6	37.8	9.2	12.2	17.5	13.3
Nearly every day	88.3	65.6	38.7	40.2	26.1	32.3	34.4	45.2	31.5	31.2	30.4	30.4

TABLE 6-21

THE FREQUENCY OF MOTHERS' STIMULANT USE AND THE PROPORTION OF THEIR CHILDREN USING DRUGS AT EACH FREQUENCY LEVEL

Mothers' Use of Stimulants						Percentage of Children Using Drugs						
	Alcohol	Tobacco	Mari-juana	Hashish	Glue	Barbiturates	Stimulants	Tranquilizers	Opiates	Speed	LSD	Other Hallucinogens
Never	68.6	37.8	10.7	9.4	5.6	4.2	6.1	8.1	2.6	4.2	6.5	4.8
Less than once a month	83.6	49.6	15.6	14.0	15.2	10.9	25.6	24.5	5.9	9.3	11.4	10.1
Every week	80.6	54.7	20.9	18.7	22.3	16.7	35.3	20.3	12.2	16.6	18.0	10.8
Nearly every day	82.5	68.6	45.5	42.5	37.5	36.4	43.7	34.2	28.3	37.2	40.4	31.3

TABLE 6-22

THE FREQUENCY OF FATHERS' STIMULANT USE AND THE PROPORTION OF THEIR CHILDREN USING DRUGS AT EACH FREQUENCY LEVEL

Fathers' Use of Stimulants	Alcohol	Tobacco	Mari- juana	Hashish	Glue	Barbi- turates	Stim- ulants	Tran- quili- zers	Opiates	Speed	LSD	Other Hallu- cinogens
							Percentage of Children Using Drugs					
Never	69.1	61.6	10.8	9.5	6.6	4.7	7.1	8.9	2.8	4.6	6.9	4.4
Less than once a month	87.8	46.8	19.2	16.9	16.0	15.2	28.8	21.6	8.0	12.8	12.9	12.0
Every week	74.5	47.3	27.3	27.3	23.6	21.8	41.8	30.9	16.4	18.2	18.2	20.0
Nearly every day	84.1	34.9	16.7	42.9	33.3	38.1	41.9	36.5	33.9	38.1	42.9	35.5

TABLE 6-23

THE FREQUENCY OF MOTHERS' BARBITURATES USE AND THE PROPORTION OF THEIR CHILDREN USING DRUGS AT EACH FREQUENCY LEVEL

Mothers' Use of Barbiturates	Alcohol	Tobacco	Mari- juana	Hashish	Glue	Barbi- turates	Stim- ulants	Tran- quili- zers	Opiates	Speed	LSD	Other Hallu- cinogens
							Percentage of Children Using Drugs					
Never	67.2	38.0	10.1	8.6	6.0	6.0	6.1	6.6	2.6	4.0	6.4	4.2
Less than once a week	80.0	46.7	15.7	14.2	9.5	9.5	15.6	18.9	4.5	8.8	10.5	6.7
Every week	83.0	59.7	23.9	19.8	19.7	19.7	24.6	25.4	10.8	15.1	17.5	14.3
Nearly every day	79.7	63.9	37.7	37.4	22.8	22.8	31.4	42.3	18.0	24.4	28.7	23.0

TABLE 6-24

THE FREQUENCY OF FATHERS' BARBITURATE USE AND THE PROPORTION AND THEIR CHILDREN
USING DRUGS AT EACH FREQUENCY LEVEL

Fathers' Use of Barbiturates	Alcohol	Tobacco	Mari-juana	Hashish	Glue	Barbi-turates	Stim-ulants	Tran-quilizers	Opiates	Speed	LSD	Other Hallu-cinogens
							Percentage of Children Using Drugs					
Never	68.6	38.1	10.8	9.2	6.5	4.5	7.4	8.3	2.8	4.4	6.9	4.4
Less than once a month	82.1	49.5	15.4	14.8	8.5	9.7	15.7	20.2	5.0	9.1	9.4	6.0
Every week	76.1	51.1	29.5	28.7	19.5	22.7	25.3	35.2	17.0	19.3	27.3	22.7
Nearly every day	88.3	67.5	35.0	37.7	26.0	35.1	31.6	42.9	26.3	32.5	32.9	30.3

ACKNOWLEDGMENTS

This project represents the joint efforts of several groups of people. The need for a study of drug use in the Nigara Counties was originally perceived by Dr. Eileen Alexander and Dr. Robert E. Washburn of the Addiction Research Foundation, Welland office. It was our great good fortune that they were able to interest Niagara College in helping with this work as a part of their policy of community involvement. We were also able to get complete cooperation from the Welland and Lincoln County Boards of Education. The planning of the research, the development of the questionnaire and the writing of the final report were collaborative efforts, but were done largely by Dr. R. Smart and Mrs. D. Fejer of the Addiction Research Foundation Research Department.

Through the efforts of the President, Dr. W. George Bowen, and Mr. John Giancarlo, Associate Dean of Humanities and Applied Arts, facilities of Niagara College were made available to conduct the study and analyze the data. We are indebted to Mr. John Calder and Mr. Paul Farr, who prepared the computer program and made the first data analyses. Mr. Gary Kitchen of Niagara College handled the laborious task of printing and collecting the questionnaires in a very short period of time. Mrs. Gail Hilyer, coordinator of the Educational Resource Technician Program arranged with the school principals the times to administer the questionnaire, and she coordinated the efforts of the students of Niagara College to administer the questionnaire. We are especially appreciative of the seventy-seven students in the Educational Resource Technician Course and the Social Service Workers Course who helped so long and so well.

REFERENCES

1. Hayashi, T.: The Nature and Prevalence of Drug and Alcohol Usage in Fort William Schools. Fort William, Addiction Research Foundation, 1968.
2. Hayashi, T.: The Nature and Prevalence of Drug and Alcohol Usage in the Port Arthur Board of Education Summer School, 1968. Fort William, Addiction Research Foundation, 1968.
3. Laforest, L.: The Incidence of Drug Use Among High School and

College Students of the Montreal Island Area. Office de la Prévention et du Traitement de l'Alcoolisme et des Autres Toxicomies, Québec City, 1969.

4. Parry, H. J.: Use of psychotropic drugs by U. S. adults. *Public Health Reports, 83*:799-810, 1968.

5. Smart, R. G., and Jackson, D.: A Preliminary Report on the Attitudes and Behavior of Toronto Students in Relation to Drugs. Toronto, Addiction Research Foundation, 1969.

6. Stennett, R. C., Feenstra, H. J., and Aharan, C. H.: Tobacco, Alcohol and Drug Use Reported By London Secondary Schools. London Addiction Research Foundation and London Board of Education, 1969.

7. Whitehead, P. C.: Drug Use Among Adolescent Students in Halifax. Province of Nova Scotia, Halifax, Youth Agency, 1969.

7

Patterns of Drug Abuse in Young Adults: An Empirical Study of Clients of a Free Clinic

John Marks and Charles Spray

Throughout the Western World, young people are increasingly turning to drugs which are designed to change the state of their mind. For many, this is a stage of experimentation, a part of the natural curiosity and the thirst for experience which characterizes the young adult and the adolescent. For many others it may be an initiation into a new culture with its own norms, its own varieties of experience and its own way of life. This is an account of a study of these drug-oriented young people coming to a free clinic designed to serve that subculture.

When Outside-In Sociomedical Aid Station began to crystallize two years ago, its planners were faced with many unanswered questions. Where do the "hippies" come from, and where are they going? What's it like to live on the streets or off in a commune? Why does a person try drugs, and how are those drugs likely to affect his life? It soon became clear that if Outside-In was to meet the needs of alienated youth in any meaningful way, answers to such questions would have to be found. For that reason, a questionnaire research component was incorporated as an essential part of the total clinic design. This chapter represents a culmination of our research efforts to date.

Located near a church-sponsored coffee house on a fringe of

Note: The authors are indebted to James Anderson, Janet Engle, Loretta Lester, Priscilla Mosser, Christine Olds, Glen Olson, Margaret Pitts and JoAnn Wood of the Portland State University School of Social Work, who collected the data of the second survey, and to Dr. Kuo Lu and Lewis Van Winkle of the University of Oregon Dental School, who performed the computer analyses of the results.

downtown Portland, Outside-In could be termed a maverick agency, since it has no organizational connections with any established governmental or health care facility. Relying basically on volunteer professional staff, the clinic offers first-contact outpatient care for medical, social and psychological problems. The population it serves is largely that of the hip community. Thus, our study population, composed of a random selection of patients from Outside-In, we consider representative of "alienated youth."

METHOD

Between June of 1968 and May of 1969, all patients seeking help from Outside-In were asked (but not required) to fill out a confidential research questionnaire. This first form sought information about the patient's family background, educational level, housing arrangements, sources of support and experience with drugs. A number of philosophical questions prompted one visiting professor to proclaim that we had invented a new treatment modality: questionnaire therapy. In designing the form we took considerable pains to exclude judgmental or leading questions. To encourage freedom and richness of responses, we offered many a fill-in blank thus avoiding the mechanistic and impersonal flavor of a forced-response format. While this first questionnaire did indeed gain the acceptance of our clinic patients, we were chagrined to find that it was far less acceptable to the computer. Responses often proved so vague, tangential, incomplete or truly so rich as to be uncodable. As a result, of 700 questionnaires reviewed, only 333 could be used for definitive study.

Because of difficulties with this first form, we gathered a collaborative research group which chose to design a second questionnaire, one which might prove more palatable to the computer and more precise in its yield of information. The resulting form differed significantly from the first in that almost all questions could be quickly answered by checking one number from a list of alternatives. Beyond the general areas surveyed in the first questionnaire, there were additional questions designed to measure the respondent's sense of numbness, powerlessness and alienation. Use of the vernacular, an element of dry humor, and hand-printed instructions helped maintain an informal and human quality despite the multiple choice format. This second questionnaire was offered to Outside-In patients between October and December 1969, during which time 276 forms were retrieved. Of these, only 42 had to be discarded mostly because of inadequate information about drug use. In this respect the second questionnaire proved compatible to both clients and computer alike, for which all of us were thankful. Information from both research forms was analyzed, compared and categorized in a variety of ways.

1. Differences between first and second questionnaire groups were noted in order to identify any trends developing during the year separating their retrieval.

2. Characteristics of our combined population samples were compared with expected norms and previously researched high school populations.

3. Different types of drug users within the total sample were defined and compared. Details of this classification should probably be described at this point.

Because we were interested in finding patterns associated with the use of different drugs, we divided our respondents into groups based on their reported use of different drugs. A regular user was defined as one who had used an agent monthly or more often or one who had used a drug five times or more. Of the total sample, all regular users of narcotics were classified in the narcotics group. Of the remainder, those who regularly used amphetamines were put into the amphetamines group. Of that remainder, all qualifying as regular users of the psychedelic drugs were assigned to the psychedelic group. Similarly, those remaining who were regular users of marijuana were put in the marijuana group, and the final residue was called the "limited use" group. We had to call it that, since in the entire study population we could find practically no drug virgins at all.

In any event this classification depends on two assumptions which you should bear in mind. The first is that one can grade the heaviness of a drug or drug habit in the same way that one sorts oranges or grapefruit—screening out the biggest ones first and ending up with the smallest ones at the other end. Under this assumption, the qualified regular user of narcotics remains in the narcotic group no matter what or how much of the lesser drugs he may have used. The second assumption is that a drug user may be categorized according to the heaviest drug he has *ever* used regularly, regardless of whether he is *currently* using that kind of drug or not. This assumption reflects the dictum—"Once an addict, always an addict"—which may have certain practical aspects for researcher and therapist alike.

RESULTS

There are some interesting contrasts between the sample using the first questionnaire and the sample using the second questionnaire. The group who said they had regularly used narcotics was proportionately about four times larger in the second sample. The amphetamine group had doubled, while the group of limited users had about halved and psychedelic users had gone down about a third. Apparently in this period of time there had been a movement away from limited use and toward the heavier drugs.

What are some of the general characteristics of the people who come to Outside-In? The characteristics we will give here are those of the entire group, not those of the separate drug groups, and they are ones which do not show differences between the first and second samples.

Overall, the people are about equally divided between the sexes. Women are as likely as men to come in for treatment. They come mostly for medical or social problems; only about one in seven comes for a problem directly related to the use of drugs. Although one in every eight has been refused services elsewhere, the majority come here as a matter of preference, usually on the recommendation of a friend.

They are a young group, most no longer adolescent but not fully adult either. The mean age is close to 20 and the great bulk are between 17 and 23. A higher than normal percentage come from broken homes. Typically, they have finished high school and have gone on somewhat beyond. About a third are presently in school full or part time, and about a third are working, most of them in jobs at which they have worked for six months or more. Almost half have lived in Portland less than a year but most come from the Northwest with about a sixth from California and sizeable representations from the Midwest and the East Coast. Most

have left home (about one in five has been married) and they
have left home at a relatively early age—around 17 or 18 in most
cases. They are, in sum, a population which is partly a mobile,
rather transient one but one which for the most part is stable in
terms of residence and in terms of what they are occupying themselves with. Neither gypsies nor stick-in-the-muds, they appear to
contain some elements of both.

What are the ways in which the groups classified by regular
usage of one drug or another differ? In making these comparisons
we are using the data from the second, more structured questionnaire. All these differences from high to low are significant at the
5 per cent level or better.

At the outset, let us say that in these comparisons we will
frequently find those who use the narcotics or the amphetamines
resemble each other in background, as do those who use marijuana
or who have only limited use of drugs. The users of psychedelics
seem to be something of a breed to themselves. All the different
groups have about the same mean age so that the differences between group are not just reflections of age differences.

First let's take a look on the sex composition of the groups. As
you can see from Figure 7-1 on percentages of females, there are
some striking differences. The narcotics group has a preponderance of males and the amphetamine group is unbalanced in the
male direction, too. On the other hand those who have regularly
used the psychedelics are more likely to be female. Apparently
being male is associated with use of the "heavies." Parry, in his
study of the abuse of medical drugs in a normal adult population,
found that males are more likely to abuse the stimulants; females,
the sedatives. Our males followed the "upper" pattern with their
preponderance in the amphetamines, but they also predominate
with the narcotics, a downer, par excellence.

Now let's look at the family background of the various groups.
Figure 7-1 shows the percentages who say that there were no
separations in their family before they reached eighteen. First,
it is worth noting that all the percentages seem low in comparison
to population norms. Comparable groups of young people in the
schools of Portland show more than 80 percent in complete families. Apparently there have been more family breakups in the

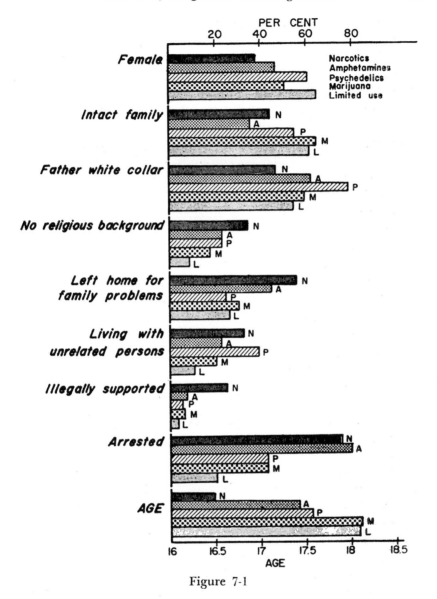

Figure 7-1

Clinic group. These breakups are most prevalent in the narcotic and amphetamine groups, least prevalent in the limited use and marijuana groups, with the psychedelic users falling someplace in between.

The drug groups also differ in the status levels of their father's occupations. The figure also shows the percent in each group who said their father did clerical, administrative, professional or executive kinds of work. It is worth noting that overall our Clinic group seems to come more often than not from the white collar strata. In terms of the overall population, their families belong to an occupationally favored group. However there are differences among our drug groups. The narcotic users have the lowest percentage of white collar backgrounds, significantly lower than that of the psychedelic users, while the limited use, marijuana and amphetamine users fall in between. However, because the clients of the Clinic are almost altogether white, we cannot link race and race discrimination to heroin use.

Religious backgrounds of the patients also differentiated the groups. Those without a Protestant or Catholic background were more frequent in the narcotics groups, least frequent in the limited use group, with the other groups falling in between, as shown in the figure. It should be noted that almost all who did not indicate Protestant or Catholic backgrounds checked instead the "None" space.

We asked the clients to rate the warmth and love they received from their parents both as a child and as a teenager. Those in the amphetamine and narcotics groups tended to rate the childhood warmth low while those in the limited use and psychedelic groups tended to rate it high. While most respondents felt they had received less warmth from father as a teenager than as a child, the amphetamine group showed greater decline in this respect than did the psychedelic group.

A rating of their perceived success with studies in high school also differentiated the groups. The amphetamine and narcotic groups more often saw themselves as having been poorer scholars than did members of the other groups. It should be noted, though, that the groups did not differ in terms of how they rated their social success in school or their general success in getting what they wanted out of life, so that the hypothesis that the users of the heavies were some kind of losers was not generally confirmed.

It is not surprising, with a decreasing warmth at home and diminishing returns at school as well, that most of these young people leave home to be on their own. But as the figure shows, the narcotics group leaves earlier, while the limited and marijuana users leave later. The narcotics group have been on their own longer, even though the five groups do not differ in present age.

It should be noted that the narcotic users also seem to have begun use of drugs at an earlier age. Typically, they start regular use of alcohol at fourteen, a year or two later start on marijuana, and then a little over a year later go on to hard narcotics. The general pattern of progression outlined above is not universal. A case will illustrate:

> P. W., at age 13, first came to Outside-In in a semi-stuporous condition after ingesting assorted nighttime sedatives obtained from a neighbor's medicine cabinet. Two years before, he had begun a compulsive course of glue sniffing, for which he had been suspended from school at one point. By the time he was twelve the patient had used alcohol, marijuana, amphetamines and psychedelics—all in a periodic binge-like fashion. At thirteen he still had not injected by needle but seemed quite interested in the prospect.
>
> From the early age of onset and the compulsive nature of his focus on drugs, we predicted that he would eventually turn to the narcotics. Within a year we learned from concerned school advisors that the patient had indeed been using heroin for several weeks.
>
> Of incidental interest in the family history was the fact that his father died at age 31 of liver complications after a meteoric career in alcoholism.

In general, the young narcotics and amphetamine users tend to be heavier drinkers than are the members of the other groups. In almost all cases of our sample, however, it has been alcohol which has started the progression toward other mind-altering drugs.

The use of alcohol is not surprising in terms of what the respondents say about their family backgrounds. About a quarter say that one or both parents are dependent on alcohol—an estimate which is much higher than the estimates for the percentage of the general population which is alcohol dependent. Usually it is the father who is said to have the problem, but when the father is alcohol dependent the mother is said, more often than not, to be dependent, too. The limited use group has the lowest rate of alcoholic parents, and the amphetamine and narcotic group have the highest rate.

Heavy drinking at home may have been one of the problems the clients had in mind when they said that they left home to avoid family problems. Figure 7-1 shows the percentage of the different groups. It will be seen that the narcotics and amphetamine groups are the ones which show the high percentages. The young people in the other groups were more likely to leave home to go into the Armed Services, to take a job or to go to school.

There may be some differences in the extent to which the groups identify with the hip counterculture. One approach to this is to look at what living arrangements people have, as we do in the figure. Those who say they are living with a group of unrelated persons are more likely to be in some cooperative or communal arrangement. It can be seen that the psychedelic group is most likely to be in this kind of situation and the limited user least likely.

The groups also differ in the way that they make their living. One of the response alternatives when we asked how the client got his support was "illegally supported" (stealing, dealing, et cetera). The figure shows the proportions of the different drug groups who chose this response. The narcotics group differs substantially from the others in the proportion choosing this alternative. We are inclined to believe this statement and not to attribute it to bravado.

The figure, for the next step, shows the proportion of the different groups who say they have been arrested. Note how the narcotics and amphetamine groups resemble each other, as do the psychedelic and marijuana groups. The limited use group stands alone with only 21 percent having been arrested.

These have been some of the gross background factors which differentiate our groups. We were also interested in attitude factors and how they related to the use of the various drugs. Three variables seemed important: alienation, numbness and powerlessness. Alienation we defined as a cynicism about other people (particularly about parents) and a rejection of the goals prescribed by the social order. To measure this we took five items from the

Isidor Chein[1] study of youthful New York heroin users which appeared in his alienation cluster. These included statements such as "Nobody really cares about anybody else" and "Parents are always looking for things to nag their children about." In a study of Portland high school students it had been found that drug users were more alienated—as measured by these five items—than were nonusers.

Numbness was suggested by Kenneth Keniston's[2] description of the typical "head." Overburdened with stimulation he turns off and develops a cool stance, muting messages both from without and from within. Since there was no ready-made scale of numbness we developed five items which seemed to tap this dimension. They included such statements as "There are days when nothing seems to matter" and "I am sure how I feel about things that affect my life."

For the third dimension, powerlessness, the sense that one has little control over one's own destiny, we used five items from the Rotter Control of Reinforcement Scale.[4] These included such statements as "Getting what you want is a matter of getting the breaks" and "When things go bad I try harder."

Our results with these attitude variables can be summarized rather succinctly: there were no significant differences in these attitudes between the drug groups. Moreover, the mean scores of the Clinic group of the alienation scale were no different from the mean score of young people in high school. This high school data came from a sampling of almost nine hundred students in Portland schools.[3] The Clinic group scored higher on numbness and powerlessness than did the high school students but the difference was quite slight—significant only at the 10% level. Apparently the decision to join the drug culture is not associated with a strong attitudinal set, despite striking differences in social background and past experiences between our clinic group and the general youthful population. It can be noted that in their attitudes toward drugs our Clinic group is quite different from the average youth. Our Clinic group overwhelmingly voted for making marijuana legal, while the high school youth were substantially opposed.

A number of background items were thought to be indicative

of these three attitudinal variables; alienation, numbness and powerlessness. In general the alienation indicants showed the most relationship. The relatively poor father relationship of the narcotics and amphetamine groups, which has already been mentioned, is one example of this. Similarly these two groups rated their happiness as a child lower than did the other kinds of users. These two groups tended to be less often members of clubs and teams, and in the case of church clubs, these differences were significant. Moreover, there were differences in the persons they chose to talk over personal matters with. Narcotics users more frequently than the other groups said they would talk over problems with nobody. All of these differences point to the narcotics and amphetamine users as loners. On the other hand there were no differences between groups in the number of close friends they said they have now and those they had in their childhood.

The numbness indicants came out almost uniformly negative. There were no intergroup differences in pressure felt from the family, interest in school, size of school, nor in size of home town (we had thought that people from big towns and big schools would have more reason to turn off).

Similarly, the powerlessness indicants—except for the narcotics and amphetamine users seeing themselves as academic failures in high school—did not differentiate between the groups. Rigid family discipline and the extent to which the family listened to the client's opinion bore no relation to the group classifications and likewise the client's perceived social and general success failed to relate to our classifications.

In sum it is the obvious kinds of social measures and relationships, not the more subtle ones, which seem to be related to the kinds of drug use. Census tract kinds of data rather than the mind picking ones seem to be the crucial variables.

Now for a moment, let us look at the drugs themselves rather than at the drug user groupings. You will recall that many of our population had taken other kinds of drugs than the one which determined their groupings as a regular user. Let us examine our total sampling about their experiences with different drugs. What have been the experiences of the Clinic group as a whole with these drugs?

They start them at different ages. Alcohol is the earliest drug sampled (85 percent of those who have used it started before age 18) and marijuana is the next one they take up, with almost 65 percent starting before age 18. Amphetamine and narcotics come next with about 50 percent starting before age 18 and with perhaps a slight priority for speed. Interestingly enough, of those who have used psychedelics, the majority have started after age 18. Is the trip a sign of maturity?

Why do they start? Most start drinking for fun, apparently knowing from observation what to expect from it. By contrast, most say they started to take illegal drugs out of curiosity. A substantial group say that they tried marijuana or the psychedelics in the hope of personal growth. Many had their first experience with amphetamines when they were using them to stay awake. Narcotics were frequently started just for fun or to relax.

Why do they continue to take drugs? Here the preponderant reason is for fun, a kind of Dionysian drive, though more of those who use psychedelics give as a reason the proper Calvinist justification, "personal growth." A lesser proportion of the marijuana users cite personal growth as a reason for their use, and eight of the thirty-three who justified their present use of narcotics do so on this personal growth basis. "How I shoot smack for fun and personal growth." It sounds like the title of a *Reader's Digest* article. A substantial number take marijuana now to relax and many amphetamine users are still taking them to keep awake. Few say they are now taking drugs because of the influence of friends, to get along with people, to go to sleep, to ease depression, to escape or because it is forbidden.

Not all the experience with drugs has been as sunny as the answers to the continued-use question might indicate. Many have had bad trips; these occurred with alcohol as well as with the four kinds of illegal drugs. Alcohol gave a higher proportion of bummers, most of them physically distressing, than any other substance. Almost a third of the bad trips came from the psychedelics where the distress almost always involved mental symptoms. The amphetamines and narcotics also produced substantial percentages of bad trips among those reporting, but in narcotics the reported effects were largely physical while with the amphetamines they were both physical and mental. The lowest percentage of bad trips came with marijuana, twenty-six out of eighty-one people who reported, and here the symptoms were largely psychological.

Another drawback of the drugs is the dependency they produce. There were people dependent on every drug we inquired about—including alcohol, marijuana and the psychedelics. Of the drugs it is the amphetamines which have the highest incidence of dependency. Almost half of those who respond say they are dependent on amphetamines. Of the eighteen instances of dependency upon marijuana, which the literature and common belief usually consider nonaddicting, two involved physical as well as psychological dependency. Here is an example of one such patient:

> M.S., at age 18, had been smoking marijuana for two years with an average daily intake of some twelve to twenty joints. Repeated efforts to abstain had been met with motor restlessness, tremor, insomnia, cramping abdominal pains and general physical and mental discomfort. Symptoms would persist as long as he stayed off marijuana—which was seldom more than three or four days, although on one occasion it was a full three weeks. To support his habit and ensure a continuing supply for personal use, the patient had worked his way up from schoolyard dope dealing to regional distribution of narcotics, as well as speed and psychedelic drugs. When the pressure and responsibilities of this position finally forced him to find a way out, he came to Outside-In for counseling. Certain that marijuana was not a physically addicting drug, he was convinced that his own apparent withdrawal symptoms must be purely psychological in origin.
>
> The patient was hospitalized for five days during which he received sedatives and a loading dose of reserpine. The latter was continued for a few weeks following release from the hospital. After several months of odd jobs, the patient volunteered for the Army (from which he was technically exempt). At the time we last saw him, he appeared ambitious, enthusiastic and drug-free.

Although twenty-seven of the narcotics group have used narcotics daily, only thirteen say they are dependent on them. Apparently dependency on alcohol, marijuana and the psychedelics is usually considered psychological. Dependency on the amphetamines and narcotics is considered physical as well.

With these kinds of experiences, it is not surprising that many of our respondents have quit some of these agents or shied away from them altogether. Many say that they are simply not interested. This is particularly true for quitting alcohol. A bad trip is the preponderant reason for abstaining from the psychedelics, while the danger to health keeps many from the amphetamines. It is the health danger and the additional fear of dependency which keeps most from narcotics. For those who are interested in legal control, it is interesting to note that few say they have quit or never started because of the legal dangers, unavailability or the expense as reasons for not indulging. Apparently, for this group, information and experience are much more potent in preventing drug abuse than is the pressure of legal compulsion.

DISCUSSION

One of the surprising things about this study was the failure of the attitude scales to differentiate between the drug groups or to distinguish between the Clinic group and the general high school population. There are several possible explanations for this.

It may be that we are simply asking too much when we take three 5-item scales and expect them to give us valid and stable measures of subtle activities. Yet in the high school group, our alienation scale, derived from Chein, sharply distinguished between those who had dabbled in drugs and those who had not, as also did the powerlessness scale, though not so distinctly. Yet on these two scales our Clinic group differed very little from the high school group as a whole.

Another possibility is that the somewhat older population cannot really be compared with the younger high school group. This may be so, but there is a tendency within the high school group for the scores on alienation and powerlessness to *increase* not decrease with age. If this tendency were extrapolated into our older Clinic group, we should expect them to feel more alienated and powerless, rather than less.

A third possibility is that on these personal attitude variables the drug-using subculture simply does not differ from other youth. They differ in their backgrounds and some of the life experiences. They differ, too, very specifically in attitudes toward drugs. But in these attitudes which we measured they are right in there with the mainstream of American youth. Having separated families, alcohol-dependent parents and leaving home early might have made their mark but would appear not to have soured them as a group.

Our total sample is certainly not a homogeneous one. The psychedelic users seem to be a relatively specialized group, more likely to be female, more likely to come from white collar families, more likely to be living in a communal arrangement. In many ways they seem like the core of the old "hippie" peace child culture, but now they are only a small part of the total drug-using culture.

The marijuana users are impossible to characterize, partly because almost everyone in our sample who uses other drugs, also uses marijuana to a greater or lesser degree.

Those who have regularly used marijuana alone seem to have more benign backgrounds than the other drug users of our sample and seem less involved in illegal activities as well. They seem able to smoke marijuana with both psychological and legal impunity.

The users of the amphetamines and of the narcotics have had the poorest life experiences of our sample. In addition to the previously mentioned background items which unite them, they contrast with the rest of our sample in being more likely to have had alcohol- or drug-dependent parents and to be out of school at present. In many ways—on both questionnaires, early and late—these two drug-using groups seem very similar. In order to find out if there were differences between the narcotics and amphetamine groups, we looked at subsamples who had used the drugs daily. Twenty-seven persons had used narcotics daily and twenty-three used amphetamines, but not narcotics, daily (it should be noted that more than half of the daily narcotic users had also used amphetamines daily). We compared them on twenty-four background items which we thought might be important and found some interesting differences, which must be only tentatively accepted because of the small size of the samples. Among these daily users, the narcotic user was more apt to be male. He experienced more warmth than the amphetamine user from his mother both in childhood and in adolescence, experienced less severe discipline and was less likely to leave home because of family problems. While at home he felt more pressure to achieve, but he felt that his ideas and opinions were less likely to be listened to. At school he felt less successful in his studies than did the members of the amphetamine group.

Perhaps these diverse findings can be summed up by saying that the narcotics user was more likely to be a boy, to have been neglected and ignored and to have suffered the usual school and conduct difficulties of "boys who will be boys." The amphetamine user by contrast is more likely to be a girl who came into conflict with her family and experienced their disapproval because she did not live up to the standards of conduct which they set for her.

In this study the amphetamines seem to take the heavy role. Of all the drugs they provided the greatest tendency to drug dependency and one of the highest proportions of bad trips. By comparison with amphetamine experience, experience with the narcotics would appear to have been relatively benign.

It is important to recognize in this discussion that there may be some people who are able to cope even with the most dangerous drugs. Of our total Clinic sample most were drug users, usually regular ones, but only a relatively small portion had come to Outside-In for drug-related problems. At least a third of them, as you may recall, were regularly employed. Most of this population would seem then to be handling their drug use fairly well. How some users can maintain their equilibrium while regularly using dangerous drugs is seen in the following admittedly extreme example:

E. W. is a 28-year-old steady blue collar employee in the transportation industry. Every day on arising he prepares a syringe full of illegally procured amphetamines, injects himself and goes to work. He is a valued employee who has logged more than six years of time with the same company. There have been occasions when he has missed work because of drug use but these have been infrequent. However, because his particular drug scene keeps him prowling about much of the night and takes a considerable portion of his income as well, the patient's wife has felt neglected enough to force a family separation. Becaus of this he has sought counseling. Nonetheless both the patient and his wife can state that since he began using amphetamines, he no longer races cars, no longer gets into beer brawls and no longer ends up in jail, all formerly frequent occurrences.

While this particular case may not qualify as a prime example of "Better living through chemistry," it *would* appear that the patient has achieved some sort of equilibrium which includes a self-sustaining, semiresponsible lifestyle alongside the continuous use of drugs.

In other ways, too, our study population failed to fit the stereotypes expected of the drug abuser. Most would appear to have started drug use for somewhat positive rather than negative reasons. Very few claim to have reached out for drugs in order to escape from some problem or to have fallen under the nefarious influence of a friend. Curiosity and fun are much more commonly ascribed motives. A similar preponderance of positive motivations emerged as reasons for continued use. Again it is done for fun, for personal growth or simply for relaxation. But why, finally, do these people stop taking drugs? Getting away from dope would appear more a matter of learning than of compulsion. This learning may come from a personal experience or from witnessing bad trips or other unpleasant results of drug use. It may come from an exposure to information gained through drug education about the special hazards of one or another of our drug practices. Or it may come from self-knowledge and the discovery of other, more interesting things to do. By contrast, fear of legal consequences at least for our particular Clinic group played only a minor part in stopping or preventing the start of drug use.

As with so many investigations, the conclusion we seem to come up with here is one that some ancient Greek had already made years before. In this case the Greek is Socrates, the conclusion being that knowledge is the key to a virtuous life.

REFERENCES

1. Chein, I. *et al.: The Road to "H."* New York, Basic Books, 1964.
2. Keniston, K.: Heads and seekers. *American Scholar, 38*:97-112, 1968.
3. Marks, J.: Study of Alienated Youth. Unpublished report to the Metropolitan Youth Commission, Portland, Oregon 1970.
4. Rotter, J. and Murray, R.: Internal vs external control of reinforcement and decision time. *J. Personality Soc. Psychol.* 2:598-604, 1965.

8

The Sociology of a Multimodality Strategy in the Treatment of Narcotic Addicts

Arnold J. Mandell

If one reviews the medical literature early in the 1900's on the subject of pneumonia, it is clear that there was a wide diversity of opinions concerning the treatment strategies of choice. The debates frequently had to do with the appropriate temperature of the patient's room, the use of chronic verus intermittant mustard plasters, recommendations as to the nursing strategies before, during and after the crisis, and ideas as to the appropriate clinically defined subgroups to which the various treatment strategies were best applied. As might be expected with the great limitation in knowledge of both etiology and treatment of this disease, there arose very spirited political positions as to the appropriate treatment strategies. Various professors of medicine from different schools in Europe and the United States maintained and taught different positions as to the treatment of choice. Following the remarkable revolution in bacteriology and chemotherapy relevant to the development of specific treatment for bacterial infections in the last several decades, we look back on such arguments as amusing. Yet, we might be able to learn something from the sociology of this early medical knowledge in that it demonstrates that when human suffering combines with professional ignorance and the expectation of expertise by the patient, there inevitably arises superstition and politicized organization of the so-called body of knowledge within which the delivery of health care in such an area must go on.

The delivery of mental-health care services over the past several hundred years would certainly appear at different times and places to be directly analogous to our pneumonia model. This appears to be the case from the early days when deviant behavior was considered to be a sign of malfunction of the spirit generated by the devil to the present day when behavioral deviance and subjective suffering is attributed to the complicated interaction of nebulously characterized internal processes. When attempting to treat psychiatric syndromes, we are caught in a welter of partially substantiated historical tradition, currently operative value systems, factors having to do with professionalism and almost trade unionism, and sociopolitical forces that have become invested in the power (financial or otherwise) engendered by the creation and running of mental-health treatment programs. Certainly the current zeitgeist in the treatment of the narcotic addict is in such a conflictual state. It appears that a number of vested interests are fighting over the junkie.

The justice establishment with its extensive parole, probation and incarcerative treatment programs appeal to the anxiety and righteous wrath of the populace in asking for more money, larger spheres of influence and greater power not only to help control the supply of illegal drugs but to use their strategies to keep the junkies within their province.

Numerous self-help groups formed initially on the model of Alcoholics Anonymous and evolving to Synanon, Daytop Village, Narcotics Anonymous and numerous indigenous worker-staffed and community-supported programs have grown immensely over the past decade. In addition to challenging the mental health profession with new models for effective social rehabilitation and producing a new kind of psychosocial adaptation for a certain subgroup of addicts with abstinence as the focus, they have created their own political action theme in the field of narcotic addiction treatment. Running principally on the "mystique of the dope fiend" (which I am beginning to feel has the same validity as the expectation that a training analyst in fact knows more about people), the self-help movement has pretty consistantly attempted to disenfranchise the medical establishment as competant to deal with these problems, created and promoted resistance to pharmacological substitutive or blocking treatment strategies, and via both demonstrated and advertised competance in the area has more or

less sold the idea to all of us that the only people who can understand or treat dope fiends are other dope fiends. This latter
promotion has led to the creation of a new career ladder for ex-
addicts. What has been begun as a rehabilitative effort for ex-
addicts appears to be a group with the same needs to maintain the
existence of their institution that any other kind of establishment
might have. Synanon's way out of the institutional-maintenance
demand was to shift formal focus from the dope business to the
"people business." Rehabilitation by self-help groups into new
carrers of creating and maintaining more rehabilitative programs
certainly must have a limit.

A third group fighting over the junkies is the medical psychiatric establishment. With the trends in psychiatric treatment
moving in the direction of more relevance to community relevance, toward lower socioeconomic groups as patients, the incorp-
oration of indigenous workers as mental-health care deliverers
and a reevaluation of professionalism within mental health contexts, it is only natural that many psychiatry departments, community mental health centers, and other such mental-health care
delivery systems would involve themselves in the treatment of the
narcotic addict. It also makes sense, following the brilliant and
innovative work of Dole and Nyswander, that the modality pushed
by such medical establishments would be a tool with which the
doctor feels most comfortable: chemical agents. Agents such as
methadone, whether in fact it turns out to be operating by blocking or what appears more likely nowadays by substitution, cyclo-
zazine and other drugs, have become the avenue with which the
medical establishment have become involved with the treatment
of the junkie. Funding for such programs are now, even at a time
of short money supply for new programs, available both nationally
and locally. A remarkable amount of staff support, research
support and other fringe benefits that come attendant on the
organization of narcotics treatment programs within a medical
context make the setting up of such organizations very seductive
indeed. It is not surprising therefore that many of the treatment
programs have not asked the question about what is the minimal
medical intervention necessary for what outcome (and why should
they—either the justice or the self-help establishments have certain-

ly not focused on the treatment evaluation) but rather have fun-
neled narcotics treatment money for use within the context of
already evisting mental-health care delivery systems. Intakes, psy-
chodiagnostics, psychotherapy, group therapy and rehabilitative
efforts have in many instances automatically accompanied drug
treatment for addicts. Very recently this kind of system has been
challenged by the number of workers, especially by Blachly in
Oregon, Goldstein in California, as well as some by Jaffe's subgroups in which the question is asked, What is the minimal interventive effort that can be made by a medical establishment in
this regard to achieve cost-benefit analysis justifiable outcomes
for narcotic addicts? In this time of sagging support for mental
health treatment, training and research programs, it has paid the
medical establishment not to ask this kind of question.

Another group that are fighting over the junkies in some
locales are the political activists with primary goals of political
and financial power for the radicalized segment of one or another
ethnic minority. By exploiting the issue of lack of drug treatment
facilities and the florid tragedy of the junkie, several significant
inroads into mental health establishments, destructive disorganization of establishment power hierarchies and occasional accession
to patronage power has accrued to such groups. As is the case
with such a focus by activists, the approximation of the formal
goals often leads to more agitation as the institutional maintenance
issues triumph over real social concern. The substantive focus of
the struggle can vary from the pros or cons of methadone treatment—who controls admission policies, who determines hiring
policy for indigenous workers—or whether or not a community
group can control the budget. The Yale Community Mental
Center is said to have suffered from such a struggle. We at the
University of California School of Medicine are just recovering
from ours. It is interesting, however that in most instances, the
activists have their own ideas about how treatment should be
conducted. The diversity of approaches proposed by these various
establishments with little in the way of hard evaluative data I am
afraid characterizes the situation with many problems being
handled by mental-health care delivery systems. Crisis intervention, psychoanalysis, group therapy, T-groups and other such in-

terpersonal interventive techniques have suffered from such a lack of treatment evaluation that most intramodality arguments are made up of platitudes rather than statistics.

I have belabored the sociopolitical aspects of the development of treatment modalities in narcotic addiction as background for my general proposition. The general statement I wish to make is that in order to stimulate, develop, integrate, maintain and get support for narcotics treatment programs in a scientific and social circumstances as I have described them, it is my feeling that a multimodality treatment system, if it is financially feasible, is the approach of choice. From our experience over the past several months in San Diego and more significantly, from studying a remarkable system developed by Jerome Jaffe over the past three years in Chicago, I am convinced that it is possible to develop a multimodality treatment system within a single administrative structure and that such a system can reduce or eliminate much of the inefficiency and destructive rivalries between the establishments that I have outlined. In addition, by developing a diverse program, it becomes possible to evaluate outcome and compare efficiencies of modalities in specific communities without operative biases. Over the next few years (in comparison to the past several decades), it will be possible to finally evolve both some idea of the efficacy of the various modalities as well as perhaps, and most hopefully, specific indications for one or another of them depending upon the type or characteristics of the addict in treatment.

The major underlying assumptions of the multimodality concept are that we are currently quite ignorant of causes and cures of narcotic addiction and that the relevant variables are probably quite heterogeneous. One, there is a marked heterogeneity in the addict population even in such subgroups as long-term, hard narcotics users. Those who make up the narcotic addict populations clearly have different reasons for initiating drug use, exhibit different patterns of drug use and have become established in widely differing psychosocial patterns in relationship to their narcotics use. Obviously then, as far as we know at the present time, such a heterogeneous group may require a number of different kinds of treatment and rehabilitative approaches. Two, we assume that there is a heterogeneity of community resources, especially the interests and orientation of various groups concerning the treatment modality of choice. Certainly community support both from the patients and their community as well as the relevant government agency is necessary to be able to create and sustain treatment programs. The multimodality treatment concept gives some piece of the treatment program with which to identify most, if not all of the community groups. The availability of a detoxification and a community run, abstinence program in San Diego reduced the paranoid opinions toward our methadone component markedly. The third kind of acknowledged heterogeneity is that of the goals of narcotics treatment. As is the case with all psychosocial intervention, goals are very much dictated by the ethics and values of the involved society. What the desirable goals of a narcotics treatment program are certainly has not been established. Is it abstinence? Is it social rehabilitation? What kind of social rehabilitation? Is it the reduction of crime? Should we focus on increasing the number of tax-paying citizens? Should the goal of the program be the constructive use of narcotic addiction as a reason for social change in order to ameliorate some of the causes of a psychosocial or socioeconomic sort which may have led to the indigenous narcotics use patterns. There may, in fact, be a choice of goals for some addicts. Recent preliminary findings growing out of our program and more definitive data from Jaffe's work has suggested that the back-to-work goal (the person's old work) may be best promoted by a methadone maintenance strategy. In contrast to this outcome, an abstinence program in a therapeutic community with reentry as a goal may lead to ex-addicts who are engaged in a new career of social action, narcotics program development or other missionary causes but who seldom, if ever, return to their previous socioeconomic arrangement. Such psychosocial character change has been noted in the Alcoholic Anoymous abstinence programs as well. The heterogeneity in available goals may require some difficult sociopolitical decision-making. In one instance, the community may desire addicts to return to their old work and generation of taxes whereas another community might regard as valuable the small but significant group of self-help oriented ex-addicts who can lead narcotics treatment and education programs in the community.

The fourth kind of heterogeneity justifying a multimodality approach is the real difference that may exist in statistical effectiveness of various modalities in different communities. That is, between ethnic groups, socioeconomic groups, geographical areas and communities what is the best treatment? Figures growing out of a unimodality treatment program like that of Goldstein's in Santa Clara (using methadone alone) say 60 percent his patients' urines are clean in six months. I like to ask in comparison to what? Historical controls using law enforcement figures are not the best we can do now. The multimodality concept allows efficacy comparisons which will lead to programs tailored to the community.

THE MODALITIES

The program we are in the process of development in San Diego is to a certain extent modeled after the one in Chicago with certain interesting and relevant exceptions. Jaffe's program in Chicago has several treatment elements to which patients were initially randomly assigned. These program elements include methadone substitution alone, methadone substitution with group psychotherapy and vocational rehabilitation, outpatient detoxification with a short-term therapeutic community and early reentry rehabilitative program and long-term therapeutic community stay with reentry a delayed goal. Our program, which is modeled after this one, has a methadone maintenance clinic, with and without rehabilitative and psychotherapeutic efforts detoxification in a hospital with follow-up by an independent Chicano group, detoxification in the hospital with therapeutic follow-up in the University program, and we are currently developing a therapeutic community. It is interesting that in exploring the specific therapeutic community organization that would be appropriate in San Diego, it became clear that the Chicano addict who represents about 60 percent of the addict population is San Diego adjusts poorly to a Synanon-type disarticulation from his family and fails to develop a useable new group identification. They refuse to stay away from their families in halfway houses; they tolerate confrontational rhetoric of the sort seen in Synanon games not at all. The combination of Macho and their dependence on the females in their family require a different kind of rehabilitative institution characterized by more deferential ritual, more respect and less disarticulation from their mothers and wives. We are currently exploring the possibility of developing a family-oriented therapeutic ambience that seems to fit most specifically the psychosocial climate of the Mexican-American addict. We were struck by the fact that Chicano methadone patients frequently brought their wives and children to the clinic and would consider living away only if their primal or secondary family was available to them.

THE STAFF

A word should be mentioned about the development of our narcotics treatment staff. Through the flexibility allowed us by innovative university personnel policies, we have been able to attract a number of competant indigenous workers led by David Deitch from Daytop Village. He is busy developing indigenous talent from the community but within the context of our department. We have been able to give job security and professional status to our indigenous workers via the development of new catgeories of University employees called Addiction Rehabilitation Conselors, or ARCS. This career ladder has various steps (I, II, III and IV) and varies from $7,000 a year to about $14,000 in salary. Funding for this program which is channeled through the University comes from various sources including county contracts, state training money, and hopefully in the not too distant future staffing money from NIMH. The University-defined job categories produce in addition to an increased sense of job security for these addiction rehabilitation counselors specialists, a fusion with the academic department of psychiatry. A fallout from this kind of enmeshing of talents has been a serious questioning of the professionalism in psychiatry and a growing knowledge on the part of the residents in training that they will be able to avail themselves in later years of nonprofessional talent when creating community health delivery programs. It appears that our narcotics treatment staff in relating to our more conventional faculty may lead to a hot bed of innovation in treatment and training in mental health delivery. I cannot emphasize too much the remarkable and important humbleness engendered in our residents when they see the sensitive, capable and effective interpersonal transactions of our indigenous workers. If the narcotics treatment problem gets cleaned up in a significant way in San Diego (where it appears as though it may be of manageable size), we hope to take the same organization and move it into the area of juvenile delinquency, alcoholism and other areas of psychiatric failure.

PROCEDURES AND PRELIMINARY RESULTS

As patients approach us for admission, they are given several interviews and rather extensive evaluation by both professionals and ex-addict indigenous workers focusing on their psychosocial status, the validity of their story and a discussion with them of their choice of treatment modality. Following this, various treatment programs are instituted and using regular urine tests and psychosocial inventories, the patients are followed. It appears that thus far in our program, somewhere between 60 and 70 percent of methadone maintenance patients after three months regularly evidence clean urines. It appears that the back-to-work rate which is about 15 percent in our methadone patients before treatment moves up to between 50 and 55 percent within three to six months of instituting treatment. The other extreme in terms of outcome is our hospitalization and detoxification with minimal follow-up (which has been carried out by an autonomous indigenous Mexican-American group who have abstinence as their major goal). Of sixty-five patients in six months who have been detoxified on our unit and followed by this Mexican-American group, only three remain clean three months later. Our own follow-up and therapeutic community data await further work. In terms of the evaluation of methadone maintenance with and without intrapersonal intervention, I have some very recent data from Jerome Jaffe's program in Chicago which I think is probably relevant. It appears that in his "holding pattern" (methadone only) program, the back-to-work rate is somewhat between 20 and 25 percent when studied over six month's time. The back-to-work rate in the methadone program, when carried out in collaboration with group meetings several times a week and some available vocational rehabilitation, doubles to about 50 percent. If this back-to-work rate is associated with the social integrative rehabilitative moves that it is in many other kinds of psychiatric disease, it appears as though more subtle measures might show even more dramatic differences.

The therapeutic community (Synanon-type) issues vis-à-vis abstinence figures is certainly a very loaded question. There is little question that this kind of thing is quite expensive, qute long term, and therefore should be looked at critically with outcome measures. I have recently had the opportunity to visit The Family at Mendocino State Hospital and see their statistics over the past year and a half. The similarity of the statistics to Jaffe's therapeutic community programs is so remarkable in spite of the clearly different geographical, social and ethnic organization of the data that I thought it would be of interest to you. It appears that in Jaffe's program, of those patients assigned randomly to the therapeutic community modality, only about one-third show up to participate. Of those that show up to participate, between 60 and 70 percent of them split within the first year. Therefore, the figure in terms of retention and abstinence in a therapeutic community is about one-third of one-third or approximately 12 percent of a general addict population in Chicago. The Family at Mendocino State Hospital with a little bit different arrangement has very similar numbers. Patients originally enter a modified therapeutic community for three months as a test of their motivation. As they enter the authoritarian structure and demands are made on them, close to two-thirds "split." Of the 30 to 35 percent that go on to The Famliy, only 40 percent remain abstinent and affiliated with The Family at the end of the year—that is, therefore, 40 percent of about 35 percent or approximately the same number 12 to 15 percent. In a follow-up of The Family, all but three of the thirty-seven graduates last year have gone on to work in other narcotics treatment programs, spawning much of the same kind of programs from which they came. This is true in Jerome Jaffe's program as well, in that the abstinent people very often involve themselves in a new career in narcotics treatment and prevention. As one begins to compare the efficacy of modalities, methadone maintenance with, for example, the very best of the abstinence program in a reentry-oriented therapeutic community, one comes to believe, at least in this early stage, that in terms of large population efficacy the methadone program is much preferable to the abstinence programs. On the other hand, I must hasten to add that the kind of addict who successfully participates in Synanon, Daytop Village or other such therapeutic community programs turns out to be rather valuable indeed, going on to educate, create and organize in a socially relevant and constructive way. As I noted previously, we will have to wait until all the statistics are in to see if the governmental agencies or social groups will be willing to support one or another of these programs. Meanwhile, however, we hope to be able to generate statistics to present to such decision-making groups.

As I review what I have laboriously tried to say here, it sounds in summary quite simple. I think one of the Chicano addicts working in our program put it very simply, saying that there are "different strokes for different folks." The implications of that simple kind of statement, however, are myriad. The ease with which a multimodality program can move into a community is so much greater than one or another of a special treatment type. The possibility of a wide variety of modalities reaching different kinds of addicts are very obvious. The gradually being realized hope of finally getting some good comparison figures for any community is emerging. I think that the multimodality concept is a very defensible approach to narcotics treatment during our time. It brings together doctors, mental health professionals, indigenous groups, community organizations and government in a very constructive way. Perhaps this kind of program will become a model for more general psychiatric treatment program delivery in the future.

REFERENCES

1. Blachly, P.: The simplest methadone blockade treatment program. Annual American Psychiatric Association Meeting, San Francisco, 1970.
2. Brill, L., and Jaffe, J. H.: The relevancy of some newer American treatment approaches for England. *Brit J Addiction, 62*:375-386, 1967.

3. Dale, V. P., and Nyswander, M.: A medical treatment for diacetyl-morphine (heroin) addiction. *JAMA, 193*:646-650, 1965.

4. Goldstein, A.: Santa Clara County Methadone Program: Details of organization and procedures.

5. Jaffe, J. H., Zaks, M. S., and Washington, E. N.: Experience with the use of methadone in a multimodality program for the treatment of narcotics users. *Brit J Addiction, 4*:481-490, 1969.

6. Jaffe, J. H.: Statement to the United States Senate Special Sub-committee on Alcoholism and Narcotics of the Committee on Labor and Public Welfare; August 8, 1969.

7. Roberts, Arthur C.: The Family. Personal communication, 1970.

9

Sociological and Economic Aspects of Drug Dependence in India and the United States

Gurbakhash S. Chopra

W hen properly oriented and kept within their normal relationship to other motives, the search for pleasure and avoidance of pain are healthy and constructive human objectives, universal in their appeal. However, if man fails in the pursuit of these objectives, he may then attempt to derive such satisfaction by artificial means. If the individual chooses to escape frustration through the use of drugs or a narcotic stimulant, he is a potential victim of drug dependence.

CASE STUDIES IN INDIA

The object of the present study is to assess the role of narcotic and habituating drugs on the social and economic life of the habitual user. A general survey was undertaken in selected urban, industrial and rural areas in the states of West Bengal, Punjab, Bihar, Uttar Pradesh and Orissa, covering a population of nearly two million persons.

For analysis, information was carefully recorded in one thousand volunteer cases. These persons gave information regarding their addiction, its source, their income, the effects of the drug, their capacity to follow their vocation and other relevant personal data. Areas with approximately equal populations in urban and rural sections of different states were selected for the survey.

The highest incidence of drug addiction was in West Bengal, Punjab and Bihar. This is not difficult to understand because these are comparatively more industralized states than Uttar Pradesh and Orissa. With developing industry comes a rapidly changing pattern of life accompanied by many previously unknown mental pressures. Such pressures have induced certain individuals to search for artificial means of fortifying themselves against depression and other psychological frustrations.

Of the cases studied, 70 percent were from industrial and urban areas, while 30 percent came from rural areas or villages. This suggests that drug addiction is primarily a problem which concerns cities and overcrowded areas. Throughout the world, there is a vast migration to large cities. In India, this has resulted in the replacement of older village social groups and close family ties by industrial and urban civilization, with its accompanying breakdown of social and family units. Due to this change, there is a potential basis for the development of drug addiction or quasi-addiction in people who are removed from their original social and cultural environment and find adjustment difficult in the new environment. New social units are established, but many times lack the personal, intimate nature of previous living situations and seem to be artificial and impersonal.

Analysis of the persons involved in this study indicated that drug dependence was more common among persons whose occupations involved long working hours and high enough wages to sustain the habit. Many workers stated that the drugs ameliorated feelings of fatigue and were used to insure a restful sleep. Individuals also indicated that drugs were utilized in order to alleviate feelings of hunger and other physical ailments, as well as to combat the effects of arduous labor. In the states with the highest level of income, there were comparatively better paid industrial populations and, therefore more of an ability on the part of individuals to afford drugs.

SOCIOLOGICAL FACTORS

Poor living and unfavorable working conditions invite the use of euphoriants and other drugs. They represent an easy and fairly cheap means of escape for those who can find no satisfaction in their work or life. In underdeveloped countries such as India, most individuals begin work at an early age. Because of this, they usually lack proper basic education and psychological development. Existence for vast numbers of persons in India is difficult and oppressive. The mere act of keeping alive may require that a person lead a physically and mentally exhaustive life of hard labor. In light of such conditions, many persons find relief and escape through various drugs.

ETHNOLOGICAL FACTORS

Opium, alcohol, cannabis preparations and various other plants have been used by man for pleasure from ancient times. The use of euphorics dates far back in most countries, with many ethnological groups showing an affinity for particular narcotic substances. There have been the opium eaters in the Near and Far East, the drinking of "soma" by the ancient Aryans, and the smoking of cannabis by several cultures, as well as the use of many other substances. These aspects of drug addiction have an important bearing upon its prevalence—especially in underdeveloped areas.

Alcohol as well as drugs are used by various ethnological groups today. However, cannabis is the most popular substance with the economically lower working classes. The psychedelics, barbiturates and addictive tranquilizers, which are widely manufactured, have no traditional background. Unlike the ancient drugs, their use is of recent origin and does not stem from traditional religious or ritualistic applications.

With modern and rapid development of communication in recent years, different groups, communities and cultures have exerted a mutual influence upon one another. Because of this, the basic patterns of drug usage have also been influenced. However, despite this intermingling of different ethnological groups and cultures the preference on the part of different races and ethnological groups for particular drugs still exists.

RELIGIOUS FACTORS

The use of wine and narcotic plants, like cannabis, for religious celebrations has been prevalent from the earliest time. It is intimately connected with the history of man's social and spiritual development. In India this practice has been traced in most of the country where it forms, or has previously formed, an integral part of religious worship. The use of hallucinogens, such as cannabis, for such purposes is universal. In recent years, especially in the Western World, there has been a renewal of the idea that drugs may play a part in achieving mystical or spiritual experiences. One finds, therefore, individuals and groups experimenting with drugs such as cannabis, peyote and LSD in an effort to establish a particular religious situation.

DRUG ABUSE IN INDIA AND THE UNITED STATES— A COMPARISON

The drugs which are commonly used in India are mostly raw and crude products. In many cases they are prepared by the habitue himself, which in itself limits their excessive consumption. Furthermore, in the case of crude forms of drugs obtained from plants, the addicts absorb comparatively smaller quantities of the active principles responsible for producing toxic effects. In the United States and the Western countries, almost all the drugs used, with the exception of marijuana, are highly purified chemical substances such as morphine, heroin, cocaine, amphetamines, Methedrine, LSD and many other newly discovered chemical compounds. Moreover, most of these drugs are taken by injection. This mode of administration brings about more rapid and intense effects. In India, most of the drugs are taken by mouth and seldom produce the intense effects observed in the United States and other Western countries.

There are also important environmental differences between India and the United States which influence the motivations leading to drug dependence. India is predominently an agricultural country with most of the population living in villages. Although the situation is changing, India is relatively free of the rapid pace of life present in the Western World, which appears to be partially responsible for drug dependence.

The motivations to use drugs are, in general, slightly different in India. Opium and cannabis drugs are often used for medicinal purposes. Good medical facilities are scarce and the majority of the population do not receive the benefit of modern medicine. Sedatives and pain-relieving drugs often are used as household remedies and habits are formed many times from such indiscriminate use. For instance, among the uneducated classes, opium is often administered to children and elderly persons for diseases and ailments of a minor nature. Opium and cannabis drugs are also believed to stimulate physical energy. These drugs are often taken by laborers and workers who must work outdoors. The author found, for instance, that the use of opium and liquor increased during the harvest season in Punjab, by over 50 percent.

DRUG ABUSE IN THE UNITED STATES

My experience of the drug abuse problem in the United States is limited. The observations recorded are general and pertain only to the youth in this country. During the year 1969, I was in the United States and had the opportunity to visit various college campuses and meet young people. One hundred of these youth were willing to discuss their particular viewpoints, and the circumstances which led them to drug usage. The relevant data is presented in Table 9-1. It appears that alienated children are more prone to drug abuse than those enjoying a stable family environment. The other contributing factors were associates, the search for new experiences, desire for mystical experience and the desire for a sense of oblivion. All the hallucinogens are capable of altering the sensations of the mind. However, it appears that marijuana, or cannabis sativa, is the most popular in the United States. This is probably because marijuana requires no sophisticated technology or complex organization structure for either production or distribution.

MOTIVATION

A large portion of youthful drug users derive from the middle to upper middle class. They are experimenters who enjoy encountering challenge and risk. Many of them feel a sense of boredom which is alleviated by drugs. Others are motivated by a rebellious spirit and a need to gain attention from indifferent and rejecting parents or other authoritative figures. Marijuana is believed by some youth to be a key to discovering hidden mysteries. This belief is often based upon the past use of the drug for religious purposes. Still other persons use drugs because they are seeking oblivion. Such persons usually take the drug for short periods only. Many of them are from maladjusted families where they have been deprived of parental love. They often have feel-

TABLE 9-1

I. Family Conditions		II. Use of the Drug		III. Other Information	
Parents both alive	70	Introduced to drug by peers	80	Criminal record—arrest	10
Parents alive, but divorced	20	Introduced to drug by older youth	15	Criminal record—minor	28
One parent alive	10	Introduced to drug by pushers	5	Criminal record—none	62
Good relationship to parents	60	Drug used—marijuana	79	Drug used occasionally	16
Indifferent relationship	25	Drug used—LSD	11	Drug used once or twice a week	64
Hostile relationship	15	Drug used—Methedrine	4	Drug use daily	20
From upper middle-class home	72	Drug used—other drugs	6	Age group—12–15 years	25
From lower-class home	28	Source of drug—theft	7	Age group—16–20 years	31
Chaotic family environment	19	Source of drug—borrowing	20	Age group—21–25 years	30
Parental neglect present	58	Source of drug—drug pushing	4	Age group—26–30 years	14
Normal family environment	23	Source of drug—parent's money	69		

ings of incompetence and inadequacy and may feel that they cannot succeed in the success-oriented American societal structure. For these reasons, they seek to drop out of what appears to be an unsatisfactory situation. Frequently, they are unable to make this personal declaration of independence without the intervention of a drug.

It is not easy to assess the effects of marijuana on personality and behavior. It may be that a particular type of behavior is caused by the drug (or other drugs), or it may be that that behavior is characteristic of those who turn to the drug, or it may be coincidental behavior. One example of such behavior is a paranoid reaction observable in certain individuals after continued use of marijuana. The danger with a drug like Methedrine is that it can cause toxic psychosis, characterized by paranoia and hallucinations. Once taken, it can produce a compulsive need for injectons for a number of days, resulting in a serious loss of sleep and appetite. The subsequent exhaustion accounts for many ill effects, such as the depression (which may last for several months) following its discontinuance.

PSYCHOSOCIOLOGICAL FACTORS

In order to understand the complex problem of rapidly spreading drug abuse among the younger generation, one must realize that religious, moral and social values are changing. These changes are due to intimate contact provided by rapid transport and extensive communications between all cultures of the world. Youth react more intensely to these changes than do their elders. One must take into consideration that (a) most adults are biologically, psychologically and socially more firmly rooted and developed than adolescents and (b) that the growing youth possesses unlimited energies which need orientation towards biological, psychological and social maturity. These important phases in the development of the youth tend to be neglected in this changing, busy world and thus produce long-term crippling effects. A similar situation can be observed at times in India where young persons, in what is now a fast-changing social environment, often find themselves in conflict with traditional thought and concepts.

The indifferent, unhappy family environment, often discovered in the United States, has resulted in changes in behavior and values and has produced individuals vulnerable to drug abuse. Thus a typical, adolescent drug abuser is a youth from 14 to 19 years of age from an upper middle-class family. He is often unstable, alienated from family, religious and home environment, and sometimes from school. His parents may tend to be apathetic, uninterested and uncooperative. Communication suffers a breakdown and complicated guilt feelings sometimes develop in the youth.

The breakdown of family bonds in Western Society are also conducive to emotional disturbances in a normal child. These factors may give rise to an unstable concept of self and confusion about the basic values of life. The absence of definite aims and values creates chaos in the young mind and may result in development of a disturbed personality. Again, drugs are sometimes utilized as a relief from this confusion.

Some of the youth, when questioned, stated that their parents and elders did not give them the proper directional guidance as far as drug abuse was concerned. Exaggerated accounts about the effects of some of the drugs made them doubt and reject the parents' advice. The young persons were also frustrated by the highly mechanized and hypocritical world in which they lived. The advice against drugs seemed often to be in antithesis to the societal values they saw in action.

There are additional factors such as the fear of modern competitive life and the problem of overpopulation. This has resulted in a change in the pattern of drug abuse in Western Society. Whereas, formerly drug addiction was thought to be a problem confined to the ghettos, at present much drug abuse is found among the intelligentsia and children from the middle class, especially on college campuses and in urban areas. It is estimated that over 50 percent of the present youth have experimented with marijuana or LSD at one time or another. Easy escape through pills and marijuana is becoming a cultural factor for the present generation.

Basically, then, the prevalence of drug abuse in the United States, unlike India and other underdeveloped countries, seems to be caused by chaotic family conditions, defective and confusing self-definitions, and rebellion against everything that represents the Establishment. The present wave of drug abuse in the United States appears to be symptomatic of a deeper problem of social upheaval in the Western World. The younger generation believes that the present American affluent society is a sick society. They are sensitive to the hatred of races and violence and to the future-oriented competitive business ethos of Americal social and economic life. The youth who use drugs yearn for more direct, immediate contact with reality, for more genuine and authentic expression of feeling and for human relationships in which the sense of separateness is blurred. Such a yearning often leads to an interest in exploring the occult, oriental philosophies and drugs which supposedly bring about spontaneity and freedom in experience and expression.

Parents of such alienated adolescents are seldom prepared to understand and cope with this nearly total skepticism and disregard for traditional values. The protestant ethic which stressed the rather somber virtues of work, perseverance in the face of difficulties and moderation, particularly in the area of sensual gratification, was basic to the personalities of most of these parents. Today, the secularization of society, with the dwindling force of religion and the work ethic, has had a more critical influence upon today's developing youth than it has had upon his parent, and therein lies an important generational conflict.

The remedy lies in education and orientation to the evolving social order with the reestablishment of viable routes of communication.

DRUG ADDICTION AS A WORLDWIDE SOCIAL PROBLEM

Drug addiction is detrimental both to the individual and to the society. Yet it is worldwide. The entire world is experiencing change. A new scientific and technical civilization is replacing the old rural and agricultural community. There is a disintegration of the old social groups. Family allegiance with the old social framework is disappearing. The development of individual personalities is now greatly influenced by movies, radio, television and other mechanical forms of amusement. Man, thus, instead of attempting to find pleasure within himself and in his relationships with other persons, resorts to mechanical methods of relaxation. This factor is responsible for the danger of possible drug addiction in persons who find it easier to depend upon these artificial substances than upon themselves.

SOCIOLOGICAL IMPLICATIONS OF THE HARMFUL EFFECTS OF DRUG ADDICTION

Psychological effects and general health hazards of drug addiction have been discussed at some length by the author in previous papers (1965). From a sociological angle, intense forms of drug addiction have effects on the individual and upon the nation.

Abuse of narcotic drugs over a long period produces psychosomatic changes and an abnormal state of mind. In addition, it affects digestive processes, perception and sexual activity. These manifestations, with slight variations, are common to all forms of drug addiction and may be slightly influenced by environment and the individual's way of life. Because of digestive debility, the absorption of the drug aggravates malnutrition in opium, Methedrine, and heroin addicts. Impairment of spatial and temporal perception, as in the case of cannabis smokers, affects the individual's working capacity.

If the control centers are disturbed, many of the normal life functions are neglected. The addict may neglect personal cleanliness and hygiene and may resort to actions prompted by his subconscious. In advanced cases, the addict may deteriorate until he becomes a burden to the state.

CONCLUSION

It is incorrect to disregard the essential consistency of human behavior, which seems to adapt itself in a similar manner to a given environment and situation. During the past three decades, the world has become more vulnerable to the spread of drug addiction, not only in the formerly backward countries where rapid industrial and economic development is taking place but also in the developed nations where other factors are also responsible. Prevention is better than cure, and if drug abuse is to be prevented, it must be fully understood.

10

Today's Drug Abuse Laws at Work

The Honorable Robert E. Jones

Instead of you just sitting there passively listening, I want you to be the judge here. I am going to describe some actual cases and have you commit yourself, not just sit there and wring your hands and say, "I wonder what I'd do?" but actually commit yourself on disposition of some specific cases.

First of all, I want to discuss some general attitudes. How many of you feel that the judges in this nation are generally too soft on criminals? How many of you think that the judges are generally too harsh? Many of you may be ambivalent. Let's refer to narcotic cases. How many of you think that the judges are too soft on the narcotics cases? How many of you think they are too harsh? [It is interesting to note that a majority of those people attending these proceedings felt that the Courts were generally too harsh on narcotics cases, although in speaking to many groups throughout our community, almost unanimously, the feeling was that drug abuses should be put in the "slammer"— that is, the law should come down hard on narcotics offenders.] As judges evaluating narcotics cases, how are we to approach the narcotics problem—as a medical problem, a mental health problem or a legal and criminal law problem? So many feel that it is a combination of both and that is probably a rational position to take. Still this is a dilemma because until recent times we have had too much of the criminal approach and perhaps not enough of the mental health approach. Of course, one of the fundamental purposes of this Institute is to try to induce looking at these problems from a more balanced point of view.

144

As a judge are you going to be pompous like the judge in Figure 10-1 or casual like the one in Figure 10-2?

You may ask, How do you go about sentencing someone? Of course, in some states the law provides for indeterminate sentences, so as judges you would just look up time provided in the statute, if you determine the case does not warrant probation, and you just read off the statutory indeterminate term. You leave it up to some mystic body—the Department or Board of Corrections—to determine when the person shall be released. A lot of people in Corrections criticize this procedure because they feel that people

Figure 10-1

"Mirror, Mirror on the wall
Who is the fairest judge of all?"

get lost in the process. Other people criticize the sentencing done by judges in setting specific terms, because of the disparity. To try to eliminate this sort of guesswork, we have been running a pilot program in Oregon for two years, consisting of a three-judge panel to review sentences. So every Tuesday morning at 8:15, Judge Dale and Judge Olson and I sit down with that week's sentences. We will have studied the presentence reports before the meeting. We have complete work-ups on these people, covering their backgrounds, psychiatric evaluations, former institutional histories, criminal records, references and so forth, and then we commit ourselves, just as I am asking you to commit yourself on the Appendix A form. So having read the case background, but having never seen the individual, except for the one judge to whom the case is assigned, we commit ourselves as to what we think would be the appropriate sentence. We then discuss the case thoroughly and then make a record of whether we changed our minds or not. The actual sentencing follows shortly thereafter (see Appendix B form). The system has the attribute of reducing

Figure 10-2

"The Court sentences you to . . . oh, four and a half years."

judge hang-ups on certain types of people or certain types of crime. For instance, some judge might be very harsh on rape cases. This was exemplified at the National College of State Trial Judges when we recently met in North Carolina. We took a rape case, and we had our sentences range from twenty years to probation. A judge from South Dakota said, "Boy, anytime I see a rape conviction, that's a 20-year sentence in South Dakota." On the other hand, an old judge from North Carolina said, "Well, fellows, I don't know what you call it in South Dakota, but with facts like these down here we call it 'rough lovin'."

Thus you can have judges that are very tough on narcotics cases. Consequently we occasionally see inappropriate sentences. In Louisiana we conducted a sentencing institute using this same type of format. Do you know what the penalty is in Louisiana for a 21-year-old to sell marijuana to a 20-year-old? Anybody guess? It's death. Anybody selling narcotics to a minor is exposed to a death penalty, but despite this they had to close down the park near the courthouse because there were so many drug sales going on. Is the death penalty a deterrent? It's an age-old argument. Remember the stories about the hangings in the old days when pickpocketing was a death penalty? What happened during the hangings? The pickpockets had a field day!

In acting as judges on these cases, we are going to take a parochial point of view, and I will refer to the Oregon laws, though I realize you come from many states. In Oregon, I think that we have the ideal disposition because we can treat sales or possession as a felony or a misdemeanor, a misdemeanor being punishable in a county jail up to one year and a felony being punishable in a penitentiary. If you treat it as misdemeanor, it can be up to one year in the county jail. If you treat it as a felony, you can imprison for up to ten years in the state penitentiary. It is within the discretion of the judge to decide what sentence to impose. Some people criticize this law saying this is giving too much discretion to the judge. We find the law very realistic because if we are dealing with a youngster who is just experimenting, we can give them a misdemeanor slap and we do not have to clobber them with a felony conviction which they will carry with them the rest of their lives. On the other hand, if we have a multiple offender, then we can handle it on the felony level. You can grant probation on any case whether it is a misdemeanor or a felony. With persons under age 25, you can send them to the first felony institution, which we call the Oregon State Correctional Institution. They have similar institutions in almost all of the states now so that you do not put the young first offenders in with the multiple hard-core offenders. Incidentally, until last year we had a straight felony law in Oregon, and Figure 10-3 fairly describes it. Note what the lawyers is saying to his client. That's what our law was, and many of the people, particularly those convicted of marijuana possession, had this same sort of expression as the defendent here does when they were so informed that they had been convicted!

What are the costs of disposition? If you are going to put someone in a first felony institution, such as the Oregon State Correctional Institution, the cost per year would be roughly what it

Figure 10-3

"Ten years. That's a nice round number . . . easy to remember."

would cost to send your youngster to Harvard for a year—$5,000. At the correctional institution they train for nineteen vocational trades. They have everything from remedial reading to other advanced courses. They have a junior chamber of commerce, an Alcoholics Anonymous, a toastmaster group, et cetera. The recidivism rate at the Oregon State Correctional Institution is unknown. Opened in 1959, at first the rate was 16 percent, but the last figure I saw was 33⅓ percent, and I imagine as time goes on it becomes greater and greater. Still we do bombard these young people with every form of institutional aid that we can muster. Now at the Oregon State Penitentiary we are warehousing them, we are providing care at a basic subsistence of about $2400 a year. Do you know what our recidivism rate is there? or our failure rate? or our return-to-crime rate? It runs about the national average of 80 percent failure. So we know if we put them in there we are going to get them back as a future customer.

The cost of supervising someone on probation will run approximately $300 per year. Your success rate on probation is 80 percent. I just received some figures from one of our probation officers, and he is running only 6 percent failure rate on his cases. Our probation officers are overloaded, of course, carrying 70 to 100 cases per month, so some of them just become glorified bookkeepers because they do not have a chance to do any real counseling; however they are very dedicated people and work very closely with us in most of our programs.

It is time for you to act as a judge. I have given you the conditions of probation in Appendix C—a whole sheet of special conditions you can order. By setting and enforcing special conditions, you can wrap a legal umbrella right over a person to keep him in production in the community.

Your first thought in sentencing should be, Can I keep this person in production? Because if you don't, you are going to be looking at the expenditures mentioned, and you are going to be looking at the failure rates mentioned. Of course, you must remember that you must isolate the dangerous offender from the community—that is, the hopeless sociopath who constitutes a danger to people in the community.

Now look at that checklist of conditions of probation, and you can see under the category for drug cases, "No Drugs." That is easy to say but hard to enforce. Next, the Federal Narcotics Commitment Program, a program that is being handled locally, essentially calls for sending addicts back to Lexington or Fort Worth for six month periods and then returning them to the community with follow-up on an outpatient basis. If the addict fouls up, he goes back for one more commitment. This program is being handled through our Alcohol and Drug Section via Mr. Wipple. Very frankly, in my personal experience with the new federal program, the Narcotics Addict Rehabilitation Act (NARA) of 1966, is that it, if used alone, has been a failure. I have not had any people successfully complete or stay drug-free on that program. They have all had to be either put in prison or put on the methadone program. We have several who are on both programs, so we have the federal after-care program supplemented by methadone, a very successful combination. We have tried Synanon with varying success. We do have some relationship with Corona in a civil commitment situation. (I used to be very strong for civil commitment.) We studied the Corona program very closely. We read about their controlling some 4000 addicts and spending $7 million a year doing it, and we looked at their success and failures. This was before the methadone program came in. We did get a new law so you can civilly commit a person at least in Oregon. The only trouble is that program has met with no success because we have no facilities. All we have done then is to provide for a mental commitment with no specially trained personnel. So it has worked no differently than our mental commitment. Some judges have required that some youngsters view drug films and study the drug literature. You know it is easy to buy literature and easy to hand it out, but is it read? You can actually require a youngster to read some of this good literature, require a report back to you as to what is understood from the reading, so you can enforce instruction.

As a condition of probation you can order various types of testing for addicts out in the community to see if they are using drugs. We also have a 1969 law providing for counseling not only for people convicted of crime, but also for people not convicted of crime. They can receive counseling under state auspices at the Alcohol and Drug Section. This completes our list.

All right, you have seen the costs of disposition, you have a list of your options. Let's see how you handle real cases.

Take the first case of Marie. She is 19 years old. She is an honor student, high school graduate and a national merit scholar. After she started Portland State University, she became involved with all forms of drug use. She used marijuana extensively. She used mescaline. She used LSD rather constantly and had some bad trips. She used speed, shooting as well as dropping. Finally, she dropped out of society as the expression is commonly used. She was no longer working. Her boyfriend was called the king of hippyland and was known as "the doctor," because he carried his own kit and claimed to have taken two hundred youngsters off bad trips with his own Thorazine®. To support themselves, she and "the king" went into drug sale, mostly of marijuana and LSD. They were associated with the more hardened criminal type, people that were involved with heroin sale. Marie, a beautiful young lady, very bright, very personable, stands before you convicted of illegal possession of marijuana although she could have been convicted of illegal sale and freely admits she has engaged in many sales of various drugs. Now I usually catch an audience by saying, How many think all possessors of narcotics should be treated as misdemeanants? Everybody usually raises their hands. How many think all sellers should go to jail? Most people raise their hand to this question. Now what are *you* going to do with this young lady? Write down your sentence in Appendix A. You can grant probation up to five years and you can fine her up to $5,000, or you can put her in prison up to ten years, or you can put her in the county jail. You can do any of those things on that probation checklist.

What would you do with this young lady? Would you send her to jail? How long? Remember she is a very pretty young lady, and the prisons and jails are loaded with very aggressive lesbians, a constant problem. All right, this is what did happen. We put her on a three-year probation and required her to do something for someone else; we sent her down to the state hospital and we had her stay down there and work on the floor doing all of the work, cleaning up and taking care of these terribly disabled people. She worked with the psychiatrists in a working environment. Later she wrote back and said it took going down there and doing something for someone else to wake her up to the fact that she had been completely self-indulgent up to that point. She had not thought of her family, nor anyone else, and it took that environment for her to realize she had been so selfish and noncreative. This young lady left the drug scene and her old boyfriend. Soon after my wife and I had the privilege of attending her marriage to another young man in which she wore a white wedding gown, which we felt she richly deserved. She has gone back and has worked in the community and she is finishing her college education at this time.

For every one of the cases that have worked out well, we can count equal numbers that have not worked out. Recently I had another young girl to sentence. She looked like a movie star, a truly beautiful youngster. Age 19, she had been involved in the manufacture and sale of speed. Her boyfriend had been murdered in a negotiation over the sale. She was completely uncontrollable at home and would not stay there. In fact I "recogged" her and she skipped that same night and we had to find her again. She is drug dependent (when I say dependent, I mean she has a constant use of the amphetamines and marijuana but not LSD). Now she is completely rebellious at the time of your sentencing. What do you do with her. It is very difficult to find an answer to this case, because it is too tough. It just presents the other aspect of it. Where is the victim of that crime? Well, we talk about crimes without victims, but here we have a person involved in trafficking of methamphetamine and I can tell you that we have had some very antisocial activity related to the use of that particular drug, including murder, rape and armed robbery.

All right, let's take another case. Let's take George. George has a history of drug use dating back three years. He has one burglary conviction. He did complete probation on that conviction. He has psychiatric problems, but they are vague. He had what I think you call a paranoid personality, not psychotic. He is actively engaged in the sale of the so-called softer drugs—LSD, marijuana, speed. (When we say "so-called," I know many of you twitch because we all know the serious consequences of at least some of those drugs.) George is 24 years old and is involved in the sale of these drugs to the minors in our local area at the various parks. We have a full vice squad report on his activities. They have been gunning for him a long time, but they only can get a conviction on possession of marijuana. Now, what are you going to do with him? Will you respond by giving him a sentence? Incidentally, I am not trying to indoctrinate anybody into any line of thinking. All I want you to do is think about the laws in action and how you would handle them. Would you give him one year and suspend everything but thirty days, dependent on the condition that he stay away from drugs? How about thirty days as a condition of probation? Incidentally keep in mind that if these people have working skills you can put them on work release; we use that a lot. Would you give him five years in prison? Doesn't sound quite so shocking under those circumstances, does it? Then you have got to look at yourself as a judge. Are you imprisoning him because of the offense or because he needs the correction? There is the problem. You know what you wrote down. Whatever it might be I will tell you historically that he was sentenced to four years in the Oregon State Correctional Institution, became a brick layer, came out, and he's now earning about $7 an hour, or whatever brick layers make. He has had no further difficulty with the law.

The average time, incidentally, that a person will serve on one of your sentences in this state, which I would say would be about average across the country, is one-third of the sentence if he is a good prisoner. So if you want someone to complete a trade at the Oregon State Correctional Institution and say it takes about sixteen months to train a person to be a good welder or a good brick layer, et cetera, you are going to have to sentence him between three and five years in order to beat the parole system and keep him down there long enough to get the correction job done. This is not meant as any criticism of the parole people because they have tremendous problems. They have 450 to 500 people down there and sometimes they have them standing in the hallway. Often they have got to make releases in order to make room for newcomers.

Let's take one more case. Several persons here know him. He is my age. He had seven prior felony convictions when we got him for sentencing on a burglary charge. All of the others are property crimes, burglary primarily, and forgery. He is a pimp, who is running one girl regularly and has others. As he describes it, he has done every despicable act known to man. He has been a hard-core heroin addict for a number of years and has been in and out of the federal programs and prison. He has had prolonged prison confinement in the past. Now the day he gets out of the federal hospital or the penitentiary, he sticks that spike back in his arm. On the last occasion, burglary, he disarmed the police officer who arrested him and there was a shooting. No one was hurt. This is the only act of violence on his record, but he was violent enough to make an attempt to escape by getting the weapon. You can sentence this man under our habitual criminal proceedings up to life imprisonment. Now what are you going to do with him? By the way, under a life term he will serve approximately on the average sixteen years in Oregon. Burglary not in a dwelling is the actual charge and the sentence can be up to life because of his prior felony convictions. Would anybody grant him probation? Would anybody put him back in prison? How many would put him in prison for life? What conditions of probation would you give? Would you recommend the methadone program? This is precisely the kind of individual we are gambling with, and place on the methadone program. Through the cooperation of Doctor Blachly, we started him on the methadone while in the county jail, and he has been on the program now for fourteen months and has not been apprehended for any further crime. He has not missed one day of work as a body and fender worker since that time, so we have identified at least one individual whose criminal pattern was drug-based.

I just made a count a month or so ago and find that last year I personally sentenced 144 felons, of which 36 were heroin addicts and 16 went to prison. So the methadone program is not a free ride out of prison. These sixteen people were armed robbers or peddlers. They had committed crimes that were not going to be solved by the methadone program or else were not allowed to be tolerated because of it. I have had twenty heroin addicts on probation on the methadone program and I have had to revoke two. The methadone program does not make a prostitute turning $200 a night in tricks into a woman who is going to go to work in an accountant's office for $80 a week. It just does not work out that way. We do not suddenly get a fine creative person over night. We have had one probationer die using Ritalin®, one go blind —the talc getting in her eyes. We have had a great number of them shooting Ritalin and speed on top of the methadone, but essentially they have blockaded out the heroin addiction. I had made it a firm policy that any person who goes back to drug sale will get the maximum—ten years. The two revoked who were on the methadone program reverted to drug sale, and they received our maximum sentence of ten years. What is our percentage of success and failure? Only time will tell.

All I can say to you is that I have been a circuit judge in the criminal field for seven years. In my opinion the methadone program is the greatest contribution to the corrections picture that has come up in a decade, and perhaps longer. It comes not from a penologist, not from a sociologist, not from a judge, not from a lawyer, but from a doctor, Dr. Paul Blachly, who has brightened the corrections picture in Oregon. It took the cooperation of other doctors, including Doctor Crothers, the Chairman of our Public Health Legislative Committee who gave our legislature the insight for looking at this problem realistically. The program also was blessed by the support of Dr. Kenneth Gaver of the State Mental Health Division. So here we have an advance, a great advance, in the law coming about from outside of our judicial or legal environment. How often this has been the case—that breakthroughs are most likely to come from outside the system. Experts within the system are too often occupied with the developed knowledge inside the prescribed boundaries of their particular discipline, so any new knowledge usually comes from the ouside. Our drug laws have been in the dark ages but now are being improved. We are being given more options and we are getting more inputs and it takes meetings like this to give more and more and more inputs. I am sure that Doctor Blachly will agree that the methadone program is just one step in a future ladder.

I hope that you have found some interest in being judges here today.

Court is adjourned.

Appendix A
SENTENCING PANEL WORKSHEET
Judge Jones

Date Set:

Defendant:

   C-

Crime Plead To:

   ORS

Penalty:

Proposed SENTENCE:

_____

_____

_____

_____

Notes:

_____

_____

_____

At the Conference (for an accurate record)

This proposed sentence (*and* your postconference recommendation) is to be entered on the sentencing judge's DATA RECORD.

Appendix B
SENTENCING PANEL DATA RECORD
Judge Jones

Date Set:

Defendant:

 C-

Crime Plead To:

 ORS

Penalty:

At time of Conference, please complete in full:

Before
 Olsen   _____

_____

 Dale   _____

_____

 Jones   _____

_____

After
 Olsen   _____

_____

 Dale   _____

_____

 Jones   _____

_____

AT SENTENCING:

Date _____

Sentence _____

_____

 Please record sentence imposed and **RETURN** this record to Judge Jones' Bailiff (542).

Appendix C

CONDITIONS OF PROBATION

1. Bench Probation—No Supervision
2. Complete High School
3. County Jail Time as a Condition
4. County Jail Work Release
5. Curfew Hours Set by Court
6. Pay Court Costs
7. Specific Companions Restricted
8. Establish a Savings Account
9. Pay a Fine
10. Maintain or Find a Job
11. No Alcoholic Beverages
12. No Car
13. No Checking Account
14. No Drugs
15. Pay Own Attorney
16. Outpatient Psychiatric Treatment
17. Release to Military
18. Restitution
19. Support Child, Family or Wife
20. Vocational Training
21. Commitment to State Hospital
22. Pay Damages to Victim
23. Return to College
24. Restrict Driving
25. Consult with a *Leading* citizen
26. For Drug Cases
    a. No Drugs
    b. Take Methadone
    c. Federal Narcotics Commitment
    d. Synanon
    e. Narcotics Center, Corona, California
    f. View Drug Films
    g. Naline Test
    h. Urine Test
27. For Alcohol Cases
    a. Attend AA
    b. No Alcoholic Beverages
    c. Report to Alcohol Rehabilitation Center
    d. Take Antibuse

11

Utopia at High Dudgeon

David W. Maurer

Editor's Note: The following is a work of satirical fiction designed to stimulate discussion, and it did.

Today I am going to discuss the new narcotics law, now in effect for more than a year, with which you are probably all familiar. However, for the benefit of anyone who does not remember all the details, I will outline it briefly a little later on.

Dr. Blachly has asked me to keep my remarks in a light vein, owing to the highly controversial nature of the subject under discussion at the Institute today. However, much as I respect Dr. Blachly's opinion, I cannot agree with him on this point. A law like this should not and cannot be treated humorously. Personally, I would favor a law making it a crime to make any jokes about addictions, just as it is a crime to make any jokes about putting bombs on an airplane. Therefore, let me speak to you seriously and from the bottom of my heart.

First, what are the provisions of this new law, admittedly written with the advice of addicts and now in effect for more than a year? Copies of this law are not easy to obtain and the new reservation for drug addicts at High Dudgeon, Arizona, has been given only minimal publicity through federal agencies. Let me sketch for you, in outline form, the highlights of the program developed under this law.

I. *Place*
   A former military camp located on 75,000 acres near High Dudgeon, Arizona.
   Buildings and facilities for 150,000 troops.

159

Renovated rapidly by two trainloads of trusties shipped in from federal prisons.

Administered by HEW.

Converted into a minimum security, voluntary-commitment, reservation for addicts.

II. *Who Goes There*

Any addict to the several opiate or synthetic opiate drugs, chief of which is heroin.

Any addict to other drugs who has formerly been addicted to heroin or who fears he may be readdicted to heroin or other opiate.

First preference given to long-term addicts who have relapsed after several periods of treatment.

Now houses about 75,000 addicts, with about 5,000 on the waiting list.

III. *Assignment*

Addicts selected

    a. when convicted on a serious drug charge, as an alternative to a prison sentence.

    b. when recruited directly by agents of the Bureau of Narcotics.

    c. on application to a federal judge for voluntary commitment.

In return for acceptance, the addict signs a contract that he will live the rest of his life on the reservation, subject to various conditions.

Opiate addicts are assured of a steady supply of medical opiates or opiate synthetics free of charge.

Addicts have patient status. No stigma attached to commitment.

Inmates who become serious discipline problems can be

    a. confined in punishment facilities on the reservation.

    b. expelled from the reservation.

    c. sentenced to a federal prison.

IV. *Modus Operandi*

Barracks subdivided for inmates who can afford privacy and want single units. Dormitories available to others.

Provisions and necessities available through government com-
misaries. These will eventually be broken up into stores and
taken over by addicts who can qualify. To be staffed by those
who wish to work.

All inmates eligible for relief funds set at the median provided by all states.

Inmates pay minimal rent for facilities.

Relief funds can be supplemented by working or going into
small business.

Transportation by bus service; no personal cars permitted.

Drug rations issued daily from round-the-clock distribution
centers.

Marriages permitted between inmates only; any children sent
out to other institutions.

Medical services provided by HEW.

Also education in trades, crafts, business, management, etc.

Treatment facilities installed if and when an effective cure
for opiate addiction is developed.

Minimal security provided by the Bureau of Prisons.

Visitors from the outside permitted on a limited basis.

Some degree of self-government to be developed under a
Director and Board of Governors supplied by HEW.

V. *Rationale*

To provide a humane form of isolation for persons suffering
from an incurable and communicable disease.

To permit a generation of opiate addicts to live out their
lives with no more restrictions than might apply in a tuber-
culosis sanitarium, a leper colony or an Indian reservation.

To take traffic in opiates out of the hands of racketeers.

To reduce the cost of addiction to society and to the government.

To free enforcement agencies to concentrate on other forms
of drug abuse.

To sustain a very slow-paced, partially self-supporting, addict-
oriented community where addicts can take refuge from law
enforcement harassment, exploitation by the rackets and the

economic problems of addiction and, at the same time stop the spread of narcotic addiction among those not yet infected.

Well, the law itself is no longer secret, but the larger question is, How did it get through Congress, signed by the President and into operation without even a hint in the *Congressional Record?* I think I have some information on this.

Just last week the Grove Press, which has initiated a new policy of giving equal time to the forces opposed to pornography, announced that they had commissioned Spiro Agnew to write a regular column in the *Evergreen Review* under the title SPIRO SAYS. . . . In this month's issue Mr. Agnew's column appeared opposite a remarkable set of color photographs by Masters and Johnson, accompanied by a glowing endorsement of new aphrodisiacs for elder citizens, written by a Supreme Court Justice, which may account for the fact that none of the newspapers have yet noticed the Vice President's debut into journalism. In his first article Mr. Agnew has really hit the jackpot, however, for he has told the story of how this drug-addict community was authorized by Congress and approved by the President. It will doubtless be widely read once it is discovered.

While I should like to read you this article in full, I shall not do this for several reasons, chief of which is the intemperence and even violence of Mr. Agnew's language, which, it seems to me, has no place in a scientific gathering such as this. Therefore, I shall paraphrase it as best I can, so you may have the facts right from the horse's mouth.

Mr. Agnew reveals the astonishing fact that this law was passed and signed into law in the course of a single day. It seems that for some months previous to this day the McClelland Committee had been holding closed hearings in which many drug addicts were interviewed regarding the type of law that would best suit their needs if and when the drug laws should be liberalized. The fruits of these hearings were fresh in Senator McClelland's mind on one day more than a year ago when he, along with most of the rest of the Senate, dropped into the Senate Dining Room for lunch.

Now the FBI has determined that on that day some person or

persons unknown had maliciously introduced into the bean soup, for which the Senate Dining Room is justly famous, a small quantity of lysergic acid diethelamide, known to the trade as LSD. The effects of this powerful hallucinogen are well known, and almost immediately they became obvious. While Mr. Agnew was not present personally, since he eats his lunch from a brown paper bag in his office, he has weighed all the facts carefully and has described them in a vocabulary which he says he has borrowed from George Wallace for the occasion. Those who know Mr. Agnew, however, may say that he is unduly modest.

It seems that during lunch, Senator McClelland arose and, perched on top of a dining table, delivered a powerful speech favoring a drug law written to the specification of addicts. This speech was received with great acclaim, and the Senator was then invited to place a motion proposing such a law, which he did off the cuff and without the benefit of notes. This was passed unanimously, except for some protest by Senator Dodd, attending lunch as a guest of Senator Fulbright, who tried to introduce an amendment forbidding all firearms on the drug reservation on the grounds that once the drug addicts defeated the Black Panthers, they were ripe to take over the country from the college students. He was ruled out of order by one of the waiters, who had also tasted the bean soup. The only other objection was a spirited protest by Senator Javits of New York, who said that, frankly, the whole thing sounded crazy to him. He was unceremoniously pushed head first into a cuspidor, but not before he had a chance to cast the only dissenting vote.

The Senate then turned its attention to the House, many members of which were already at lunch and voting enthusiastically with the Senate. It was voted to send out pages and round up as many more Representatives as possible so they could complete the voting right there. Meanwhile, President Nixon, says Mr. Agnew, had heard that Congress was in joint session in the lunchroom, and because he felt there must be some urgency, passed up the underground tramway and took off across the Capitol ground in a golf cart. As he pulled up to the Senate lunchroom, he was astonished to see Senator Margaret Chase Smith leap gracefully from a second-story window with an open parasol and float gently to the lawn. Mr. Agnew says that she then smiled happily at the President, who reports that she said, "Mr. President, I can fly!" The President replied, "I see you can, Senator," and hurried into the lunchroom, for now he suspected the worst.

When he entered the lunchroom, he relaxed immediately. The entire Congress rose and cheered, then began singing "For He's a Jolly Good Fellow," some of the senior members leading the singing from the table-tops. Before he could inquire into the nature of things, he was seated at a table, a waiter was summoned, and he was urged to have some lunch. "Let me clarify this," Mr. Agnew quotes him as saying, "I never eat anything over here except your wonderful bean soup. Bring me a small bowl, please." This was done forthwith, and by the time the President had learned the nature of the proceedings, he was very much one of the group. Senator Mike Mansfield was just making a speech committing the entire Democratic party to vote for Mr. Nixon as President in 1972, when a quorum was declared for the House; Senator McClelland again described the nature of the bill without benefit of notes, and the House passed it by voice vote. Senator Mansfield then ceremoniously presented it, jotted on the backs of several envelopes, to the President, who by now was vigorously shaking hands with old friends and enemies alike and mentioned the fact that he knew just how Senator Margaret Chase Smith must have felt. He asked for an umbrella and headed for an open window, but Senator Mansfield urged him to sit down and sign the bill, which he did with a great flourish, after which he presented Senator Mansfield with his own solid gold fountain pen as a momento of the occasion.

Then, according to Mr. Agnew, Senator Stennis arose on top of a table. He was marking a large peace-sign on his forehead with a lipstick which he had found unaccountably reposing in his vest pocket. He complimented both Houses on their joint work several times and proposed a bill which, he said, all Congressmen, as well as the President, needed for their self-protection. He outlined this bill briefly, and it very sensibly provided that any Congressman who ever dared to describe or even refer to the proceedings of this day should be declared guilty of a felony, the penalty for which would be total disclosure to the news media of all his sources of income, certified by the FBI and the IRS. An amendment to exclude the House because of its traditionally secret method of voting was defeated on the grounds that, since the vote was unanimous, no one could reasonably deny voting for the measure, except, of course, Senator Javits.

At this point Mr. Agnew mercifully draws the curtain over what could have been a distressing scene, as the Secret Service moved in with a crew of doctors shooting Thorazine like mad. He is careful to add, however, "Although I was not present, I have gathered my facts carefully. Had I been present, this could never have happened. I would never partake of LSD, even if I did not know what I was taking. . . ."

Mr. Agnew does further note, however, that J. Edgar Hoover, without being consulted on the matter, gave him this comment: "You see how those subversives and radicals have infiltrated Congress. Only Senator Javits had the courage and red-blooded patriotism to stand alone against them. He deserves a lot of credit." Mr. Agnew finds it difficult to reconcile this statement with what Senator Javits told him. "I certainly do not deserve any credit for my stand," said the Senator. "It was just a matter of the bean soup. I noticed that it contained rather large chunks of pork, and so did not order any." So much for Mr. Agnew's account.

What have been the public reactions to this experiment after nearly a year of operation?

First of all, there have been many protests from bleeding hearts and do-gooders who deplore the isolation of drug addicts from their friends, families and cultural pursuits. Second, there have been critical blasts from the CLU over possible violation of constitutional rights. Third, the American Medical Association has gone on record as opposing the idea of a reservation, since it allegedly violates the doctor-patient relationship which physicians have so carefully cherished with drug addicts for many years. I am sure that you have all seen these items in the papers.

Incidentally, it had been expected that users of other drugs might organize and demand a similar law, but so far this has not materialized. The general public seems to have shown little interest in the reservation so far, the psychology being that it does not matter what is done with drug addicts as long as they are kept out of sight and out of trouble. Meanwhile, rock festivals and other large spontaneous gatherings suggest that users of pot, acid, speed and the barbiturates are working out some kind of reservation program on a free enterprise basis, insecure and peripatetic as that program may presently be.

However, there have been more tangible reactions on the part of various state, local and government agencies, not to mention many unofficial organizations who have an interest in drugs. From these recent news clippings I note the following:

Cleveland, Ohio, *August 1.* The entire detective force of this large mid-Western city staged a demonstration in front of City Hall at noon today carrying signs protesting the lack of addicts who can be recruited as stool pigeons. One sign read: "A little information is better than all the police science in the world." Another said: "No Junkies—no Stoolies. Give us back our Stoolies!" Police Chief Moohey Baloheney, Cleveland's ninth police chief in the past year, intimated that he might resign if the plainclothesmen could not be mollified. "They've just got too much on me," he complained.

Washington, D. C., *August 5.* Several officials in the Justice Department today conceded that there is an active lobby in Congress to persuade that body to amend the no-knock law in connection with narcotics arrests. The Justice Department, together with the Narcotics Bureau, says it is necessary to provide legal immunity for officers to plant bags or capsules of heroin on suspects in order to be able to train agents in the proper methods of search, seizure and arrest. The spokesman, who requested that he not be identified, said, "We would plant only very small quantities. And an equal number of blacks and whites, Democrats and Republicans would be selected by computer so that there would be no racism or political partisanship involved. Just so they have long hair. . . ." Said another official, "It is so rare to find an authentic heroin junkie on the street that we can't train our officers properly. You can't train an agent on grass. Those potheads simply aren't dangerous enough."

Chicago, Illinois, *August 7.* The National Association of Insurance Underwriters, in convention here, today announced that they are recommending across-the-board cuts in urban insurance rates covering burglary, theft and vandalism. They cite nationwide reports indicating that claims in these areas have dropped dramatically in the past six months.

Washington, D. C., *August 8.* The FBI announced today that its records show a dramatic reduction in the crimes of theft, burglary and vandalism in places of business across the country. "This is the first time in history," said the FBI spokesman, who declined to identify himself, "that the FBI has announced a decline in any kind of crime anywhere." When this reporter asked him if his office had been influenced by yesterday's announcement of the National Association of Insurance Underwriters, he replied, "No indeed. The FBI does not collect its statistics on crime from anyone who knows anything about it."

Atlanta, Georgia, *August 2.* Federal officials at the Federal Penitentiary here have requested the right to transfer long-term, hard-core incorrigible convicts to the Arizona reservation known as High Dudgeon. It has been reported, they said, that there are no behavioral problems on the reservation, since the most hardened types of criminals spend most of their time in rocking chairs dozing or, if they desire some action, knitting. The Justice Department has ruled that problem convicts cannot be transferred to Arizona unless they are currently addicted to opiates. The Warden at Atlanta promptly withdrew his request saying, "That only happens at Leavenworth."

Portland, Oregon, *August 5.* The Methadone Block Program for sustaining of drug addicts with very small amounts of methadone administered daily will cease to operate shortly, according to Dr. Paul H. Blachly and Dr. Samuel Irwin, of the University of Oregon Medical School. This was a pioneer project which attracted nationwide attention as one of the few therapy programs which kept the addicts free in society and working at jobs. "Seems as if they all developed a methadone habit and volunteered for the reservation in Arizona," said Dr. Blachly. "We tried everything to keep them happy, like flavoring the methadone with raspberry, strawberry, dingleberry, vanilla, Schwepps, juniper juice, and the like. But strangely enough, all

they wanted was an increase of their daily dosage of methadone.
It is hard to understand the fascination which plain, unflavored
methadone had for them. Since we felt that it would be unethi-
cal to increase their dosage again, they have all gone to Arizona."

Pine Ridge, South Dakota, *August 10.* After three days and
nights of powwowing among the Isantee, the Oglalla, the Lakota
and the Hunkpapa Sioux, Chief Shunka Wakan Witk, spokesman for the Oglalla, announced today that the entire Sioux
nation planned to depart later this summer by motorbus for
Washington. The Sioux are disturbed, he told this reporter
through an interpreter, that drug addicts have a better reservation than any Indians ever had. "The Sioux intend," said the
chief, "to stage a massive sit-in at the Bureau of Indian Affairs
until satisfaction is obtained." "What will you say to the Bureau
of Indian Affairs?" he was asked. "Maka chan pagmiamia tipi
wasichun luzahan mazaska maniyapi. Washtelaka," he replied.
The interpreter refused to translate the Chief's message, saying
that his vocabulary was too earthy for publication when ren-
dered into English. Secretary of the Interior, Walter Hickel,
when contacted in Washington, said that he had heard that the
Sioux were coming. "This is more advance notice than Custer
had," he said. "They will simply have to sign up in advance and
wait their turn. We are having a lot of demonstrations here this
year. . . ."

Washington, D.C., *August 12.* After several postponements,
President Nixon today met with a contingent of twelve Dons,
or Mafiosi, who are the heads of the forty Cosa Nostra "families" throughout the United States. The conference was held
on the White House steps, since the Secret Service insisted that
they should not be admitted to the Presidential Office. Scores
of Secret Service men, armed with submachineguns, were de-
ployed across the White House portico. The meeting was closed
to the press, although many reporters and photographers viewed
it from behind police lines. Later a presidential aide gave news
releases to newsmen.

"The Mafiosi came," he said, "to complain that the market
for contraband heroin has been ruined by the government reservation for addicts at High Dudgeon. This has placed them at
a tremendous economic disadvantage, they said, and they
pleaded with the President to abolish the reservation and restore
the free enterprise system to its rightful place in our economy.

Their spokesman intimated that if the heroin traffic were eradicated completely, the Mafia would be forced to step up their activities in prostitution, the numbers racket, gambling, violent crime and even assassination. At this stage the President spoke firmly and with great conviction, and he has authorized a direct quotation:

> Gentlemen, he said, No one has been a stronger champion of the free enterprise system than I have. I do not want to see anyone's business ruined by government competition. But let me make this perfectly clear. I am doing what is right. It is right because it is required by law. We can buy opium direct from Turkey and Iran far cheaper than we can buy it through your agents. And it is pure, strong, uncut opium, certified by the Department of Agriculture. So my advice to you is to go back to your olive-oil importing business, your resort hotels and your banks in the Caribbean, and try to eke out a living in some honorable way. Besides, he added, after that last election in New Jersey I am convinced that your rumored political clout is a myth.

After this the Mafiosi, all impeccably attired in morning clothes and top hats, each with a white carnation in his buttonhole, filed grimly off the White House steps and departed in their waiting bullet-proof Cadillacs. . . ."

12

The Viewpoint of the Bureau of Narcotics and Dangerous Drugs on Legislation

Michael R. Sonnenreich

M y topic is really not to tell you what the Bureau of Narcotics and Dangerous Drugs has proposed but rather what the Administration has proposed, since the new law is an Administration bill. Before I go ahead and get into the area of legislation, I first want to talk about what prompted this legislation. When the Bureau of Narcotics and Dangerous Drugs was organized in 1968, the old Bureau of Narcotics was moved out of the Treasury Department and the Bureau of Drug Abuse Control was moved out of the Department of Health, Education and Welfare, and both entities were joined in the Department of Justice. At that point we were involved in an organizational streamlining so that we could find out just what the Federal Government was doing in this area of law enforcement and how best to make it effective. After we put the whole thing together and looked at it, we turned our attentions to the most important aspect of the problem which was not just organization of manpower, but ensuring that our legislative and legal tools were in order so that we would have something that was (a) credible, and (b) workable. With this in mind, we turned around and started working on the drug laws, and as I am sure many of you are aware, they were just a tremendous hodgepodge of laws that ranged from laws established in 1914 dealing with narcotics through marijuana in 1937, through opium poppy import/export controls. In short there were some forty laws, all of which were directed at singular problems, all of which were enacted either because of public outcry or because of a need felt by the Congress to do something about each specific problem that arose. The result has been a hobgoblin. We had a situation where there were penalties that were not in phase internally with each other. We had information that was not currently scientifically acceptable. We had, in short, a system that was not something that we could turn to with any sort of logical pride and say, this is an integrated system of law that is a workable, fair system of law. So we decided to change it.

The first thing we did was to identify what the problems were. We found two major problems. First, there was a lack of credibility among the public, especially among the young people, as to the penalties, especially with regard to marijuana. However this concern not only applied to the young people, it also applied to everybody who was a student of law or who had any idea of what the law was about, because these penalties were not in phase with the rest of the federal criminal code, so that whether or not you felt marijuana or any of these other drugs were dangerous or not so dangerous, their criminal impact still did not comport with other penalties that we were prescribing for manslaughter, white-slave traffic, espionage, the giving of state secrets and other serious crimes. So we felt that we were obligated to conform these penalties to the federal criminal code, which is what we attempted to do.

We also recognized that we had a second problem—a problem that was germinating in the sixties, but which really bloomed at the end of the sixties—and that problem was the ready availability of so many new, legitimately produced drugs on the market. We are a pill-taking culture. We constantly see this fact visibly presented to us in television commercials. As a result, America has been pill-popping at an alarming rate. So we felt that not so much from a criminal aspect but more from a regulatory aspect, it would be very important if we could at least find out how many of these pills are being produced, where they are going and determine methods for keeping down the supply, which was often exceeding the legitimate demand. This second problem was also focused upon in the federal bill.

At the drafting sessions, the first question that was raised was, Why not treat the entire drug area? Another issue that was raised was the fact that people have been constantly saying that law enforcement in this area does not work. A large portion of the populace simply does not accept the criminal sanctions. This is not the way to solve drug abuse: the answer is education, the answer is rehabilitation, the answer is research and the answer is in some part, law enforcement. Well, as draftsmen, we have no quarrel with these feelings. Our response was that in talking to the Department of Health, Education and Welfare, sufficient education and rehabilitation legislation was already on the books. The major question here was the implementation of federal funding for these programs. It is the feeling of the Administration that the states themselves are the ones that can better deal with the current problem, if they have Federal funding and if they have Federal direction and assistance in the areas of research and long-range rehabilitation programs. So what we decided to do was to keep rehabilitation and research programs out of the bill as much as possible and treat them separately under the Community Mental Health Centers Act and the Narcotic Addict Rehabilitation Act and focus on what we considered to be the most out of phase part of the drug area, which was the law enforcement aspects and the penalties. This does not mean that we do not recognize the fact that education plays a vital role, as does rehabilitation and research. The question is one of priorities, and law enforcement was the one that was most in need of reform right now.

The federal bill is a rather long bill. It was introduced into the Congress on July 15, 1969. It has wended its merry way through the Congress, starting with hearings on September 15, 1969. My opposite number, Mr. Chayet, has also followed this legislation with great interest. We have gone through the Senate process; the bill passed the Senate. We have gone through the House process and the bill was reported out of the House committees; the only thing that prevented it from being passed by the House at that time was the fact that the House adjourned. It will have to go back to the Senate because there have been some changes in it, but we anticipate that we will have a new federal law either some time in September or early October of 1970.

The bill has four major aspects, and I do not want to belabor them all since the bill runs some 120 pages now, most of the substance of which is highly complicated. For persons not familiar with the bill, it just does not make sense to discuss it at great length, but there are four areas that are very important.

The first area deals with the listing of the drugs themselves. Too often in the polemics on drug abuse we talk about narcotic drugs, we talk about the hallucinogenic drugs, we talk about marijuana with some people calling it a narcotic and others saying it is not a narcotic, which I might add it is not. What we have tried to do is look at each drug as a drug, trying to get the emotionalism away from these trigger words by analyzing the drug scientifically and looking at its effects on the community, so that we can pattern regulatory and penal controls on that particular substance. We have categorized the drugs in schedules by drug name, not by class of drugs. What we have tried to do is to build in some flexibility. One of the problems we have with drugs such as marijuana is that the current state of knowledge is far different than the state of knowledge in 1937. We wanted to have some administrative flexibility so that, within the general parameters established by the Congress, drugs could be moved up and down the schedules in order to tighten or loosen regulatory controls or move them out of the schedules and decontrol them if necessary. New drugs could be placed into the proper schedule without having to constantly go back to the Congress and say, well here is a new drug, it is an MDA, it is an hallucinogenic, let's add this to the list. It just does not make sense to require new legislation for each new drug. The current knowledge on new drugs and the development of new drugs is so swift that we are talking about hundreds of drugs constantly coming up that perhaps should be controlled or drugs that are presently controlled that should be decontrolled. The feeling was that the system would be improved if it were placed in administrative hands, so we put it in to the hands of the Attorney General and the Secretary of Health, Education and Welfare. Using their expertise in terms of the gathering of information and the Secretary's expertise in the terms of looking at the medical and scientific information, they determine whether or not a drug should be controlled, whether or not a drug should have tighter regulatory controls or whether we should just kick it out of the schedules. Maybe we should not control a certain drug at all; the question there, of course, when you get down to the final judgment, is one of legal sufficiency, so of course the Attorney General would be responsible for establishing that in court. The feeling is that we have not built a structure where we can respond only to current scientific information, but we can also respond to what is actually happening in the street. We can administratively respond to new legal definition that comes down from the courts in terms of what constitutes "capacity" or what constitutes a "crime," so that in that manner we can deal effectively with a drug problem.

Now the second part, which I feel may be rather cut and dried for most of you, but which is extremely important, is the business about the regulatory controls over the legitimate industry. This area is important because of the estimates which are constantly presented to you, such as "13 billion dosage units of amphetamines and barbiturates are produced legitimately and 8 billion of them are unaccounted for this year. We do not know where they went." Well, these are estimates, very, very rough estimates, since we do not really know how many are produced because we have no way of identifying how many have been produced. One of the important aspects of the regulatory provisions is to find out who is producing drugs, how much is being produced, how much is going into the legitimate market and what is happening to the rest of it. We also have a problem in that unlike the heroin which is coming into this country from other countries and causing us a problem, we are exporting our technical know-how on these other drugs and causing problems in other countries. So this presents not only a national problem but an international one as well, and we have got to meet that. We have designed a series of provisions so that the Federal Government will monitor what is going on in the industry with these controlled substances. It is not unlike the kind of system currently used to review the trucking industry or to monitor television or radio stations. It is intended to get information, and these provisions provide the way we feel we can best gather the information.

The third area that is of maximum importance, in my judgment, is the penalty area. Now this is something that we have fought up and down the line. The Federal Government and the position of the Administration is that we must make a very, very clear distinction between trafficking—those people that engage in trafficking or proselytizing these drugs—and those people that are in possession of these drugs for their own use. Now from the federal point of view, the possession offense is a *de minimis* offense from our standpoint in terms of law enforcement. It is economically, from a managerial sense, the most time-consuming and the least effective if our goal in terms of law enforcement is to cut off the supply of drugs. You do not do that at the lowest level, which is the consumer level. You do it at the top where it stops the flow of the drugs and is far more effective. Our position was also based on the fact that you have a wide variety of people who are using these drugs, ranging from the people who are addicted to heroin to the kid in a college dormitory that because of peer pressure, or anything you want to call it, decided he is going to smoke marijuana. We felt that, as a possession offense, this should not be treated in the same category as a felony in the same way that a trafficking offense should be. Therefore the federal bill, which has the support of the Administration and, I might add, has the support of both Houses of the Congress in this area, treats the first offense of possession of any drug, regardless of the drug, as a misdemeanor—that is, possession for one's own use. By that I mean that the penalty under federal law would be a minimum of zero and a maximum of up to one year. It also provides for suspension of sentence and for probation of sentence. It also permits the judge, in his discretion, to provide first-offender treatment. That means that if the judge has before him an offender that he thinks has a good chance of being rehabilitated or being a nonrepeater in the sense that one crack at the judicial system is enough, the judge can impose conditions other than putting this person in jail. If the person fulfills the conditions, the judge can then hold him not guilty and expunge his record. Now we think this is important because of the statistics that we get. The best statistics that were available are from state arrests, and we find that the average age for the people arrested on possession offenses is about 21 years of age, and we find that the vast majority of these people, some 98 percent, are first offenders. Now, forgetting just the issue of drugs, but looking at the entire system of criminal justice, bear in mind that for these people this is the first time that they have ever walked into a courtroom other than for a traffic ticket. The system has to be flexible enough and credible enough so that everyone can look at the system and say, I can get a fair shake. The penalties, the procedures, the sentences fit me, they do not just fit some hypothetical guy but they could also fit me. That is the reason why we feel so strongly that there should be maximum flexibility at this level, so that people who are arrested the first time for a possession offense have a chance. After discussing it with the judge—we assume that judges are reasonable people, some are, some are not, we all know that—there should be an opportunity for the judge not to criminalize this person for the rest of his life. There is also a provision in the bill which provides that if a person is on probation for possession, at the end of the probation, if the judge does not expunge his record, the person can petition the court and require that his record be expunged. Perhaps I had better explain that. Once a record is expundged, for purposes of getting a job—that is, for purposes of ever having to answer on a form, Have you ever been convicted of an offense?—the answer is "No" and you are not guilty of perjury. There is, of course, one record that is kept, and that is the court record which is nonpublic and cannot be released except to judges in subsequent cases. The reason for this is if the violator commits a second offense, he cannot have his record expunged again, and the Court has to be advised of that fact. Now that is the way the bill treats the simple possession case.

For trafficking offenses we have eliminated all the minimum mandatory sentences primarily because we just do not have minimum mandatory sentences for other offenses in the federal criminal code. In addition, we are once again putting the discretion, and we belive rightly so, back in the hands of the judge and not tying his hands and saying you must sentence this person to a minimum of five years. This way we feel that the judge can exercise his discretion from zero up to the maximum term of trafficking. The maximum term for trafficking narcotic drugs is as yet unsettled between the two Houses—the Senate said twelve years and the House has said fifteen years. For marijuana or the other depressant and stimulant drugs, the penalty is zero to five years and Congress is in agreement as to that. We feel that the judge will now have the ability to make a better, more rational decision about how to properly treat the person brought before him.

Now we have a third category of penalties that we felt were also necessary. These deal with what we call the professional criminal and the continuing criminal enterprise. We recognize that we are dealing with various types of people that are involved in the drug traffic. One large group makes up the organized criminal elements, and these people are not going to be rehabilitated. They are not usually junkies in the sense that they are using drugs, but they are commercial operatives, dealing in illicit traffic, mostly with heroin. You are not going to take one of these people, put him through a vocational training school in prison and have him come out work on an assembly line for $150 a week. If released, this man is going to go back and he is going to take his tax-free $2000 or $5000 a week income, and he is not going to stay away from the criminal drug traffic. So, for these people we feel that the pendulum tips more in favor of incarceration. It is intellectually unappealing. Many people cringe at it, but the fact is that society does have some rights, and we would like to insure that these people stay off the streets for a while. For these people we do have a minimum mandatory sentence. The penalties for persons that are involved in continuing criminal enterprises—that is, those involved as supervisors of operations dealing in five or more people in the drug trade these same people have large sums of money that somehow they cannot account for, nor have they ever reported them on their income tax form— may be sentenced to, from a minimum of ten years to a maximum of life. They receive a mandatory fine of $50,000 and they forfeit all their property either directly or indirectly used criminally by them. We feel that something has to be done with these people for the protection of society. This is not the college kid, this is not the occasional distributor of drugs, this is not even the middle level drug trafficker. These are the higher-ups that you only get a crack at once, and we feel that we should have some strong penalty against them. Now the penalty may not deter them, but the prison term will if we catch them. We are not really talking deterrence here, and I think you had better understand that. What we are saying is that we recognize that these people are going to traffic in these drugs and it is our job to go out and catch them. If we catch them we want to make absolutely certain we can put them away for a long period of time. So we are not discussing deterrence and that is not the primary intent of that penalty.

The last area, reviewed rather briefly, includes the enforcement powers that have been put into the bill. Some of these enforcement tools have perhaps caused the greatest amount of controversy in the entire bill, for example, the enforcement powers called quick entry or no-knock. The no-knock provision has been amply discussed in the Senate and in the House. From all indications it is going to be discussed once again when the Congress reconvenes, since there are many, many people that feel that the no-knock provision should not be part of the law. There are of course, many people that feel that it should be included. I think that you should be aware of one thing: no-knock entry is not a unique or new concept. It is a concept that is lodged in English common law. It is a concept that is presently being used in thirty-one states and has been for some time. The concept of the no-knock in this bill will require the policeman, not to merely enter on his own motion or judgment, but to go before a judge and explain why he needs a special warrant to enter without announcing authority and purpose. If he can convince the judge of that need, by demonstrating that he has probable cause to believe that an offense is being committed and that in addition, he has probable cause to feel that there is a danger to the life and limb of the officer or that the evidence would be quickly and easily destroyed, then he will get the special warrant. The officers executing the warrant will then be authorized to enter without announcing their authority and purpose. However, do not mistake this with the initial authority of obtaining a search warrant. The Constitutional requirements for getting a search warrant were never diminished but were, in fact, somewhat strengthened, and the judge still has the final authority in issuing the search warrant. So whatever your personal feelings are on it, I hope that you will look a little bit beyond what is stated in the newspaper and actually study what the no-knock provision actually is, because, quite honestly in my own personal feeling, I think that there is no Constitutional problem involved. The Supreme Court has reviewed this area and they do not seem to find a Constitutional problem. I think it is more a visceral one, it is something that either offends you on an emotional level or it does not offend you, and I think that both sides have equally good points, but I think that if you are arguing it from a Constitutional point of view, it would stand the test of scrutiny.

Finally, I would like to give you some idea of what we are also doing at the state level. When the President sent his message up to Congress last July 14th, after first mentioning the need for new federal legislation in this field, he then stressed a need for new state legislation, because many of the gross inequities that we find in the existing penalty structures originated in state laws and because there is no real consistency among the states in the penalty area. So we proposed and drafted a model state bill. We also decided at that time that we should work with the National Conference of Commissioners on Uniform State Laws if they would have us, and they did. In December at the White House Governor's Conference, the Attorney General announced that we were working with them. We have since visited almost every governor of every state, over forty-six to date, to discuss the model law. We also met with the National Conference of Commissioners in St. Louis in August. At that time they approved the model state act, declaring it a Uniform State Act, which will mean that as soon as possible, the Commissioners of every state in the Union will go forward and try to get it passed in their own state, so that we will have uniformity around the United States. There are two points I should like to mention about the model state act. The issue of no-knock came up during discussions on the model state act, and the decision was made to delete no-knock, so the Uniform State Act does not contain a no-knock provision. There were also extended discussion on doing something that the Commission rarely does, and that is to recommend a penalty. The decision was made, in the light of the federal direction and because of the feelings of many of the Commissioners that for simple possession, the maximum penalty for a first offense shall be a misdemeanor. This action caused a great deal of controversy because they have never done it before, but it was accepted by the Conference as a whole, therefore a first offense simple possession is a misdemeanor in the Uniform State Act. That, of course, tracks the federal bill in the sense that it would apply across-the-board for any drug. So that is where we stand as far as the state law is concerned. There are forty-nine out of fifty state legislatures meeting in January of 1971, and we feel very optimistic that with the passage of the federal bill, the states will follow with their uniform act and we can get some sort of consistency in application of the law, especially in terms of the penalty structures for these drug offenses.

13

Alternative Viewpoints Regarding Drug Legislation

Neil L. Chayet

My first involvement in the drug situation was in 1964, one year after I graduated from Harvard Law School, when I innocently returned to moderate a debate between Doctor Timothy Leary and Doctor Norman Zinburg before the Harvard Law School. Since then, a great deal has happened. I am extremely disappointed with the law in the area of drug regulation, and think it can only be characterized as a total failure. As a lawyer it bothers me to say that, but I think it is true. We have done very little which could be termed positively constructive. About the only thing that we have done, clearly done, is that we have probably created 100,000 felons below age 30, and I think that is a conservative estimate. Throughout the country we now have 100,000 criminals, 100,000 felons—people who have had no previous criminal records but who have been arrested on various charges of possession and who have become felons.

The problem of course goes back to the Uniform Narcotic Drug Act and as Mike Sonnenreich has mentioned, the Uniform Act was promogated during the 1930's; It was a rather unimaginative piece of legislation which did not include any recommendation with regard to penalties and merely looked at things in terms of sale and possession, et cetera, and let the states fill in the various penalties. All substances were treated pretty much as a narcotic. As new drugs came along through the years they were merely added to the definition of narcotic; thus, marijuana and LSD, were all added to this comprehensive definition. Even though it is recognized that these substances are not narcotics, they are treated as such in most of the states which are still functioning under the Uniform Narcotic Drug Act. Some of the penalties are absolutely unbelievable, and when Mike Sonnenreich mentioned the discrepancies in the state levels, he was certainly not kidding. My own state, for example, punishes those caught in the presence of marijuana without knowing it, the penalty being a five-year sentence in the state penitentiary—that is, five years imprisonment for being in the presence of a narcotic drug, which includes marijuana, *without knowing it.* To *knowingly* possess marijuana only carried a 3½ year sentence. I am sure there is a reason for that—there must be—I have been looking for it for five years now and have not found it. We are trying to change this law.* Finally our Supreme Court did come down just a few months ago and say that it is a bit harsh to give someone five years when they did not even know they were in the presence of the drug, and the court held a person must have knowledge, but it may be presumed that a person had knowledge if he is in a room where there are drugs, and it is up to the accused to prove that he did not know it. This seems to me to be just a slight reversal of our standard concepts of justice, which declare you are innocent until you are proved guilty, but we see many reversals in this areas of late. Sale of a drug in Massachusetts is punished by ten to fifteen years for first offense. So a college roommate in a dormitory who hands some marijuana to his roommate can receive up to fifteen years and twenty to forty years for a second offense. You may think that is harsh, but Georgia punishes doing the same thing by offering mandatory life for the first offense and death for the second offense (and nothing said about a third offense). I note that very recently the states of Washington and Oregon (while still functioning under the Uniform Narcotic Drug Act) have, as of about a year ago, separated out marijuana so that while, for example, to possess a narcotic drug in Oregon carries a $5,000 fine or ten years in prison, for marijuana, there is an alternative penalty which can be given: $5,000 or one year and it is deemed a misdemeanor. There is also the alternative

---

*Subsequent to this speech, the Massachusetts law was changed to require that the person in possession had knowledge.

penalty of $5,000 or ten years which remains in the Uniform Act, but at least there now is an alternative for the court to choose.

Are people going to jail for these long terms on the state level? For the most part they are not. What is happening in most of the states is that there is a great deal of plea bargaining going on. For those of you who are not attorneys, plea bargaining is the process by which you plead guilty in return for a recommendation of mercy by the prosecutor or a recommendation that you not go to prison but that you receive a suspended sentence and be placed on probation. This is what has happened to thousands and thousands of young people throughout the country. They have been facing twenty, thirty, forty years of penalties if you add up the state and the federal penalties. They go into court, plead guilty and are placed on probation for a year or two, which means they have to call a probation officer every few months. When they do call the probation officer, after a few months, he often requests that they do not even call any more. They have so many real criminals to deal with without the addition of the marijuana offender. Consequently the youngsters feel they have beaten the system. The question is, have they in fact beaten the system? I feel that they have not, and they find this out very quickly, for the first thing to be lost is their driver's license. The next thing they have to do is go through life answering "Yes" to the question, Have you ever been convicted of a felony, and if so, what kind? The answer is "Yes, a narcotics felony," and that is going to stay with them and prevent them from practicing law perhaps, prevent them from practicing medicine, prevent them from voting, prevent them from going into the armed services and in many ways interfere with their lives. This was brought home very clearly to me in a case of four dental students who were charged with possession of LSD. They purchased the LSD from a girl who was regularly supplying the dental school. It bothered me that they made the purchase because as I often ask the question, How do people know that what they are buying really is LSD or what they think it to be? We know from monitoring the drug traffic that 30 percent of what is purchased is not what it is supposed to be; it is either oragano or cereal or strychnine or something else. Many of the deaths from drugs (we have had forty in Massachusetts; there have been over four hundred this year alone in New York) are caused either from the overdose from improper cutting of these drugs or from a foreign substance. Many deaths in Massachusetts have been caused by talcum powder which apparently is not absorbed by the lung; people think they are buying heroin and it turns out to be talc and they are dead a few hours later. So it troubled me that these dental students, with their knowledge of pharmacology and so forth, which they would be obtaining in school, would just buy this substance. However, it was LSD and they chose very carefully. They chose a most secluded area. Of course how were they to know that there was a horse show in progress on the adjoining acreage and that there was an exhibitionist running around there and that this day the police decided they were going to get this fellow by sending in an extra squad of men to fan out into the adjoining acreage. Well, these dental students took the LSD—they had eight capsules, they took four and left the remaining four in an open briefcase. They were contemplating the beauty of the water, or whatever you do under the influence of LSD, and everything was going smoothly until one of them had to go to the bathroom (I gather that going to the bathroom under the influence of LSD can be a problem). One of them left the group, went up over the hill, took off all his clothes and began going to the bathroom, whistling as he did so. At this moment, through the woods came a rooky patrolman, searching for an exhibitionist. He found what he thought surely must be the exhibitionist of all times. He walked up to this fellow and said, "What are you doing?" The fellow looked back at him and said, "Well, what do you think I'm doing?" The officer, having a sense of humor, said, "Well, do you always whistle?" The way the fellow put it, he said at this moment it was as if his mind left him and went up in a tree and watched this naked idiot talking to this police officer. Then he suddenly realized he had to save his three friends. Now if he had just gone and gotten into the patrol car and done nothing else, that would have been it, they would have never found the three friends. But he began yelling their names at the top of his lungs and the officer, not really knowing what to do with this youngster, handcuffed this fellow naked to a tree and ran after and got the other three, and thinking he was hallucinating himself, he called for help. This story was told on the witness stand and it was just unbelievable.

I wrote to the Board of Dental Examiners asking the hypothetical question, which I said I knew would be very unlikely to ever arise, but what would happen if four dental students were ever arrested. The answer came back very quickly. In all probability, they would not be permitted to take the state exam; they would not be permitted to take the national exam; and that would be the end of four years of college and three years of graduate school. Now I do not know how you feel about that, but I merely say to you that the problem of going in and pleading guilty and getting put on probation is just the beginning of the problem, and that is why I am so concerned that we have 100,000 felons going around. I guess we will be seeing some cases in the near future also of people who want to practice law and whose board of bar examiners feel that if you are convicted of marijuana or LSD possession, you are not fit to be a lawyer. I am sure we will be seeing some cases where people seek admission to these professions, even though the drug offenses remain on their record.

The parents of these four boys came to town and exhibited classic reactions. One father was angry and would not talk to me. He saw this as my fault, my mistake, my law, and I represented everything that he was against and that was it—complete animosity. The second kept asking, "Isn't there another boy with the same name [and it was a very long complicated name], isn't there another so-and-so in the dental class at the school. There must be. This couldn't be my boy." He never believed that it was really his boy. The other two fortunately were able to carry on logical, rational communication with me and proceeded to trial. The judge wanted to make an example of these boys because he said we cannot have dental students and medical students doing this, but finally after a lengthy speech from the Dean and everybody else that I could come up with, he did continue the case without a finding, which is the only result that would prevent a conviction. This also makes the law look ridiculous, because here you have crimes carrying many years in penalties and the case is continued without a finding as if it were a parking violation. How does that make the law look in the eyes of young people or in the eyes of anyone.

There is a lot of talk about reducing marijuana possession to a misdemeanor; you heard Mike Sonnenreich say that is what the Federal Government is going to do and I am all for that; we have got to get rid of the felony penalties. Remember we still have the same problems because many employers and many professions are now not asking any longer, Have you ever been convicted of a felony?, but they are asking, Have you ever been convicted of any crime other than a parking violation? And if so, what kind? So I really do not think this solves the problem. My own feeling is that the criminal law does not belong in the area of possession, it belongs in the area of trafficking where it can be very helpful. The civil law can be helpful in dealing with possession. I do not think we gain anything by criminalizing huge segments of young people. When you reduce the offense to a misdemeanor, you might bring about the result of a harsher enforcement of the law than if you left it alone as a felony, because in the states where they have five- or ten-year felonies, nobody is going to jail. One or two people are serving twenty years for simple possession of marijuana that I know of. I believe that there is one in the state of Washington and there is one, or was one, recently in the state of Virginia. Still most people do not go to jail. However, if you reduce this offense to a misdemeanor and you have a penalty of six months, or as in Nebraska, seven days, and in California, up to a year, young people do go to jail. I question whether anybody who is convicted of marijuana possession ought to go to jail, because all he is going to learn there is that there are a lot of different drugs than marijuana and there are a lot of ways to make money with them. I cannot see how anyone is going to be helped by being sent to jail for simple possession of any drug.

The point I was going to make as far as states such as New Jersey, Massachusetts and about a dozen other states in the country is that they have mandatory reporting statutes. This means that at the moment a young person or any person feels he is getting sick or that he needs help with a drug problem, he goes to a physician. The physician must immediately report him to either the police or the public health agency, depending on which state he is in. In New Jersey, it is the police who must be directly informed; in Massachusetts, the public health department must make it immediately available to the police. This constitutes a mandatory breach of the physican-patient relationship so that when a person goes for help, he is reported immediately. Name, height, weight, date of birth, name of the drug—and we wonder why people are not seeking help in the outpatient units of various hospitals around the country until they are at death's door. Why are they going to the outside fringe groups, the self-help groups, the groups outside the Establishment? Because they are afraid of the Establishment. They want help and they do not feel they can get it within our school system, within our established medical system. I submit that we have got to change this, and I think that these laws which force this mandatory breach of a professional relationship, whether it be with a teacher, a social worker or a physician, are improper and must end. Perhaps we will make out better in an individual case, we will apprehend somebody or cut down on the trafficking to some minute degree, but the harm we will work on society in general, it seems to me, is just not worth the cost.

The federal law operates on top of and concurrently with the state law, and not instead of the state law. This was brought home very clearly to me when I gave a speech at Wayne State to the medical alumni, five hundred very eminent physicians and their wives. The fellow who spoke before me decided he wanted to keep his audience awake, so he handed marijuana out to everybody in the audience, and they were smelling it and passing it around. I began my speech by telling them what they had done —they had committed felonies ranging up to thirty years in both the state and the federal prison. When they held the marijuana and looked at it, they violated the Michigan possession law which is eight to ten years in the state penitentiary. They also violated the federal law which is two to ten more years in the federal penitentiary. When they handed it to their neighbor, they violated the Michigan transfer law—fifteen to twenty years in the state penitentiary. They violated the federal law on transfer of marijuana without a tax stamp which carries a minimum mandatory five-year penalty in the federal penitentiary, which means that you cannot be put on suspension or be given a suspended sentence. You must serve five years or the parole period of at least three years in the federal penitentiary. The audience thought it was very funny when I began, but when I finished they did not think it was so funny. Everybody walked out of there feeling a little bit different about the marijuana and drug laws, and I did not think it was so funny either when I read the headline in the paper the next day that five hundred medical alumni committed felonies at Wayne State. I left immediately thereafter.

As for pushing, we all hear that we must kill the pushers and not be so tough on the users. The question must be asked, What kind of pusher? There are two kinds of pushers in the world—the smart pusher and the stupid pusher. I always end up representing the stupid pusher for some reason. The smart pusher is the importer. He takes a minimum of risk. He brings the stuff in, sells it to the middleman who takes all the risk and makes the contact with the police and sells it to the ultimate user. I had one case that I will never forget, the case of a young fellow who sold to a police officer. The police officer had made errors in his cover, and anyone would have known that it was a police officer to whom he was selling except my client. Well, he made the sale on a Friday, and the officer a federal agent, was extremely pleased. He said, "Could you get me some more." The fellow says, "Sure. I can get all you want." He called up the smart pusher who was still in town, the importer, and said he needed some more for this fellow—"We got a great customer here." The fellow said, "I don't like it. It sounds to me like there is something wrong." Of course my client put his hand over the phone and said to the agent, "He thinks there is something wrong. Now isn't that ridiculous." So the agent said, "Let's send a cab for him." Now it was alleged, and I could never prove this, but it was alleged that the driver of the cab was also an agent. I have reason to believe it was true. This cab was dispatched. They picked up the prime importer who was not so smart after all, because he figured that if a cab came he would go. He made the transfer of the substance to the middleman who gave it to the police officer and both were arrested at gunpoint. The middleman was arrested and charged with a violation and was indicted for the sale on Friday. He was also indicted a second time—a separate indictment which came up before a separate judge—for the sale on Saturday. It was the intention to try this fellow and convict him on the first offense which carries a minimum mandatory five-year sentence and convict him of a second offense which carries a minimum mandatory ten-year sentence. I repeat that this is a young man with no previous criminal record whatsoever, and he is about to go away for ten years. That disturbs me and I felt maybe here is the case that I would be able to appeal. In many other cases, the statement is made by the prosecuting attorney that there will be a recommendation of probation if the person pleads guilty and this offer must be accepted. Everybody wants to be a test case until they are arrested. After they are arrested they do not want to be a test case any more; they just want to be rid of this process, and the attorney for the accused cannot take a chance of turning down an offer of probation or suspended sentence in the hopes that he will succeed on appeal. If I lost, the fellow would go away for five, ten or fifteen years. But in this particular case you cannot be placed on probation. Sale of marijuana under the present federal law (which is about to be changed) carries a minimum mandatory sentence which remains a no-probation and no-suspended sentence. Many people in law enforcement make a great deal of this discretion. I would say, "Fine," if you have the right judge or if you have the right prosecutor, but if you have the wrong judge, the wrong prosecutor, the wrong police officer, people are going to be very badly hurt by these present laws. In this case, discretion was used and the charge of sale was dropped against this individual, and he was tried or he was allowed to plead guilty of possession. We did have a bit of a problem in the courtroom. Ordinarily when one goes in for a guilty plea, it is a very routine matter. In this case, the judge began to cross-examine this young man. Did anybody make you any promises? Did anybody make you any deals? Of course, the answer is "No." No promises, no deals, because we tell the client that he may still go away, even though he may receive probation for possession and even though the sale charge has been dropped, he still could go away for two to ten years for possession. The client invariably asks, however, "Have you ever seen a person go away when the U. S. attorney has recommended probation?" my answer is, "No, I never had." But this fellow was being cross-examined for forty-five minutes and the judge said, "I've had it with these marijuana cases. I'm going to send you away. Do you have any last words?" After they propped up my client, who tried to speak after what seemed like hours, but really only a few seconds, he finally said, "What will I do about my wife, she's pregnant?" The judge took a five-minute recess, verified the pregnancy and came back and accepted the recommendation.

How do we change laws? We realize we have problems with the law. We all realize that no matter what side of the picture we are on. How do we change them? Well, Timothy Leary has one way. He gets arrested for various crimes and then he appeals to the Supreme Court. Now in one case he was driving into Loredo. He had some marijuana in the car and drove across the bridge to Loredo, then drove back from Loredo into the United States with the same marijuana in the car and an agent looked in and saw a shred of marijuana on the floor. (If an agent looks in your car and sees marijuana on the floor or counterfeit money on the seat or guns, that is not illegal search and seizure, because he is merely looking in and that is not an unreasonable search.) So they ordered everybody out of the car and they vacuumed out the car. Now if you vacuum out Timothy Leary's car, you are bound to come up with something. They did find about a half an ounce of marijuana. They also found another half an ounce on Susan Leary, his daughter. They did not say where they found it, but they only said in the opinion that they found it after an in-depth personal search. Dr. Leary said on the stand, I believe, that he ordered her to get rid of the marijuana before they ever went near the bridge and she of course, disobeyed. (These kids just will not listen to their parents any more.) In any event, he was convicted and received the maximum under the law. Thirty years in prison and a $30,000 fine. His first appeal was based on freedom of religion. He said, just as the native American Indians in California can use peyote, so should all of his followers, who are Hindus, be able to use marijuana to facilitate their belief in Hinduism. The Court went through the cases clearly, including the Woody Case in California and showed how careful controls were used by the native American Indians. They described how one person never took any peyote and he administered it to the others, nobody was allowed to leave the reservation. They actually worshipped the drug. Without their drug, peyote, there would be no religion, and the Court found that there was just nothing like this in Dr. Leary and they threw this appeal out. The second appeal was a very interesting one, and it was successful in part. This is the case which invalidated the tax stamp mechanism. The federal law allowed one to possess marijuana, or even to import it, and to transfer it legally if you bought a tax stamp. You might try to get a tax stamp sometime. It is an interesting experience. What happens is if you ever were to get a tax stamp, the federal law also requires that the Federal Government who sold you the tax stamp immediately notify the state authorities that you have just bought a tax stamp. Possession of marijuana under the state law is illegal so you have just been forced, Leary said, to incriminate yourself by the federal law, because when you get the tax stamp you are immediately arrested by the state authorities. This argument was successful. For all intents and purposes the marijuana tax act is dead.

Another way to change marijuana laws was tried in Massachusetts in the longest marijuana trial in history—about eight weeks—during which every expert and pseudo-expert on marijuana in the entire world came to tell the judge what they thought about marijuana. This was the case which tried to question the merits of the law. Is it not a cruel and unusual punishment to send a person away for five years for being in possession or being in the presence of a drug such as marijuana? I think that is a good question. It is a question I have a lot of trouble with when kids will ask me, "Well how come my father can have his five martinis and get absolutely stoned drunk every night at dinner and if I go near marijuana they can put me away for five years?" It is a tough question to answer. However the Court did find that marijuana was a dangerous drug and in the judge's opinion, if you just plugged in the word "alcohol" instead of the word "marijuana" you would come up with a perfect description of alcohol. However he still felt marijuana was a dangerous drug and refused to change the penalties. It seems to me that legislation is the way we are going to have to go—not in the courts. That is why this federal legislation is extremely significant.

There was one reason I was sorry to see the tax stamp mechanism go and that is because we tried to do marijuana research in Boston. Now here is a drug being used by between fifteen and twenty million people right now, this week, and there were only two research projects until 1968 in this history of the United States. One in the 1920's involved a group of prisoners from the Canal Zone and another in the 1940's was the LaGuardia Report which was an excellent study and which showed that marijuana was not all that dangerous as people had thought it was, and as a result you could not buy a copy of the LaGuardia Report for many years. I think we are in agreement that through the whole Department of Justice, the whole Federal Bureau of Narcotics, the Anslinger days and until very recently, there was a great deal of repression of research. This is why we are concerned about the difference between the law enforcement approach to the drug problem and the health, education and prevention approach which I do not think are incompatible. This is the battle we have been waging this year in talking about the federal legislation. But at least when you had the tax stamp mechanism, you went to the Government and asked for a tax stamp, you could hold the marijuana and possess it legally under the federal law. So we went and we asked for a tax stamp. It took us eight months to get a tax stamp. When it finally came through, after eight months of hassle and a trip to Washington, we were finally federally empowered to do research for a drug being used by fifteen to twenty million people. Most researchers would just have given up, which is why research has not been done over the past thirty years because it has been just too much of a hassle to do it. Finally we received the tax stamp. The Federal Bureau was very cooperative, the new bureau, and said, "Well, where are you going to get the marijuana?" We did not want to tell the researchers we were thinking of buying it on Charles Street. We just did not feel that that was professional. So they said, "Look. We'll send some up. We have six tons which we have seized. We can't even burn it any more. It will turn on the whole city of Washington, if we do." They sent up the marijuana. As it was in transit, I had a terrible thought that we were all going to be arrested, because possession of marijuana for any reason, research or otherwise, is illegal under the laws of the Commonwealth of Massachusetts and under most state laws. I remembered the meeting early in the morning with the researchers who tried to talk me out of doing anything about this saying, "They will never find out. Let's go ahead." I had a feeling they already knew and that they were just waiting for some nice headlines of which we had seemed to have more than our share in Massachusetts. Well in any event, I decided to take the bull by the horns and write a letter to the Commissioner of the Boston Police asking his permission to do a marijuana research project. I wrote as follows: "Dear Commissioner McNamara, This is to request your permission to do a marijuana research project at Harvard and Boston Universities at such-and-such a time at such-and-such a place. May we have your permission? Very truly yours." He wrote me back saying, "Thank you very much for informing me that you are about to commence a marijuana research project at such-and-such a time and at such-and-such a place. Very truly yours." That is a real problem. What do you do with a letter like that? The state police said "absolutely not" and it was only with the help of Elliott Richardson that we were able to proceed with the research.

Well, there we are. Where are we is really the question? We have got some federal legislation coming up. Doctor Blachly mentioned before that Mr. Sonnenreich and I have gone different ways. Well, we really have. Now what is the argument all about? Doctor Blachly knows well what it is all about because he is a member of the Committee for Effective Drug Abuse Legislation, which was formed last year, believe it or not as a result of Mr. Sonnenreich's comments. He appeared at a symposium in Rutgers, and everybody said, "How can you do this?" For at that time the Justice Department had submitted a bill which not only was a terrible bill, because of what I will tell you about in a minute, but even had the same penalties that are in the law now, the same minimum mandatory sentence for marijuana transfer, et cetera, all the way down the line. Mr. Sonnenreich got up at Rutgers and said, "If you are so upset, why don't you organize about this and do something about it," knowing that we never would because scientists just cannot seem to organize effectively. The Committee for Effective Drug Abuse Legislation was formed at a meeting of the Salk Foundation February 1970 a few days after the bill passed the Senate of the United States, 82 to nothing. Here we had a bill that went for 82 to nothing and the penalties had fallen down by that time; they had been dropped to a reasonable level, and the penalty structure was pretty good. It is still pretty good today although it certainly could be a lot better. What the bill did was just to take the entire drug problem from beginning to end and deliver it lock, stock and barrel to the Attorney General of the United States and remove all meaningful powers from the Secretary of Health, Education and Welfare and from anyone who was interested in a health and education approach to this problem. For example, the Attorney General was given the right to review research protocols with schedule I substances, which would include marijuana, so that every time a person wanted to do research with marijuana he not only had to go to HEW, he also would have to send the research protocol to the Attorney General who would review it to make sure that this legitimate researcher is not going to divert the substances into the illegal market. Now that is ridiculous. Of course it is easy to write laws to come down hard on the physician and on the legitimate researcher. These are easy people to go after. It is tough to go after the Mafiosa and the people who are handling the drugs at those levels, although the Justice Department is making some headway there. There is a law enforcement role here. Why do we have three times the number of amphetamines that we need for medical use in this country? Why do they get exported to Tijuana and re-imported into illegal channels a few days later? Why do we have professional companies turning out 78,000 doses of LSD per hour on professional pill-making machines? Why do we have bathtubs full of methamphetamine being made in illicit laboratories all around the country? Now these are real law enforcement problems. The Justice Department is moving against these and of course it is a tremendous challenge to do anything in these areas. Still why do we have to deliver total control over drugs to the Attorney General in order to accomplish these legitimate enforcement aims. For example, the Attorney General in the original bill had the power to classify substances. Now the Secretary of HEW could give his advice, but the final decision was to be made by the Attorney General. That is a health problem. The question is how dangerous are these substances to the individual and to society? Should the Attorney General be sole arbiter of the fact? I do not think so. There were other problems with the bills. In the new bill which has just been reported out, that is H. R. 18583, there have been many changes. Now the Secretary of Health, Education and Welfare is able to exercise veto power over whether or not a substance should be a controlled dangerous substance on the basis of medical and scientific reasons. That is an appropriate approach. All research involvement of the Attorney General has been removed, and it has been sent back over to the Secretary of HEW where it belongs. There have been many other changes. The bill is a good bill and we are prepared to support it at this time. In my own personal opinion, I wish we could go further with civil penalties instead of criminal penalties but that is for the future.

We know that we have failed in our homes and in our schools to meaningfully communicate with young people. We know that. That is the whole problem, and in all of these workshops which are going on around the country, we have got to change the attitudes of teachers before we even reach the kids. We have got to change the attitude of parents before we can reach the kids, so that we can once again stimulate meaningful communication.

The dichotomy of whether you treat people as criminals or sick persons is a real problem. I had one case where a fellow was arrested for possession in Massachusetts. While he was waiting trial (and while I was trying to prevent him from having a record because he had no previous arrests), he was arrested for possession in another county. At that point I gave up. He was fined and he decided that he would leave Massachuetts because it was an unjust, unfair state, and he would go to a nice state like Florida, where justice meant something. When he left, he had with him, of course, 15 pounds of the finest marijuana you could find in Massachusetts. Naturally his first contact in Florida was with a Florida State trooper. He was arrested for sale and faced twenty years of prison in Florida because of his past record in Massachusetts. His mother who was all upset called me. "What are we going to do?" she asked, screaming and sobbing. I said, "Look. We've got to get him bailed out." And we got him bailed out. "We've got to have him returned to Massachusetts." We got him returned to Massachusetts. "We've got to get him to a hospital. I don't know what else we can do because he's going to get the twenty years down there as sure as can be." I got a call later that day from the state hospital which said, the boy was really sick—a latent schizophrenic. I called the mother and said, "I have good news for you. Your son is a latent schizophrenic. He's not going to get the twenty years." There was a long silence at the other end of the phone. The mother finally ended up yelling and blaming me for her son's problems—Why didn't I let him go to jail? Why did I make a mental patient out of him?

So this is where we are. Above all else, we must realize that the young people of this country are our most important asset. We have got to remember that as we legislate in this most crucial area.

14

Discussion

Neil L. Chayet and Michael R. Sonnenreich

Blachly: I would like to get my dig in first, and that is to point that the newspapers recently have been giving some publicity to the attempt to discourage opium growing by the Turkish farmers. When asked about opium abuse in Turkey, the farmers say, "Well, we have no problem with opium abuse. Nobody seems to be addicted here." I am also told that there is little problem with abuse of marijuana and opium in Mexico where it is also grown. If people do not abuse drugs in those locations where they are grown, does this not have implications for legal controls of drug abuse?

Sonnenreich: I would like to hold on that particular point until we get into the questions and answers, but I would like to make one point that I think just has to be said, and I know once again that it is not appealing. It is very nice to talk about education, rehabilitation and research, but the fact of life is, and it is something that you had better be very very cognizant of, the state of the art is not such that you can effectively rehabilitate large numbers of these people. I do not know how you rehabilitate a marijuana user, a chronic user or somebody on LSD. I do not know what the scope of research is in this area that will give us the answer. It does not mean that we do not try to find the answer, but let us not delude ourselves by using words like education, rehabiliation and research and find ourselves five years from now in the same credibility gap that one finds with law enforcement. We are using these as alternatives and we are constantly discussing them as the "right" alternative. We do not have the answers; yet to talk about meaningful discussions on the drug issue when most parents cannot discuss almost anything with their children is to beg the issue, because you are not going to have a parent sit down and meaningfully reach his child on the subject of drug abuse unless the parents can meaningfully reach his child on a host of other problems. I think you have to be aware of the fact that this is not something that is going to come about in a very short period of time. I have seen the seminars. I have seen the workshops. I have seen the mandatory drug abuse information required in junior high schools and high schools and the discussions at the college level. In many instances realistically, it is a farce. You are talking, but the kids are not listening. So that, sure, you are doing education but the question is, are you doing it in a meaningful way? My answer is, and I am giving you a personal opinion here, that I do not think we are even at the starting gate in knowing how to reach these people. This does not mean that we should not work on it, but do not play these points up as the panacea for the drug problem because they are not the panacea. We cannot produce results with them yet, and until you can produce results, do not back yourselves into a corner where you are going to turn around and have the same thing said of these programs which do offer hope, long-term hope, as has been said of law enforcement.

Another point that should be made is that no matter how horrendous, past state and federal laws were, nobody is questioning that, do not go and start arguing the point emotionally. Neil is quite good at this. The important thing is to look at the thing somewhat dispassionately and recognize that you are not talking about marijuana. Marijuana is a part of the problem. It is one strand going down the system. You are talking about possession, and you had better talk about possession of every drug. If you are talking about victimless crimes, you had better start facing the major issue, and that is if you do not want to have possession offenses for marijuana, you had better realistically recognize that you cannot have them for other hallucinogens. This is a legitimate point. This is something that realistically you have got to come to grips with. To just say, well, let's get a hold of marijuana. Let's solve the marijuana problem. You are not solving the marijuana problem or anything, because intellectually it is false. You have got to meet the full issue head on, and if you are going to meet that full issue head on, you have got to recognize that you are talking about an expanse of drugs. This may be an end result. It may be that from a law enforcement point of view, from a social point of view, you want to wind up with no possession penalties. By the same token you may not want to. It is something you have got to recognize. You must also recognize another important fact —that you are not just talking about all the drugs. You are talking about a criminal system of justice. You are talking about the administration of justice and the things that you do in regard to the drugs, if the penalties are in conformity, if the system is in conformity with the rest of your criminal code, then you have got to go one step beyond that and examine your criminal code. You have got to say, "Does the system respond?" The criminal law just does not respond in the area of drugs but responds across an entire width of prohibited acts, acts that society says are "no-nos," and you have got to make darn certain that before you are willing to just talk about the drug problem, you had better examine your system and see maybe if you cannot improve the general system of criminal justice as the Chief Justice of the Supreme Court stated, and many others have stated since and before, that is in a drastic need of some change. We need people not to look at the little pieces, because what you are doing if you are looking at just the drug scene and not at the whole picture—how people go through the court system, what happens in bail and in sentencing, and what happens when you throw the guy in the pokey—is exactly the same thing that was done in the past years with marijuana, heroin and the opium poppy—you are taking little pieces of the problem and saying, "We have solved it." You have not solved it. You have just taken that piece and moved it out of phase. I strongly urge everybody not to get bogged down with cliches and platitudes and the single issues of a drug, like marijuana, and start looking at it in terms of the total system. I think in fairness you have got to do this if you really want to get at the problem.

Blachly: Neil, would you like to respond to that for a minute?

Chayet: Mike, let's just look at the last point you raised—the question of the administration of justice. I understand that the County Court in Los Angeles County is running one-third of its criminal court docket on drug and drug-related cases. In Boston,

I know it is more than one-fourth. Do you realize what that means
to the administration of justice? Not only are we having really no
impact, no constructive impact, on the drug problem by the use
of the criminal law, but we are absolutely crippling the system
and preventing the rapers, the murderers and the robbers, from
being tried; they are all going to get tried sooner or later, but
we have absolutely choked the courts beyond belief because of
the drug problem. The drug problem is no longer a little part
of the problem. It is a big part. If you are going to say, let's wait
until we can reform the whole criminal justice system before we
can turn to a part of it, mainly the drug problem, I am afraid it
is going to be too late. I do not think you really mean that because
you have been working on the drug problem for the past two years
and I do not want to think that the past two years of your work
have been wasted. I do not think that it has. As for the question
of the criminal law, what is the role of the criminal law in this
area? That is really the crucial question. In my opinion, the
criminal law is extremely harmful in this area. Now this is not to
say that the law is useless in the area. The *criminal* law is useless.
We have a legislator in Massachusetts who recently said, "Look,
here's the solution. We make two ounces of marijuana or less
legal. Anything over two ounces, send him away." That was his
solution. Headlines and editorials followed along with a great
deal of public comment. This is a very questionable approach,
because there are a lot of people in this country who are not using
drugs because they are illegal. Now I think it is, of course, good
not to use drugs if you can possibly avoid such use, and anything
which encourages people not to use drugs I think is a good thing.
Although the law cannot govern private morality, I think it can
lead the way and set examples, and if we do have a lot of young
people who are not using drugs because of the law, that is fine.
However the minute you step over and use the criminal law instead of the civil law (and there are some very effective ways
that the civil law can be used in this way) and criminalize this
individual, this young person, who has no previous criminal record, you destroy him in many different ways. You destroy his
family. You effectively prevent any credibility, any communication with the system because he sees it for what it is, and I do not

think we want to do that with 100,000 of our young American people.

Chayet: I have the document which has just been adopted by the Uniform Commission of State Laws. Can I shift over to Mike for one minute and ask him to explain it a little more. He has got one advantage that I do not have. You see the Justice Department sends him around to all forty-six governors and makes sure that he goes to the Uniform Commission meetings, whereas I spend most of my time with physicians and scientists. So I would like to have him say a little bit more about a Uniform Law. I am totally opposed to the present federal law because of the abuse of the criminal law in the way it is being used. However, as a political decision, which I have to make too because, if I decided to say let's use only the civil law instead of the criminal law, our group (Committee for Effective Drug Abuse Legislation) would lose all of its effectiveness, and we have been effective because we have not gone way out on a limb. We have worked within the system. We have made meaningful changes. I would say as a political reality, the bill is the best we could have done, the best we could have hoped for, and I would support its passage, looking towards further amendment to the system in future years. I expect my reply on the state bill would be the same as long as we can keep going and keep looking at it and not do as we did back in the 1930's, pass the law, give total powers to the Federal Bureau of Narcotics and never let anybody look at it again.

Sonnenreich: Let me explain what is going on. As for the state bill, the Uniform Act will not be available because of printing. It just passed two weeks ago in St. Louis. As soon as it is ready, it will be widely distributed. It is distributed through the National Conference of Commissioners on Uniform State Laws and to get those you ask Frances McKay in Chicago and they distribute it, we do not. As to whom I am visiting, I am visiting the governors as a result of the White House Governor's Conference. I am really surprised that he did not mention another state which imposed for possession count, a 1500-year sentence. It seems that in one of the states, the jury is the one that sentences, not the judge, and the particular law is written such that there is a minimum but there is no maximum. So what the juries are now doing is they are vying with one another to see who can impose the harshest penalty. What happened is the record penalty set in this state for possession of marijuana was 1000 years, which of course is very good because the man is eligible for parole in 330 years. Then another jury came down and they felt that they were not going to be out done so they set up 1005 years, and three weeks ago another one just decided to really grab the bull by the horns and go for 1500 years. They did not want to go in these increments of five years each, which points out how ludicrous the law can be if put in the wrong hands. The state bill is a bill that pretty much now tracks the federal bill that was reported out of the House which Neil does support even though he recognizes that he is going forward into bigger and better things. The Federal Government cannot tell the states what penalties to establish. The Conference went out on a limb—and this was the big argument—by specifically putting a penalty in for possession as a misdemeanor, which I think was a major step forward in terms of the Conference. The thing that is most important is that it tracks all the provisions in terms of regulation, research and granting immunity. Many of the things that Neil was concerned about have been resolved in both the federal and the state bill in terms of the fact that the law specifically states that anybody who is authorized by federal law to conduct research is automatically allowed to possess it lawfully and distribute it within the scope of his research. So you cannot get in trouble with the kind of letter Neil mentioned from the Chief of Police of Boston. What it has also done is preempted the field in this area in terms of the federal law. Nobody can be brought into any state or federal, civil or criminal hearing or before any state or Federal legislature to disclose names of research people. Thus what we have tried to do is to bring in some consistency, and we think quite realistically. As a result of this we are going to get greater uniformity in the states, but we are going to run into the problems in the states as to the penalties. I think that Neil's viewpoint is a viewpoint shared by some but not a lot of people. That is subject to argument. The answer, as I see it, when legislatures begin to discuss the bill is that if they are not going to focus on the parts that dovetail in with the federal law, they are going to focus on penalty.

Now the intent of this is an obvious recognition that 100,000 felons do not result from the federal bill. In terms of possession offenses in the federal law, we have not made possession offenses since January of 1969, so the problems that you are getting confronted with are state problems, and the way to resolve them is quite simply by dealing with your state. The thing that is interesting about it is that laws are not made in a vacuum, and I think, as Neil and his group discovered, you can effectively alter a system, bring your viewpoint forward and get some action. You are as entitled to lobby as anyone else is entitled to lobby, to get your point of view across or at least present your point of view. So it is there and it is on the record, and I think that this is the thing that is most important when you are talking about criminal laws and legislation. You have got to get up and be heard. It is one thing to go outside and talk to your friends and say, well I think this law is terrible. It is another thing to get up, spend your own time, get yourself organized and do something about it, and I think that if you feel strongly enough about it, this is the time to do it, because almost every state but one meets this year. Rather than say, my point of view will not be heard, this is the time to get up, give your point of view, pro and con. I guarantee there are a lot of people who feel the other way. The thing I think you have got to recognize in this area is that those with opposing views are as entitled to as much respect as you are in terms of your viewpoint. However, you had better be able to logically meet their point of view, because just arguing on the basis of "they're wrong, I'm right" is not going to solve the problem for you.

Question: By your own figures, approximately eight billion dosage units of drugs go into illegal hands. Yet when you explained the laws and from my interpretation, the only penalties or the only thing that the Federal Government appeared to be doing against the drug companies was monitoring and informational. Yet the penalties for marijuana can range from anywhere up to five years. Can you explain to me how this happened?

Sonnenreich: There are three types of prohibitive acts in the federal law. There are the Prohibitive Acts A, which deal basically with illicit trafficking; Prohibitive Acts B, which deal with commercial traffic; and Prohibitive Acts C which deal with essentially fraud provisions. We have two ways of dealing with the legitimate concerns that get these drugs out of the channels of legitimate commerce. One is very simple. Do not allow them to produce. Drug companies have to be registered by the Federal Government to meet the criteria that are enumerated in the Act. If you want to talk about a club, I see no better club in the world to make conformants than to tell a company, whatever the name be, you are out of business. If you are out of business, you are in bad shape. The other thing is we do have a tier of penalties, both civil and criminal, that apply to them for willful acts committed in violation of the law. Now these penalties run from heavy fines, which of course hit the companies in their pocketbooks, to penalties for misdemeanor penalties for willful violation and for second offense felonies. So we have a tier system. Most people are not concerned with it and that is the reason I really did not mention it, but make no mistake about it, you have got a tier of penalties and a tier of different approaches. The most effective approach that we feel, in terms of the legitimate industry, is the fact that the companies have to register annually and obtain registration from us.

Let me also make this point. One of the reasons we have got so many problems is that the Federal Government has no way under existing law to deny somebody his registration. They can register as a right, and there is no way we can remove it. The new bill does give us this ability to remove a license, and in effect we feel this is going to be fairly effective. Large companies, like Eli Lilly and Smith, Kline & French, cannot afford to have their registration revoked, and I might point out that what happens is that when the federal registration is revoked, they are out of business because the state government follows the Federal Government in this area. I hope that answers your question.

Question: Do you feel that the drug problem could be better handled by civil law as opposed to by criminal law?

Chayet: I do not feel that you can more effectively deal with the drug problem with the civil law than the criminal law. I merely feel that the costs of the criminal law are so high that we must find an alternative for it. That is my position. I do not mean to say that we can more effectively cut down on the problem and supply or demand or possession by the civil law, but at least we will not be criminalizing large segments of people, and at the same time we will not be legalizing various substances which we do not really know that much about. I could see, for example, the marijuana law used this way. Again, Mike says that you should not talk about the marijuana problem but about the whole drug problem. I think one way we might be able to reestablish some credibility is to deal with the largest segment of the problem in terms of numbers, the greatest of which is the marijuana problem. We might well enforce the first marijuana offense similar to a traffic offense. Now a traffic offense is handled as follows: You are not arrested for its violation. You are given a citation for it. You come to court and there is a special docket, neither criminal nor civil. There is a special docket for these cases. Now if society does not want to relegalize marijuana or if they were to remove all penalties, which they may perfectly rationally refuse to do at this juncture, it seems to me it could move enforcing the law as a civil offense by citation rather than by arrest. The individual who came into court could either be treated some, although few, very sick people who use marijuana need treatment, so this would be a very important role of the law for people who are in fact ill or, if the person were not ill, he could be fined $50 or $100, or whatever is appropriate. For a second offense, the penalty could be the same, with perhaps a higher fine or other special conditions. You might want to make it a criminal offense at some time, you might not. If the individual failed to pay his fine or failed to show up in court, then it could become a criminal offense. It seems to me that this method at least removes the element of automatic criminalization and the marring of a person's record for a long time. Now that is one use of the civil law. The second concerns what to do with the addict? I think the civil commitment of the addict, if properly implemented, which I do not feel it really has been in California and in New York, can be very useful. However commitment should only be used if you have an addict who is a danger, an imminent physical danger, to himself or to the community. I feel you ought to be able to civilly commit that person. If you are going to try and remove all addicts from the streets and put them in concentration camps merely because they are addicts, I think that is self-defeating, but I do think civil commitment does have use. With regard to sale of drugs, I think sale of marijuana could be retained as a misdemeanor. The thing that troubles me most with this idea is that you are still forcing an individual who wants to possess marijuana (which we have made a civil penalty, a civil offense) into the criminal element, the underworld, the subculture, to gain the drug. I think that it is this forcing him into the underworld which brings about any relationship which may exist between marijuana use and harder drugs use; I think a life style is being set when the individual goes into the criminal element. Now you say, well why don't we regulate marijuana like alcohol so we will not force these individuals into the criminal element, then you are still left with the question, what do you do with the 16-year-old? Are you going to allow them to use it properly. That is a difficult question, but I feel, again, that the costs of the criminal law are so high that we ought to be able to take a little bit of thought and construct a different process. By making possession a civil offense, we may still maintain it as an illegal act, and those kids who are going to obey the law (and there are many now who are obeying it) will still continue to obey it, if it is put forward in the correct framework.

I hear Wisconsin has done this and I would be very happy to see how it works out. Another thing has been tried (and should be followed-up) in Holland where they have set up centers, houses or places where people can go to smoke marijuana legally. That is also an interesting concept.

15

Drug Abuse and Crime

David W. Maurer

A t the beginning of this chapter it should be clearly understood that there are exceptions to almost every statement contained herein. Generalizations in the area of drug addiction and its relationship to crime are not only difficult to make but often unreliable after they are made. At the same time, generalizations offer a temptation, not only to sensational journalists but to medical men, enforcement officers, the judiciary, criminologists, researchers and others who, the public assumes, may speak with authority. Once a sweeping statement is made and quoted or paraphrased in print, the public tends to accept it rather than to examine it critically; these generalizations accumulate in the form of public opinion, the result being that the public not only holds lurid beliefs about drug addiction as a causative factor in crime but is prepared to believe reports that are even more lurid, at the same time rejecting or ignoring conservative statements based upon direct scientific observation and experience. Exaggerated statements, on the one hand, and too conservative disclaimings of causative relationships, on the other, are equally misleading.

Furthermore, with the general increase in crime (or the publicity regarding crime) and in the number of drug users, the public tends to associate narcotics with this general increase, perhaps with some justification. However, this loose cause-and-effect association

Note: Acknowledgments are herewith extended to my collaborator, Victor H. Vogel, M.D., for his contributions to this subject as we treated it in Chapter VIII of *Narcotics and Narcotic Addiction,* 3rd ed. Springfield, Charles C Thomas, Publisher, 1970.

may be the basis for some fallacious conclusions regarding drugs and crime.

In the light of modern sociological research, we are learning to recognize two large classes of criminals—the professional and the nonprofessional. The nonprofessional is usually a member of the dominant culture (that large segment of our culture which pays the taxes, makes the laws, establishes the schools and in general supports the institution of organized legitimate society), and when he seriously violates the code of the dominant culture he may be tried, convicted and sentenced, all of which gives him a criminal record. However he is not accepted by the professionals, nor does he have access to their *modus operandi*.

On the other hand, the professional usually belongs to a subculture which is antithetical to the dominant culture. There are many of these criminal subcultures, some existing on the fringes of the dominant culture, some imbedded solidly within it and some definitely outside it. These subcultures have a set of values entirely or partially opposed to those held by the dominant culture. Most of these subcultures are very ancient, having migrated into Europe in the late Middle Ages and to North and South America from the seventeenth century on. There are close bonds connecting members of any given subculture, as, for example, pickpockets, and, in turn, looser but very real bonds connecting all professional pickpockets with all other thieves, of which there are dozens of varieties, all parasitic on the dominant culture.

Members of these subcultures may conform to some of the tenets of the dominant culture, but in the main they have their own mores, ethics and traditions. When they violate the code of their subculture, they must pay the penalty, often ostracism or death. When they violate the code of the dominant culture, they are processed by the courts and penalized the same as nonprofessional from the dominant culture. I have studied several of these subcultures in some depth and present here only a superficial delineation of the relations of criminal subcultures to the dominant culture.

Narcotic addicts form a very recent subculture, originating in America with the opium addicts of the late nineteenth century who congregated because of the social aspects of opium smoking. Since smoking was introduced by the Chinese, who not only had the supply of opium but the equipment and techniques for smoking as well, a small, essentially noncriminal subculture appeared wherein smokers from all walks of life gathered regularly. Although some criminals frequented these groups, largely concentrated in centers of Chinese life, they were mainly composed of people from the dominant culture and did not become predominantly criminal until after 1914, when the Harrison Act outlawed the drugs as well as the addict.

Today drug addicts inhabit a rather tightly organized subculture, supplied with drugs from the underworld and at the same time exploited by other criminal subcultures which prey on the addict. Also, the addict's subculture is infiltrated with criminals from many other subcultures, driven there in order to secure and use drugs. Members of the dominant culture who are addicted are also driven to the subculture of the addicts sooner or later and become a part of the so-called underworld.

The addict's subculture, while neither so ancient nor so homogenous as, say, the subculture of thieves, is very large and highly organized from coast to coast and even on an international basis, and it has already developed a discernible behavior pattern as well as a highly specialized language. As soon as the addict finds the means—almost always illegal—of raising the large amounts of money necessary to support his increasing habit, he becomes a criminal, often a professional or pseudoprofessional, even though he may have originally been a solid member of the dominant culture. After a while, these addicts become indistinguishable from the other criminals who populate the addicts' subculture.

This shift from the dominant culture to the criminal subculture is dramatically illustrated by the shift in the use of opiates by addicts. In 1914, all addicts used opiates or cocaine, with morphine and opium being the most popular. A few used heroin, only recently introduced from Europe and, until the advent of the Harrison Act, as legitimate as opium, morphine or cocaine. In 1937, 50.7 percent of the opiate addicts received at the Lexington Federal Hospital used morphine, a legitimate prescription drug. In 1964, only 9 percent used morphine, the rest having adopted heroin, a drug long outlawed but now the drug commonly used by most criminal addicts. Of course, this is only one of several variations in the use of drugs, not all of which show so clearly the development of the addict's subculture to one predominantly criminal.

Throughout this chapter, then, when we speak of the *criminal narcotic addict,* we mean one who has gravitated—either from the dominant culture or from some other criminal subculture—to the present subculture of the addict and who regularly employs some form of crime to support his habit. Most of his drugs now come from underworld sources. By the term *legitimate addict,* we mean one who is still a member of the dominant culture, who has no connections through which to obtain drugs from the underworld and who does not support his habit by crime, even though he may technically violate the narcotic laws in the course of obtaining and using drugs. A nurse who diverts drugs from medical sources for her own use is a good example.

Among the folklore regarding drug addiction and crime, we frequently encounter the belief that holdup men, murderers, rapists and other violent criminals take drugs to give them courage or stamina to go through with acts which they might not commit when not drugged. Some years ago cocaine was thought to be used for this purpose; but today when almost no addicts take cocaine by itself, there is a popular tendency to credit heroin (the accidental resemblance of the word "heroin" to "hero" has possibly had some influence) with this capacity to motivate and sustain a criminal during crimes of violence. It is believed that drugs stimulate sex crimes, make people vicious, cause moral degeneration and convert otherwise peaceable people into maddened, desperate criminals. Undoubtedly, one factor contributing to the perpetuation of these beliefs is the tendency of some criminals to claim, in court, that they are not responsible for their acts of violence because they were under the influence of drugs; this parallels the tendency, much more common, to claim consideration for a person committing a criminal act because he was under the influence of alcohol. However, in the case of alcohol, many people are familiar with its effects, often including members of the court, and because its use is widespread, there is a tendency to make allowances for criminal behavior by drunken persons, despite the well-established law to the contrary. On the other hand, because drugs are not so widely used and because their effects are not familiar, the drug (whatever it may be) often is credited with effects on human behavior which cannot be scientifically substantiated.

As far back as 1935, Dr. Lawrence Kolb of the Public Health Service wrote a classic analysis of this problem, and anyone seriously interested in drugs and crime should read Kolb's updated article as background material.[4] Most of his conclusions are as valid today as they were then, although the general picture of drug addiction in our society has changed considerably, and there are new drugs to be reckoned with, not all of which fit Kolb's pattern for the opiates and cocaine.

There is a close and definite connection between drug addiction and crime, although that connection is not what it is generally supposed to be, and with some exceptions, there seems to be little evidence to show that drugs, per se, motivate violent crime. While many nonviolent crimes, and occasional crimes of violence, are committed by underworld addicts, these crimes are usually committed in order to get money to buy drugs and are not generally the direct result of any physiological action of drugs on the human organism or the human personality. It should also be noted that drugs are often taken by persons already suffering from various mental disturbances ranging from mild psychopathy to, in rare cases, advanced psychoses. There is a general tendency, especially among police officers, to mistakenly conclude that the erratic or criminal behavior of these persons is the direct result of some mysterious criminogenic narcotic, never identified but firmly believed to account for their behavior.

DRUGS AND THE CRIMINAL PERSONALITY

Although not all abnormal people are criminals by any means, many professional or habitual criminals are demonstrably abnormal, with the preponderance of professional criminals showing strong psychopathic tendencies. However, it should be emphasized at the same time that a high percentage of psychopaths are not only noncriminal in behavior, but also that many of them achieve considerable success in contemporary society. In America, the frontier was made to order for the psychopath; with the physical frontier gone, many of the attitudes of frontier days linger on, and there is still a place for the psychopath in industry, in the professions, in business, in politics and in some of our law enforcement agencies. As long as these psychopaths stay out of illegal activities (by however narrow a margin) and posper, we often accept them as pillars of society; once they reach a certain level of wealth and position, it is no longer proper to recognize their psychopathy. Many personalities who would be classed as psychopathic by psychiatrists have indeed contributed much to the world of science, the arts, military achievement and industrial development, for almost always the psychopath has drive; at the same time, many of them, under the guise of constructive activity, have cause irreparable social harm.

Therefore, I wish to avoid the assmuption, too often encountered these days, that all personality traits which can be roughly classed as psychopathic are "bad," that all narcotic addicts are psychopaths and that all psychopaths are criminals or potential criminals. One finds all types and kinds of personalities using drugs, ranging from substantial and successful professional people to the very dregs of the underworld. All addicts are not criminals in the broad sense of that word, although technically and legally they are so classified, for they violate the narcotics laws whenever they possess drugs to support their habits; in fact, some state laws are so written that addiction itself may be a crime punishable by imprisonment. However, everyone who thinks about the nature of crime at all must go beyond the rather facile definition of crime as a violation of the law. Most of us are law violators every day of our lives; few of us are criminals. Although it is difficult to define crime as such, it is important to remember that there must always be in everyone's mind—and this especially concerns those who must enforce or administer the laws—a distinction between the law violator and the criminal. A criminal may be defined for the purposes of this chapter as one who preys on other people or social institutions habitually and consistently, without regard for the ethical, moral and legal code accepted by ligitimate society.

Regardless of the legal implications, a drug addict who is otherwise a respectable member of the dominant culture cannot be regarded as a criminal simply because he uses drugs. For instance, a competent attorney who has been an alcoholic and who is enabled to carry on an ethical and successful practice only because he has shifted to small amounts of morphine daily is not a criminal. He has an unfortunate personality defect. There are a few such addicts in most communities (medical men, lawyers, businessmen and so on). They seldom become police problems. However, Smith, Ellinwood and Vaillant reported that 61 percent of opiate addicts studied progressed from experimentation to daily use and physical dependence in less than a year with only 11 percent using opium for more than three years without reaching full addiction.[10] If we drop morphine momentarily and consider alcohol, some readers will be able to recall successful surgeons who do not go into the operating room without taking a substantial amount of whiskey. These surgeons, too, have a personality defect, but their technical skill, their social position and their ability to keep their addiction to alcohol under control removes them from any criminal classification; in fact, many people would take the position that if they have to have whiskey to perform first-class surgery, they should have it. However, when the same surgeons have to take narcotic drugs, people are less tolerant, and the surgeon is technically a law violator; if he comes to the attention of the law, he may become a technical criminal with a prison record.

All this discussion leads us up to a single point: Both the professional criminal and the drug addict tend toward psychopathic personalities. Because both classes have a preponderance of psychopaths, there is an area of overlap in which both drug addicts and criminals are prevalent; this is probably the primary reason that most narcotic addicts, especially those with long records of recidivism, concentrate in the underworld. At the same time, there are addicts who are neither psychopaths nor criminals, just as there are many professional criminals who are not addicted. However, the number of psychopaths who are both addicts and have a life pattern of criminality is too large to be ignored.

There are several schools of thought regarding the influence which narcotics have on a life of criminality. It appears to me, in the light of many years of observation of addicts, along with close contacts with many local, state and federal enforcement officers, that an increasing percentage of addicts gravitate to the addicts' subculture from other criminal subcultures—thieves, card and dice hustlers, shoplifters, prostitutes, short con men, forgers, grifters, short-change artists, pimps and others.[6] It is notable that these come from subcultures in which the tradition is one of non-violent crime or from those lower-echelon criminals who live by their wits. Few professionals appear from the subcultures of the *big con*, the *heist* (holdup and bank robbery), the *heavy* (safe-crackers and bank blowers) racketeering or extortion, to name only a few examples. It is remarkable that very few of those who control the traffic in drugs above the peddler level become addicted, and the number of those who do take to drugs dwindles rapidly as one goes upward through the powerful hierarchy which organizes and directs the traffic on a national and international basis.

On the other hand, several studies of large numbers of addicts have been made by researchers connected with the U. S. Public Health Service, notably Dr. M. J. Pescor, who studied 1,000 cases,[9] and Dr. Laurence Kolb, who reported on 225 cases selected because they were basically criminal over and above any criminality necessitated by obtaining drugs, and Dr. Victor Vogel, who reported on a large number of juvenile addicts admitted to the U. S. Public Health Service Hospital.[11] Doctor Pescor shows that 75 percent of the addicts studied had no criminal records prior to drug addiction, and Dr. Vogel's survey showed that 67 percent of the juvenile addicts studied had no criminal records prior to addiction. Dr. Kolb's study is only partially relevant here for the reason that he deliberately selected 225 addicts whose criminal status was well established before addiction.

Perhaps addicts during the 1930's and 1940's represented a higher incidence of people who did not come from criminal subcultures and hence were not, in early life, involved in crime. Also, narcotics were much cheaper then, and it was quite possible for an addict to support his habit for a long time by legitimate employment. Today there is increasing evidence that young addicts are involved in crime, usually of a minor variety, previous to addiction or coincidental to addiction.

Some idea of the complexity of this problem can be gained by examining one set of arrest records for 1963 from California. In that year, a total of 7,932 persons (adults and juveniles) who had no prior drug record were arrested. Of these 32.6 percent had no previous police record, 43.4 percent had a minor police record (probably a heavy percentage of misdemeanor charges), 18.2 percent had a major police record (probably a heavy percentage of felony charges) and 5.8 percent had been in prison.

In interpreting these figures, we must remember that first of all, these persons were arrested; figures on convictions are not available, but the total number will be substantially lower. If we consider also that 32.6 percent had never been arrested and 43.4 percent had been arrested (but not necessarily convicted) for minor offenses, we have a total of 76 percent who can hardly be said to have been established in a life of crime before their first drug arrest. This does not mean, however, that some of them had not been on drugs for some time without being arrested. The figures of 18.2 percent (major arrest record) and 5.8 percent (prison record) gives us 24 percent who may be said to have become closely associated with crime before their first drug arrest. However, again, we do not know how many of the 18.2 percent were convicted, how many of the 18.2 percent and the 8.5 percent had used drugs without being detected and how many of the total number arrested had committed various crimes without being detected before their first arrest.

We will return to these differences of opinion regarding addiction and crime in detail later on. They are sketched at his point only to show that those who have spent many years in contact with drug addiction do not necessarily agree on the specific relationship between crime and narcotics, although all of them would readily concur in the belief that such relationship exists and that it is very important in the overall picture of law enforcement and crime prevention. Furthermore, no one who has had experience with addicts will deny that profound personality changes occur after addiction when the addict is pressed for drugs; a person who was originally of the highest moral character will

lie, steal or commit forgery to secure drugs. How far these criminal tendencies extend beyond the necessity for supporting his
habit is, of course, open to question. At the same time, criminals
of a various and violent type frequently shift to nonviolent criminality after addiction to opiates. Many addicts seem to be quite
reliable in all matters where their supply of drugs is not concerned; many others appear to have lost all moral values and
become unreliable in all areas of behavior. Meanwhile, the relationship of specific drugs to criminal behavior will be considered.

DRUGS AND VIOLENT CRIME

Generally speaking, different drugs have different effects upon
the human being; also, specifically, different drugs vary within
limits in their effects on different individuals. Furthermore, the
effects of the same drug are sometimes different upon normal and
abnormal personalities. Therefore, when we generalize about
drugs, we must keep these three levels of difference in mind; for
every generalization, it is always possible to produce numerous
exceptions, a fact which does not simplify the problem at hand.

First, all the opiates and their synthetic equivalents have a
depressant effect, varying with the quantity taken, the length of
time the addict has used them and the type of personality involved. Although the psychopathic personality (including the
so-called addiction-prone type, whether or not the individual is
a criminal) unquestionably experiences more intense euphoria
from the opiates than does the so-called normal personality, this
euphoria is of short duration and is so intense that it inhibits any
type of physical activity, either criminal or noncriminal. The
secondary effects of opiates are in the main so pleasant and so
soothing that any violent psychopath will be deterred from following any impulses he may have to commit violent crime; he is
robbed of ambition and the capacity for aggressive action to the
point that he is eventually content with a life of idleness. This
fact is well illustrated by the fact that so few men on the heavy
rackets (holdup men, safecrackers, professional killers, et cetera)
are addicted to opiates. In theory, as Dr. Kolb has suggested,
crimes of violence could be reduced if psychopaths could be supplied with enough opiates, on a regular schedule, to keep them

thoroughly addicted. However, I must emphasize that this is an entirely theoretical hypothesis.[8] While some addicts do commit crimes of violence and while there are, with increasing incidence, cases of individuals on the heavy rackets who are in some degree addicted, these are exceptions to the general rule that opiates inhibit tendencies toward violence. Mental conflicts are resolved; lethargy ensues; the individual gets a sense of power and ease which he does not normally feel; again and again, psychopaths state that opiates make them feel "like a king." The contrast with his usual personality which the psychopath experiences is so great that he feels, by comparison, "happy" and wishes to continue this synthetic form of adjustment. The effects of opiates are, in general, exactly the opposite of the effects of alcohol, which tends to reduce normal inhibitions and to release aggressions.

Opiates have been observed to have several other effects upon those who are criminally inclined. First they usually tend to increase suggestibility, although the reasons for this increase are not as yet fully understood. Theoretically, therefore, opiate addicts are open to suggestions from others to commit violent crimes and are more likely to act on these suggestions; actually, however, the sense of well-being and satisfaction with the world are so strong that, coupled with the depressant action of the drug, the individual is less likely to commit aggressive or violent crimes after he is addicted, even though he habitually or professionally did so previous to addiction. Second, there is a marked expansion of the personality, a feeling that the addict is "on top of the world," that he can accomplish anything, that success is his, that everyone likes him, that he likes everyone else and that he is an important person. This inflation of the ego, however, is offset by lack of will power and great reduction in the capacity for action. This ego expansion is notably present in psychopaths and notably absent in addicts who have stable personalities. In the words of Kolb: "Both heroin and morphine in large doses change drunken, fighting psychopaths into sober, cowardly, nonaggressive idlers." Third, opiate addicts retreat even farther from reality and live inwardly; they gradually withdraw from all normal activity not associated with the support of their habit and eventually devote their entire lives to securing drugs. While they regularly perform criminal acts to secure drugs, these acts are usually nonviolent. However, within the past ten years there appears to be an increase in the crimes of burglary (especially of drugstores) and robbery committed by opiate addicts, and although this increase is slight percentagewise, it cannot be ignored. Fourth, the reduction or elimination of sexual desire tends to remove the opiate addict from the category of psychopathic sex offenders, even though he might have a tendency to commit sex crimes when not addicted. In fact it is well known that some homosexuals use opiates because drugs inhibit sex desire and remove them from conflict with society.

The effects of opiates on criminals or potential criminals, however, is not all beneficial. While these drugs may inhibit the more violent psychopaths, they put pressures on the personality which even well-adjusted persons cannot withstand. Because of the irresistible need for drugs, the bank robber who no longer has the courage to commit armed robbery usually becomes a conniver, a thief, a derelict who will turn to any trick not involving much effort or aggression to obtain money. However, with increasing frequency he may, when threatened with loss of his supply, commit armed robbery to obtain drugs. Furthermore, every addict, regardless of whether or not he is a psychopath, will turn to crime if necessary, and the volume of petty crime committed by addicts of all kinds is very large. However, there is no evidence to date which shows that opiates in themselves have the power to convert anyone into a criminal; the assumption is that, theoretically, if opiate addicts did not have to pay the very high prices for bootleg drugs or violate the law in many ways to get them, they would not present a very great problem insofar as crime is concerned.

This principle is well illustrated in the methadone blockade programs which are being instituted experimentally in a number of large cities. Heroin addicts, often those with a long criminal history, are given small oral doses of the drug methadone daily. Present results indicate that the methadone (itself a synthetic opiate) substitutes for the heroin in such a way that the heroin addict can no longer get the euphoria from heroin and settles for the relief from the withdrawal syndrome which methadone provides. He is thus freed from the terrific drive to acquire more heroin and, no doubt with considerable relief, relinquishes the frenzied nonviolent criminal activity necessary to support a heroin habit. Regardless of any other questionable aspects of the methadone block programs, including the production of a whole new class of methadone addicts, it has become obvious in the short time that these programs have been operating that heroin addicts simply give up crime as a means of supporting their heroin habits. All communities experimenting with the methadone block program report that significant percentages of the heroin addicts involved have given up crime and are working at regular jobs. How complete and permanent a solution this gives to the heroin problem remains to be seen.

While opiates or their synthetic equivalents are, at present, the drugs of choice among most of the criminal element, with heroin leading the list, other drugs are also used. The barbiturates and amphetamines are increasingly used by criminals in much the same way that they would use alcohol. This implies the heavy dosage demanded by this type of addict, often in combination with alcohol. While these drugs do not motivate specific criminal acts, they do induce irresponsible and even psychotic behavior. Addicts brought into mental institutions for observation are usually completely out of contact with reality. They suffer from delusions and hallucinations, frequently of a paranoid nature. They may have to be restrained because of their violent and assaultive behavior. Furthermore, most of these drugs are so readily available at low prices that addicts are not forced into crime to buy them. Those barbiturate addicts observed under controlled conditions became so thoroughly incapacitated that they could not stand and walk unaided; they became confused and disoriented; they lived in a stupor. However, there is one special type of crime that has increased spectacularly with the use of barbiturates; that is suicide, and the statistics now being collected in various cities where the problem has come to the attention of public health officers show that suicide from self-administered barbiturates has increased by several hundred percent during the past few years. By way of interpretation, it should be added that many deaths from self-administered barbiturates are probably, in the last analysis, accidents caused by the impairment of judgment of the intoxicated addict and that there is no way of knowing how many persons who committed suicide from barbiturates would have committed suicide by some other means had the drugs not been so easily available.

So far as we are able to determine, cocaine, marijuana and the amphetamines have a more significant relationship to violent crime than do the opiates and barbiturates. The use of stimulants by criminals has increased markedly in the past five or six years.

At one time, cocaine was taken straight by many addicts and was used frequently by criminal psychopaths. The effect of cocaine is exactly the opposite of the opiates. While of course it does not "addict" in the sense of producing physical dependence as do the opiates, it does produce a powerful emotional dependence and has all the other qualities of a dangerously addicting drug. Kolb[4] has summarized the relation of cocaine to crime very succinctly:

> Cocaine stimulates both mind and body and up to a certain point increases confidence and courage. Beyond the point of maximum stimulation, it produces uncertainty, fear, and anxiety. A criminal who takes cocaine is for the time being more efficient as a criminal unless he takes too much. The drug does not arouse criminal impulses in anyone, but it enhances the criminals' mental and physical energy so that he is more likely to convert his abnormal impulses into action. Beyond the point of maximum stimulation, criminals as well as any other types of character become suspicious and fearful. They run away from imagined enemies, usually the police. They are in a paranoiac state, and in this state of fear might commit some act of violence if cornered. In the cases studied, addicts in this state have walked all night to escape imaginary policemen who peeped out from behind every tree; they have looked into bureau drawers, under beds, in match boxes, and through keyholes for police. One attacked with a hammer a laundry bag in his bathroom, under the delusion that it contained a policeman looking for him. Persons in this state are, of course, dangerous, but any crime they might commit would be due to the frenzy of fear. Such a person would be incapable of planning and committing a deliberate murder or of holding up and robbing a bank.

In this connection, it is interesting to note the rumors prevalent that the Communist Chinese were "hopped up" with opiates to prepare them for furious, reckless military attacks against the United Nations in Korea. As a matter of fact, we could wish nothing better than to have all enemy soldiers addicted to opiates, for nothing would so diminish or remove their fighting spirit. An excellent example of the effects of opiates on the will to fight and resist was seen in the deliberate application of opium and opiates by the Japanese to help subdue the Chinese population during the Japanese occupation in the years just before Pearl Harbor.

Today, addicts who take straight cocaine are rarely encounted. However, many opiate addicts mix cocaine with morphine or heroin in what are known as *speedballs*. They get some of the drive from the cocaine, but rely on the sedative effects of the opiates to cut down on the stimulant effect of the cocaine and to offset the delusional state described above. The amphetamines are now used more widely than cocaine as the stimulant to mix with opiates, and this mixture does not appear to incapacitate the criminal for aggressive, well-organized action as does cocaine or heroin alone.

It would be a mistake to conclude that no addict to the opiates or stimulants mixed with opiates will commit a crime of violence. There are too many instances to the contrary, and the number of narcotics agents who have been shot during the course of duty is very reliable evidence that some addicts will react violently. However, in order to maintain perspective, we should note that the number of Treasury Department agents shot in the course of arresting narcotic addicts is smaller than the number in a different branch of the same department who have been shot during the course of apprehending moonshiners. Of course, most criminals commit acts of violence without contact with any drug. However, most opiate addicts are nonviolent, and the popular concept of a drug-crazed criminal running amok or operating with superhuman cunning or cruelty is more romantic than accurate.

One outstanding enforcement officer with a long record of effective service has commented that the only injury he ever suffered in the course of duty was being bitten on the finger by an addict whom he was trying to prevent from swallowing a supply of drugs. "Flight rather than fight" still seems to characterize the majority of addicts.

When we talk about marijuana, we are handling a subject about which there is more controversy than there is about the opiates and cocaine, probably because there has been less opportunity to study objectively its relationship to crime, especially in this country where its consumption is relatively recent compared to the use of opiates. However, any remarks concerning the relationship of marijuana to crime should be prefaced with the note that marijuana is a form of hashish, a most dangerous drug in its unadulterated form. We get the word "assassin" from the Italian *assassino,* which in turn is derived from the Arabic *Hashshashin,* meaning one who uses hashish; this etymology reflects rather accurately the cultural pedigree of the drug, which has been known for centuries to release impulses toward violence. It is still used in the Middle East to prepare warriors for combat or massacre, since some individuals, intoxicated to the point of delirious crisis on hashish, are reported to become reckless, bloodthirsty and savage.

Like everyone elso who observes marijuana addicts, I have also formulated some opinions based on many years of experience. My position, with all due respect to other researchers, is, first, that while marijuana is a dangerous drug, its importance in the United States as a factor in violent criminality has been somewhat exaggerated by journalists and some law enforcement agencies. Second, we do not know of any objective study showing a direct or causative relationship between marijuana and violent crime in a significant number of cases. Third, although marijuana addicts manifest many undesirable and antisocial tendencies which will be discussed later, it has not been my impression from contact with many hundreds of marijuana users that these people are violent criminals; on the contrary, most of them appear to be rather indolent, ineffectual young men and women who are, on the whole, not very productive; a high proportion of them are devotees of various schools of modern music. An increasing number tend to be "square" and to belong to the Establishment. While there may be occasional violent psychopaths who have used marijuana, who have committed crimes of violence, and who have, in court, explained their actions as uncontrollable violence resulting from the use of the drug, these are exceptions to the general run of marijuana users, who, while they may be petty thieves (unless they have an income or work for a living), become "criminals" chiefly in that they violate the narcotics laws. Most habitual users suffer from basic personality defects similar to those which characterize the alcoholic.

Marijuana is not possessed of any mysterious power to force people to commit acts which they would not otherwise perform. Like alcohol, marijuana is an intoxicating drug which releases inhibitions; the actions resulting from the release of inhibitions are as varied as the underlying personalities and impulses of the person concerned. *In vino veritas* is a wise old proverb; the same thought applies to marijuana, which tends to release personality, not to change it. Whatever you are before you smoke marijuana, the drug will only make you more so. By direct action, neither alcohol nor marijuana produces criminal activity, and criminal acts may result only insofar as the inhibitions operating on the personality are removed. Thus, well-balanced people under the influence of the small amount of cannabinol contained in one or two marijuana cigarettes would not be expected to commit violent crimes; psychopaths who smoke consistently or in quantities sufficient to intoxicate them might be expected sooner or later to become violent. We see this phenomenon regularly in connection with the consumption of alcohol. Normal people who take wine with their meals or drink a highball before dinner do not usually engage in brawls; such people, even though thoroughly intoxicated, usually remain affable, though their behavior may be silly or even disgusting. The psychopath, however and we all have one or more among our acquaintances, often tends toward belligerence with the first few drinks and, with continued drinking, moves toward complete and uncontrolled violence; the dockets of police courts are crowded with these cases every morning and, of course, hundreds of others are kept out of court by good fortune or the handling by friends, who excuse his fighting and brawling on the grounds that he has had too much to drink.

There is an important difference between alcohol and marijuana, however. Alcohol tends to impair motor coordination so that when an advanced state of intoxication is reached, the drinker cannot plan and execute any enterprise very effectively—whether it is criminal or not. Marijuana does not so rapidly produce motor incoordination, which means that the marijuana smoker may more frequently carry through criminal tendencies into action or perform impulsive acts more effectively than the alcoholic, whose motor incoordination prevents full and effective execution. This difference becomes very important when a marijuana user operates a car, for cannabinol distorts time and space concepts radically; at the same time, the addict does not show the symptoms of intoxication as readily as a driver might show the effects of alcohol.

Furthermore, marijuana increases the suggestibility of those who use it, although we do not have any studies comparing it with the suggestibility induced by alcohol. Nevertheless, it is known that the marijuana smoker is, while intoxicated, notably more open to suggetsion than he would otherwise be. If this influence is in the direction of criminal behavior, then marijuana smokers exposed to that type of influence are more likely to participate than when they are not intoxicated. This response to suggestibility is characteristic, in varying degrees, of all users of hemp products and may account in part for the widespread reputation which cannabinol has as an aphrodisiac, although it has been shown that none of the hemp products, including marijuana, have an aphrodisiac effect beyond which may be communicated by suggestion.

It has been the experience of Dr. Bouquet and others who have investigated the use of hemp that people begin to use it in the belief that it will preserve, improve or maintain their sexual powers. Because there may be strong expectations in that direction and because of the suggestibility induced by the drug, there may be some influence on the sex life of the individual; however, this is only temporary when it occurs at all, and the hashish addict soon becomes sexually inverted, losing all interest in sexual activity. In fact, in the East, mendicant monks and friars have used hemp from the earliest times, and still do, according to Bouquet,[2] who quotes Mohamet Shirazi Kalenderi's writing as follows:

Their object in using this drug is, in addiction to their pleasures in the visions it engenders, to dry up the seminal fluid; they thereby diminish the inclination to sexual pleasure and can the more easily avoid libertinage.

Said Theophile Gautier, one of the French intellectuals and artists who became hemp addicts during the late nineteenth century: "A hashish addict would not lift a finger for the most beautiful maiden in Verona."

Likewise, marijuana has achieved an undeserved reputation as an aphrodisiac in the United States, although it has been observed that it enjoys this reputation largely among people who do not use it and have not seen it used. In this country, it is largely used by young people from age 14 or 15 to age 25, an age span during which no aphrodisiac is needed to stimulate sexual interest. However, the tendency of marijuana to lower the inhibitions and increase suggestibility may lead to loose sexual behavior, especially if used in the atmosphere of a sex party. It is also sometimes "pushed" by prostitutes or peddlers to older men with the promise that it will increase virility, and these men may, to some extent, experience the suggested or expected effect. I have not encountered any marijuana addicts who admit deliberately using the drug to stimulate sexual interests, although some say that they have no objection to engaging in sexual intercourse while they are high. Marijuana tends to increase all sensual reactions, sex included. It would seem that from the point of view of public health and safety, the effects of marijuana present a very minor problem compared with the abusive use of alcohol and that the drug has received a disproportionate share of publicity as an inciter of violent crime.

At the same time there is little doubt that prolonged or excessive use of the drug results in hallucinatory behavior and mental deterioration. Any dean in a large university could, if he would, give an impressive list of students withdrawn from school in any year "for medical reasons," most of whom have been hospitalized or turned over to a psychiatrist as a result of excessive use of marijuana. Most of these students have the delusion that they are doing superior work as an added fringe-benefit of smoking pot.

The possible relationship of marijuana to campus violence has not been objectively studied.

Unlike alcohol, however, marijuana forces its users to associate with criminal peddlers to secure it, and it is often used in an underworld atmosphere. Probably the most dangerous aspect of marijuana is the fact that it so often, especially among young people, seems to lead to the use of heroin. The reason for this cycle of marijuana to heroin or heroin plus cocaine is not yet fully understood beyond the fact that environment and propinquity make for a desire to graduate from marijuana to opiates. It is possible that marijuana in some way conditions the user for heroin. This same cycle has been reported by Bouquet in the Near East and in Africa, although there heroin tends to replace hemp in many more mature addicts, and the use of hemp by teenagers is not epidemic as marijuana is in the United States. It is also true that millions use marijuana without going on to heroin.

DRUGS AND NONVIOLENT CRIME

While drugs may not, per se, be a known primary cause of criminal behavior, there is a very close secondary relationship between drug addiction and crime, especially that of a petty and nonviolent nature.

There are undoubtedly some addicts who support small habits throughout their lives, who work regularly at their jobs and who never show any tendency to become criminals of any sort. There are other who have sufficient funds—or close contact with supplies of medical drugs—so that they can support larger habits without financial embarrassment and do not become involved in any sort of criminal activities except the violation of the narcotics laws. There are many thousands of medical addicts (persons suffering from very painful or incurable diseases who are kept for months and even for years on opiates or opiate synthetics without showing any tendency to become criminals in any sense of the word); these people are supplied with medical drugs at very reasonable cost, and their habits are carefully managed by their physicians; many of them do not realize that they are drug addicts and will continue to be until they die. While many of these persons are quite ill and even bedfast, others are ambulant, and, as long as they get their proper dosage of drugs, feel little pain or discomfort; these addicts do not present any police problem.

However, the drug addicts considered in this chapter do not fall into the categories listed above, and sooner or later they become very real police problems. The life of these addicts follows a pattern which might be schematized about as follows:

First, the potential addict begins to take very small doses of some addicting drug, let us say morphine or heroin. He either does not realize what the drug will do to him or he knows that others have become addicted but believes that it will never happen to him. It is not uncommon to interview physicians who should be thoroughly aware of the dangers of addiction, yet who have started taking small amounts of morphine in the firm and conscientious belief that they will never become addicted. On the other hand, it is even more common to encounter underworld characters who have been introduced to heroin by other addicts who have seen the disintegration of the personality which goes with addiction and yet play around with the drug fully confident that they are immune. *It cannot be repeated too often that no one is immune to addiction.*

Second, the addict notices that the amount of drug he has been taking does not "hold" him, and if he is addiction-prone, he no longer experiences the intense pleasure which he felt in the very early stages of the use of the drug. If he has been "pleasure-shooting" (taking small doses at intervals of several days or several weeks), he notices that he must increase these in size to continue to get any pleasure from the drug; eventually, of course, he will also increase the frequency until he is taking a shot four to six times daily. This inevitable increase in dosage (when opiates are used) is made necessary by the development of tolerance.

Third, as the habit increases in size over a period of weeks or months, the addict who must buy his drugs from bootleg sources finds that more and more of his money goes for drugs and that he has less and less for the other necessities; in fact, other things come to mean less and less to him, and he becomes heavily preoccupied with simply supporting his habit. As he uses more and more drugs, he becomes increasingly incapable of performing his work steadily; any interruption in his supply causes immediate and disabling illness, and any accidental or intentional overdosage puts him "on the nod" so that he is too drowsy and lackadaisical to work. He loses time, becomes inefficient and may lose his employment. With this, his income diminishes or is cut off completely, and he becomes desperate for drugs. He may have already turned to crime in the early stages of drug use because of the heavy expense involved or because he was not employed when he started on drugs.

Fourth, it becomes obvious to him that he must have increasing amounts of money on a regular basis and that legitimate employment is not likely to supply that kind of money. (It is not unusual to interview addicts who spend from $20 to $60 per day to support heroin habits.) They must steal two or three times this in merchandise to realize the cash they need. Therefore, some form of crime is the only alternative. Sometimes the addict (if he knows something about medical or nursing procedure) forges some prescriptions. Sometimes he forges checks. More often, he starts to steal—from his home, from the relatives, from his employer, from strangers. If he lacks skill in thievery, forgery or embezzlement, he soon develops it under the pressures of addiction. During this period, he may or may not establish contact with underworld people or professional criminals. Girls take rapidly to prostitution but also may become thieves. Some addicts, on the other hand, like nurses, pharmacists or physicians, build up very large habits without knowning anything about the underworld drug traffic and without going beyond the forging of prescriptions or the theft of narcotics which have very small value on the legitimate market; these addicts are not typical, however, and most addicts not only become acquainted with narcotics through the underwold but depend on the underworld market to supply their needs and utilize underwold methods to support their habits.

While most addicts run afoul of the law sooner or later, those with an underworld background are usually in more or less constant conflict with it. If they are professional criminals, they usually have connections with the "fix" whereby they receive police protection for a fee or for acting as stool pigeons; however, when this fails or when they become involved with the federal law, they may go to jail or to prison. While narcotics are available in many jails and prisons—for a price—the chances are that at this point the addict has his first experience with kicking the habit, usually "cold turkey." If he is a stable individual, regardless of whether or not he is a professional criminal, this first experience may be his last, for once he realizes the full implication of drug addiction as it applies to him, he may be sufficiently chastened to get away from drugs and stay away from them. On the whole, I believe the trauma of withdrawal distress in jail, without any assistance, either medical or psychiatric, has a bad effect on both stable and unstable personalities and seems to increase the chances for relapse.

If the individual serves time among a jail or prison population, he is exposed (despite the best effort of prison authorities) to all sorts of crime, degeneracy, graft and abnormal behavior. If he is not already engaged in the rackets himself, he has every opportunity to learn about them; if he already has a racket of his own, he has some status and is rapidly inducted into circles where he can learn much more than he already knows. Furthermore, narcotic addicts in prisons tend to congregate together, and the conversation inevitably centers about narcotics, so that the pleasures of their use are constantly in the minds of those who talk about them. Employment in jails is often inadequate; educational programs are frequently rudimentary at best; and there is little or no opportunity for rehabilitation, except in more advanced prisons. In fact, many prisons today do little except give legitimate society temporary protection from the psychopathic and the criminally inclined, meanwhile all too frequently turning out graduates and postgraduates in professional crime.

When the addict has served his sentence, he is at the crossroads. If he is a stable personality accidentally addicted, he may get a job, seek new types of associates, stay away from narcotics and make good in the legitimate world. Everyone associated with prisons and institutional management has known such cases. They are to be admired. However, the odds are usually against such rehabilitation by the bootstraps, for a jail or prison record is hard to shake off; detectives and narcotic officers regard a man once convicted in a narcotics case as a "violator," and he may be picked up, arrested for questioning, his employment interfered with or pressure put on him to become an informer against persons he knew in prison or against other outside violators. The fact that a man has been a narcotic addict stigmatizes him socially to the point where he may find it hard to secure any type of legitimate employment. This stigma is in part justified, since narcotic addicts as a class have the reputation of being thieves, liars and petty criminals; in part it is not justified for most employers fail to consider individual cases. Gradually, a better parole system, especially as sponsored by the Federal Government and by several states, notably California, is improving this situation. It would seem, in fact, that a carefully supervised and humane parole system following hospital treatment for addicts is one of the very important factors in rehabilitation. It is inevitable that however sincere an addict's intentions are, if he cannot secure legitimate employment, he must live in some way so he rapidly drifts to the underworld fringe.

If he already has a record as a professional criminal when he is released, he usually has no thought of legitimate employment (except as a token fulfillment of his parole, if any) and goes right back to the rackets. Professional criminals do not reform; they may "pack the racket in" temporarily for good reasons, but they do not change their whole way of working and living; they have become used to easy money and do not like to adjust to the scale of living which an ordinary legitimate income would give them. The professional regards arrest as inevitable but depends on bribery and "the fix" to protect him in the long run from doing much actual time. He has come to regard the law as simply another form of racket which shakes down the criminal and preys on him, without ever putting him entirely out of business. To those professionals who are addicted, narcotics usually constitute only one of a number of vices. These people philosophically accept the fact that they will relapse, and they usually do. Strangely enough, the experience of withdrawal illness seems to have little effect in deterring the addiction-prone personality from going back on drugs. In fact, criminals who are addicts have usually relapsed many times. The established recidivist addict with a long criminal history presents one of the most discouraging problems in the treatment and rehabilitation of narcotic addicts; there is a saying amongst them that the only cured addict is a dead addict, and there may be much truth in that statement. However, observation of this class of addicts over a period of years shows that now and then an apparently hopeless case stays off drugs for a surprisingly long period, especially after passing middle age. Eventual reversion to drugs, however, is the pattern of the underworld addict, and exceptions are notable.

In the underworld, certain professions seem to show a much higher percentage of addicts than others. The incidence of addiction is very high among shoplifters, pickpockets, the pushers of counterfeit money or forged checks, and professional thieves of all types. There is also a high incidence among some types of gamblers and prostitutes. This can be partially explained by the fact that prostitution or thievery is the easiest method of securing money when the addict is pressed. Aggressive or violent crime is not required to steal from a store or to prowl hotel rooms; even poor thieves can steal some money or pawnable merchandise, and the work can be done at will, with the addict knocking off at will. Also, the tensions developing among people who must commit many small separate acts of thievery, any one of which may land him in prison, tend to make the use of drugs a quieting, stabilizing factor. However, the high concentration of addiction among thieves in general may have deeper underlying psychological explanations and merits sesrious study by criminal psychologists. Prostitutes usually find the opiates agreeable because they deaden the physical and psychological stress. Sometimes they are addicted and kept on drugs by a pimp, who thus tightens his control.

Criminal activity is almost the only avenue open to people to whom drugs have become the most important thing in life. The cost of supporting a habit in the United States is, however, very high at the present time, and only criminals—or someone with a high legitimate income—can support a large one. A three-handed mob of pickpockets will, for instance, need about $600 to $900 per week for "junk money" and must pay an average of $100 to $200 a day or even more for police protection when they are so operating; this is a very conservative estimate. That is, they must steal from $1,500 to $2,000 per week before they can even begin to make money for their own living expenses, which, with a road mob, will run quite high, since "class" mobs travel first-class all the way. Therefore, they must have a high gross income, "class cannons" averaging around $12,000 each per year, over and above all expenses.

Eventually, most addicts with an underworld background— and some without it—become involved in the narcotics traffic. This is exclusive of the violation of the laws committed in the course of buying, possessing and taking the drug and usually involves trafficking with other addicts. Most addicts are very sympathetic toward others who need drugs; hence, they give away or sell, on occasion, some of their own supply. Other addicts, knowing that they may be out of drugs themselves, find it convenient to addict several other persons (preferably of some income or standing) who can be depended upon to help out in a "panic" or when funds are low. Addicts without "connections" purchase drugs through other addicts who are known to the peddler— sometimes for a share of the purchase, an activity known as "copping." Addicts who depend on medical drugs use every known form of deception, including theft and forgery; if they are dealing with physicians who they know are also addicted or engaged in the abortion racket, addicts may use this knowledge as blackmail.

Although there are exceptions, drug addicts as a class have a reputation for being stool pigeons and informers. In short, there is no limit to the conniving, scheming and petty crime which goes on among addicts themselves.

Eventually, however, every underworld addict is put into the position of being a peddler, if only momentarily when he sells or gives some of his supply to another addict. Some addicts try to avoid being a peddler, even temporarily, because they believe, with some justice, that the law will be harder on a man who sells drugs than it will be on one who only uses them. However, many addicts use their own addiction as a sort of security to both purchaser and wholesale dealer and support their habits either partially or wholly by peddling drugs to other addicts. This addict-peddler is the real link in the chain of supply from wholesale to retail levels, and he must protect himself from both sides as best he can. He always constitutes a risk to the dealer who supplies him and always runs the risk of being "fingered" or turned over to the law by addicts who make purchases for the law or by undercover agents who are sometimes addicts or pose as addicts. Furthermore, neither addicts nor peddlers are above using the law to settle personal grudges or to eliminate competition by turning informers. As a means of self-defense, many peddlers keep on hand a few "hot-shots" (capsules identical with heroin capsules, and perhaps containing enough heroin, or other drug to be injected, to pass a taste test but loaded with lethal doses of cyanide of potassium). Sometimes uncut heroin is used, which is lethal even to a heroin addict. When a customer is known to have turned in a peddler or is even strongly suspected of having turned stool pigeon, he may be given one of these capsules mixed in with his regular purchase. The fear of these "hot-shots" is well established among addicts.

While many peddlers are addicts themselves and most of them are underworld characters, a few peddlers are not addicts, and some make their living in other ways, merely supplementing their income by selling some narcotics on the side. This type of peddler is restricted largely to the medical and nursing professions and to pharmacists, drugstore employees or veterinarians who have access to addicting drugs. Usually these nonaddicts are not underworld characters and often they continue their activities for long periods of time without coming to the attention of the law. An increasing number of these nonaddict peddlers operate in the Los Angeles-San Diego area and in several East Coast cities, but their numbers are small percentagewise.

As soon as we leave the level of the small retail peddler and go to the dealer or wholesaler (of which there are often several categories), we leave addiction behind, as a rule. The dealers, the big men behind them and the men running the highly organized smuggling activities which provide bootleg drugs from Mexico, the Near East and the Orient are not usually addiction-prone personalities, nor can they afford to be addicts. They are aggressive, resourceful, unscrupulous mobsters. These men have very large incomes from the so-called syndicates which dominate the illicit importation of drugs; they tie in with other large syndicates, such as those controlling gambling and, until recently, prostitution, and often purchase protection from the same political and police sources which protect other highly organized rackets. Basically, the so-called Mafia or Cosa Nostra is probably the most powerful of these syndicates. They are expert smugglers, with every facility for carrying on their work, including private planes. Most drugs are smuggled in by passenger or freight ship or by air from the Mediterranean area and the Near East, while those from Mexico are often smuggled through by air or in cars, some of which have many ingenious secret compartments built in. The actual smuggling is seldom done by the ringleaders in person because of the risk involved; sometimes the people who carry the drugs in do not know what they are carrying, but more often the man who brings the drugs in is very well aware of the racket and makes his living at it. If a dozen or so of these racketeers in the higher brackets could be apprehended and convicted, the illicit drug traffic would be dealt a sound blow; on the other hand, enforcement against the small addict-peddler will always be expensive and inefficient as long as the major pipelines for smuggled drugs are open. The small time peddler can always be replaced quickly by another addict greedy for the income and the guaranteed source for drugs but it is not easy to replace a kingpin in the smuggling rackets. Steady enforcement, however, is paying off, and everyone who has observed the drug traffic operate knows well that without the law enforcement work which has been done consistently in the past and which is now being done, the present upsurge in drug addiction could spread to gigantic proportions; in fact, without constant enforcement, addiction could conceivably engulf a substantial proportion of our society.

Of course, the profit in illicit drugs comes from "cutting" or dilution. As an example of how this works, 3 oz of "pure" heroin sold in Riverside County, California, was traced through its various stages, its ultimate value upon resale to addicts being $60,480. This figure is arrived at as follows: Dealers had in their possession 3 oz of heroin which is guaranteed to be at least 70% pure. Before the dealers sell this heroin, it would have been cut into 9 oz at 23½% pure, which is the usual degree of purity when sold by the ounce in this country. The purchasers of these 9 oz will, in turn, cut them into 27 oz at 8% purity. Before resale, these 27 oz will be divided into grams, which amounts to 756 gm, still at 8% pure. The purchasers of the 756 gm at 8% pure will cut them to 1,512 gm at 4% pure. These 1,512 gm will be divided into 15,120 capsules which will sell at a minimum of $4 each, and the total value of the original 3 oz is the figure listed above, $60,480.

The largest shipment of "pure" heroin ever taken by federal agents was 209 lb. confiscated from a Mafia-backed operation in Columbus, Georgia, in December 1965. The wholesale value of the drug was placed at $2,800,000 and the retail value at $100,000,-000. The size of this shipment not only gives some idea of the number of addicts necessary to support such a market but also shows why drugs interest big-time criminals.

In addition to the large smuggling syndicates, there is, especially since World War II, a considerable amount of smuggling by individuals who are not in the racket but who travel back and forth from areas where drugs are produced. These people range from merchant seamen through migratory laborers (largely on the Mexican border and to a lesser extent on the Canadian borders) to military personnel and persons who have official business for the government or for various import-export companies. These individuals discover that they can rather easily bring in packets of concentrated narcotics and sell them for a neat profit to a "drop" or agent for the wholesalers, often a "right" barkeeper on the waterfront. While these individuals account for considerable illicit narcotics, they would not be able to bring in enough to supply the illicit market if the big syndicates were put out of business; however, every such free enterprise smuggler constitutes a potential big-time racketeer if and when the circumstances are propitious. Some cooperative action through the United Nations (although not enough so far) plus rigid law enforcement at the ports of entry tend to curb this individual traffic somewhat, but not to stop it. The devices used by smugglers are as diverse and ingenious as the human brain can make them and are too numerous to be described in detail here.

It should be noted also that some synthetic drugs are being manufactured in Europe (especially Germany) for the illicit market, and it has been reported by reliable sources that there are some illicit laboratories now operating in the United States for the refinement of opiates and the synthesis of opiate-equivalents. While this illicit synthesis of drugs in this country has not yet become widespread, it could become so if smuggling channels were cut off to a degree which caused the market to suffer.

There is an even larger problem posed by the legal synthesis of opiate-equivalents, which seem to have some medical advantages over the opiates refined from natural opium. If these are widely accepted and used by the medical profession both here and abroad, the market for the legitimate products of opium could be ruined. At that point, the entire legal opiate production of countries like Iran, Turkey and Yugoslavia might be without a market; production there already far exceeds the world's medical needs. In these countries, the production and refinement of opium is a very important part of the national economy; any substitution of synthetics would probably force much more of their production into illicit channels and might flood the world markets with illicit drugs on a scale never before experienced. Therefore, it is important that the United Nations work out a plan for the international control of opiates which will protect the medical supply of opiates and at the same time not ruin the national economy of any single country. Some progress is already being made in this direction.

Counterfeiting also goes with the wholesale illicit drug traffic, where the duplication of tax stamps, labels, etcetera, may facilitate large sales to dealers or transportation of narcotics through legitimate channels. Within the past few years, parts of the Middle-Atlantic and Southern States have been flooded with large shipments of fake morphine (consisting largely of heroin hydrochloride and brucine, an alkaloid which has been added to give the characteristic morphine reaction in case anyone with a knowledge of pharmacology applied the nitric acid test) put up in tubes labeled as morphine tablets for hypodermic use. The labels, tax stamps and names of reputable pharmaceutical houses had been well couterfeited, and the containers were excellent imitations of those used by pharmaceutical houses. Many other such counterfeitings have been encountered by the Narcotics Bureau, some of them (apparently originating in the Philippines) being excellent imitations of the labels used by pharmaceutical houses who put up medical morphine for the armed forces and appearing to be surplus stores or diversions from the Medical Corps. These tablets contained no narcotic whatever. The strength and reliability of medical narcotics is, of course, well known to addicts, even though most of them depend on the bootleg market; therefore, medical drugs, apparently sealed in their original containers and stolen from legitimate sources, would be in great demand and would command premium prices in both wholesale and retail markets. Some of these counterfeit tablets traced through the markets by narcotic agents sold for from $1.00 to $2.50 per grain wholesale in lots of several hundred tubes at a purchase and reached the retail market at prices up to $7.00 per grain; as standard medical morphine, it would have been worth about 16¢ per grain on the legitimate pharmaceutical market.

To summarize, then, addicting drugs do not appear to be the direct cause of crime, with the possible—and we must emphasize the *possible*—exception of cocaine, the amphetamines and hemp. In fact, the effects of the opiates are, in general, to make an individual less aggressive and more sedentary; they unfit people for the commission of acts of violence, even though those persons might be naturally so inclined. The stimulant drugs have a different action, and stimulants can cause delusions leading to murder. Marijuana is a potent disinhibitor which may, by breaking down inhibitions, release the psychopathic personality for criminal acts; its position as a direct influence on crime is not as yet fully evaluated, but it can be dangerous.

In order to keep drug addiction and its relation to crime in perspective, we might compare it with the use of alcohol, which is sufficiently common to be familiar to everyone and at the same time socially acceptable. If we accept conviction and imprisonment under the federal laws as being indicative of serious infraction of the regulations governing both narcotics (including only those drugs at present federally controlled, but not all those now considered addicting) and alcohol, we see that in 1950 there were 2,304 commitments to federal prisons for violations of the liquor laws (including illicit manufacture, sale, transportation, violations of federal laws in the legal whiskey business, etcetera) and 2,029 commitments for violating the narcotic laws, including

the Marijuana Tax Act. No figures are available on the total state
and local violations. Approximately four out of ten of the marijuana violators were users, and seven out of ten of those convicted
in connection with other drugs were addicted. While no statistics
are available on the percentage of alcoholics among liquor law
violators, I am in a position to say that the incidence of alcoholism
is very high among moonshiners, and, of course, the possession and
consumption of illicit whiskey is a federal crime comparable to
the use and possession of narcotics.

If we accept the suspiciously conservative figures of the Bureau
of Narcotics, we see that there were 57,199 known addicts to hard
drugs in 1965 in the United States, but if we read any daily newspaper, ranging from small towns to large cities, we readily see that
the police courts are busy with crimes connected with and resulting from the overconsumption of alcohol. Reports of drunken
driving, rape, murder, fighting, domestic trouble, etcetera, in
which liquor plays a prominent role, have become commonplace,
and the public accepts them with a shrug. However, if one defendant appears in court and pleads that his conduct was the result
of the habitual or chronic use of drugs, there is a sensational and
even hysterical interest in his case. On the whole, narcotics and
narcotic addiction do not seem to present any greater hazard to
public health, safety and established social institutions than do
alcohol and alcoholics, yet it is characteristic of our culture that
we accept a major problem in alcoholism casually, while we become very much aroused over a narcotics problem involving only
a fraction of the number of people. Perhaps the explanation lies
partly in the fact that everyone is familiar, either from observation
or experience, with the effects of alcohol, which is taken socially
and out in the open. Narcotics, on the other hand, are almost
always taken in secret, and the general public is totally unfamiliar
with their use and with the effects they have on people. Because
of the sensational stories written about drug-crazed addicts, most
people feel an uncontrollable fear of any kind of addict under any
circumstances. The average citizen who would brush off a drunk
on the street, or perhaps even help him out of harm's way, would
probably experience fear and shock if he were approached by

someone whom he knew to be or even suspected of being a drug addict under the influence of drugs.

This retreat from reality characterizes much of our thinking about all social and criminal problems. We tend to ignore serious conditions until they get out of hand; then, when they are brought to public attention (usually very dramatically), drastic laws are passed (often in a hurry), and people relax with a sense of smug well being because a law has been enacted which will take care of everything. Meanwhile, we have become not only the most thoroughly law-ridden but probably also the most crime-ridden of all Western nations.

The relationship between narcotics and crime is not an isolated phenomenon, but a part of the entire pattern in a culture where crime is accepted as one of the major industries. While some three hundred federal narcotic agents may do a heroic job of attempting to enforce the federal law, and this may to some extent keep the drug traffic under temporary control, we cannot expect these men to eliminate either the tendencies toward addiction or the criminal enterprises which flourish along with addiction, often protected by the same political machines which sponsor other types of graft and corruption. As long as we support a mammoth underworld in which professional criminals can purchase police protection very much as anyone can buy fire insurance, as long as integrity tends to handicap persons seeking or holding public office, and as long as the legitimate citizen hides his head in the sand, the narcotic rackets will continue to flourish. Decent citizens must not be surprised when narcotic addiction invades their own homes through their own sons and daughters for their own lack of participation in their own government at a local level and their own failure to assume moral and social responsibility will have been partly responsible. A society is no better than its people, and our society can be improved only by a concentrated movement to develop better individuals. This may take a long time.

REFERENCES

1. Anonymous: Imitation morphine tablets in the illicit traffic. *Bull Narcotics, 3*: (2)4, April 1957.

2. Bouquet, R. J.: Cannabis, *Bull Narcotics, 2:* (4)14, Oct. 1950.
3. Kolb, L.: *Drug Addiction. A Medical Problem,* Springfield, Charles C Thomas, 1962.
4. Kolb, L.: Drug addiction and its relation to crime. *Ment Hyg, 9:*74, Jan. 1962.
5. Maurer, D. W.: *The Big Con.* International Library of World Literature. New York, 1963.
6. Maurer, D. W.: *Whiz Mob: A Correlation of the Argot of Pickpockets with Their Behavior Pattern.* New Haven, College and University Press Services, 1964.
7. Maurer, D. W.: Utopia at High Dudgeon. Presented before the Western Institute for Drug Problems, Portland, Oregon, August 19, 1970.
8. Maurer, D. W.: The subculture of the criminal narcotic addict. In *Drug Abuses Data and Debate,* edited by Paul H. Blachly, Springfield, Charles C Thomas, 1970.
9. Pescor, M. F.: *A Statistical Analysis of the Clinical Records of Hospitalized Drug Addicts.* Supplement No. 143 to the Public Health Reports. Washington, D. C., U. S. Government Printing Office, 1943.
10. Smith, W. G., Ellinwood, E. H., Jr., and Vaillant, G. D.: Narcotic addicts in the mid-1960's. *Public Health Reports, 81:*403, May 1966.
11. Vogel, V.: Our youth and narcotics. *Today's Health, 29:*24, Oct. 1951.

16

New Approaches to the Use of Drugs in the Treatment of Drug Addiction

H. F. Fraser

HISTORICAL BACKGROUND

The initial approach to the control of addiction was a pharmacological one. In 1929, a drug addiction committee was set up within the division of medical sciences of the National Research Council. This committee thought that the most promising approach to control of addiction was to seek a drug with pain-relieving capacity similar to morphine, yet without its addictive properties. Under the direction of Dr. Lyndon S. Small, a laboratory was established at the University of Virginia to synthesize compounds that resembled the phenanthrene nucleus of morphine. Although several hundred compounds were synthesized, and were pharmacologically evaluated at the University of Michigan by Dr. Nathan B. Eddy, none of them were satisfactory in separating the properties of analgesia and addiction liability.[1]

It was not until some twenty-five years later that a significant breakthrough occurred with the synthesis of propoxyphene by Pohland and Sullivan.[2] Propoxyphene is a central acting analgesic capable of relieving mild to moderate pain and having substantially less addiction liability than codeine.[3] It has been widely accepted by the medical profession.

Another drug which has shown quite a good separation between analgesia and addiction is the mild morphine antagonist, pentazocine (Talwin®).[4] Other such agents that have met with less acceptance by the medical profession include ethoheptazine

241

(Zactirin®), methotrimeprazine (Levoprome®) and mefenamic acid (Ponstel®).

Regarding new agents for relief of cough, there has been a partial separation of antitussive and abuse liability. L-propoxyphene has been marketed for this purpose but has attained only limited medical acceptance. Dextromethorphan (Romilar®) is an effective antitussive, but there have been isolated reports of abuse. In the case of antidiarrheal agents, more success has been attained since diphenoxylate[4] (Lomotil®)[5] has attained quite wide medical acceptance and has very limited abuse capacity, at least when marketed in combination with atropine.

An attempt was made to develop a sedative and/or hypnotic type of drug that would have pharmacological effect similar to a barbiturate but with little or no abuse potential. Considerable success has been attained, since meprobamate is an effective sedative and/or minor tranquilizer and has much less abuse potential than barbiturates. Other drugs that have attained wide medical acceptance in this area include chlordiazepoxide (Librium®) and diazepam (Valium®). These agents are effective minor tranquilizers and have very low abuse potential.

In summary, it may be said that science has successfully developed pain-relieving agents, antitussives, antidiarrheal drugs and sedatives that are clinically effective, yet possess much less abuse liability than their former counterparts.

Despite these medical discoveries, the problem of drug addiction has not decreased but has enormously expanded, particularly in the past several years. One must conclude, therefore, that the pharmacological approach to controlling addiction is incomplete. Further evidence of the incompleteness of this approach is the fact that the major patterns of drug abuse in our society are associated not with drugs medically administered, but with such agents as tobacco, alcohol, marijuana, heroin and LSD.

BIOLOGICAL AND OTHER VARIABLES INVOLVED IN CHARACTERISTICS OF PERSONS WHO ABUSE DRUGS

Definitive studies have been conducted on narcotic addicts, alcoholics and criminals. Hill and his collaborators[6] at the U.S. Public Health Service Hospital at Lexington, Kentucky evaluated

270 hospitalized narcotic addicts, using the Minnesota Multiphasic Personality Inventory test. They determined the profiles of (a) a teenage group, (b) a white group and (c) a Negro group. The diagnostic categories included hypochondriasis, depression, hysteria, psychopathic deviation, masculinity-feminity, paranoia, psychosthenia, schizophrenia and hypomania. In this study, only 4½ percent of the addict profiles were classified as normal. The principal abnormality was a considerable accentuation in the psychopathic deviate scales. It is interesting that the profile of the teenagers was similar to that of older addicts with long exposure to drugs. This suggests that in these teenagers, abnormalities existed prior to addiction, rather than the idea that addiction provoked a change in their personality pattern. In a related study, when the profiles of two hundred narcotic addicts were compared with those of alcoholics and criminals, the patterns of all three groups were very similar and could not be differentiated except in minor qualitative aspects of certain deviations.[7]

Another feature of drug abuse in the United States is that the pattern in respect to age is similar for delinquency and drug abuse. Addiction and delinquency are most conspicuous during the late teens and the twenties; after thirty-five the incidence drops off remarkably. The reason for this is not known.

The author is not aware of any current studies which delineate accurately the behavioral patterns of the large group of young people in our society who have started to abuse marijuana, amphetamines, opiates, barbiturates or other drugs.

MECHANISMS INVOLVED IN DRUG ADDICTION

In the development and propagation of drug abuse, biological evidence points to the fact that certain people possess hereditary traits which make them prone to abuse of drugs. This has been borne out by animal studies. For example, Nichols[8] noted that among a group of rats, certain ones liked to drink a morphine solution while others were not attracted to it. He therefore selected for breeding, rats that were addiction-prone and addiction-resistant insofar as their liking for morphine was exhibited. After several generations of selection, relatively pure addiction-prone and addiction-resistant strains were developed. When these two strains were mated, he again obtained a mixed strain comparable to the strain initially observed.

Similar observations have been made in experiments with rats[9] and monkeys.[10] In the monkeys, a catheter was placed in the right side of the heart and attached to an apparatus which permitted the animal to self-inject a drug by pressing a lever. A variety of drugs were used. Not all monkeys became voluntarily addicted to morphine, but some apparently liked the sensation and promptly increased their daily doses. Certain drugs like cocaine were so well liked by the monkeys that they pressed the bar until they had grand-mal convulsions; as soon as they recovered, they were back pressing the bar for more. In fact, some of the monkeys took so much cocaine that they killed themselves, and it was necessary to program the injection of cocaine so that the maximum dosage could be controlled. In this connection, it is noteworthy that the drugs abused by man — alcohol, barbiturates, amphetamines and narcotics — were abused by the monkey. On the other hand, drugs which man does not abuse, such as chlorpromazine, nalorphine (a morphine antagonist) and mixtures of morphine and nalorphine, were not abused by the monkeys.

We may conclude thus far from experiments in animals that certain individuals are addiction-prone and that there is considerable specificity for drugs that are abused, even though these have a wide gamut of pharmacological action from severely depressive agents to potent central nervous system stimulants.

An important factor in drug abuse is the availability of the agent. In order to abuse opium, it is necessary to cultivate the poppy plant; heroin, barbiturates and LSD would not be abused if they had not been synthesized and marketed. An additional factor is whether there has actually been an exposure of the animal or the individual to a given drug. In the case of naive monkeys, it was quickly learned that although certain monkeys rejected morphine by the intravenous route, when morphine was arbitrarily administered to them daily, they readily became dependent on it and behaved as addiction-prone monkeys.

In this connection, Yanigita[11] has demonstrated in monkeys that when drugs were given orally via a tube to the stomach, difficulty was encountered in getting the monkeys to associate pressing the lever with receiving the reward, since there was a delay in absorption of the drug. However, if the monkeys had previously experienced dependence on morphine, barbiturates or other drugs, they were much quicker to recognize the subjective effects of drugs in subsequent intragastric tests. These experiments of Yanigita probably have important implications insofar as man is concerned, since apparently exposure to one agent with known addiction potentialities predisposes to abuse of another agent of a similar capacity. However, it is necessary that the experiments of Dr. Yanigita be extended, for example, to whether smoking marijuana would predispose to abuse of narcotic agents.

SOME SPECULATIONS RELATIVE TO THE USE OF DRUGS IN TREATING ADDICTION

It is important to realize that a considerable proportion of our population — possibly 10 percent — is prone to drug abuse. Because of this, drugs with an addictive potential should not be freely available to such persons. For example, in 1949 and 1950, Dr. Isbell and I conducted extensive experiments on LSD in narcotic addicts at Lexington. These individuals were very sophisticated in their exposure to nearly all types of drugs. Provided the dose of LSD was properly titrated — that is, not too large or too small — the narcotic addicts described LSD as being similar to cocaine. On a preference basis they rated heroin first, cocaine second, and LSD third. As a result, we predicted that LSD would be rather widely abused should it become available to addiction-prone persons. Some fifteen years later, when LSD became available to the addict population, its high abuse potential was fully confirmed. Thus it is important to prevent individuals being exposed to potentially addictive agents when this is possible.

It has been demonstrated in animals that exposure to one addictive agent makes the animal more readily addicted to other agents with similar qualities. Although it is dangerous to extrapolate from correlations in the case of narcotic addicts at Lexington, 85 percent of these addicts stated that their first exposure to drugs was smoking pot. Since you can also say that 100 percent of these addicts drank milk as infants, the argument could be advanced that milk predisposes to heroin addiction. However, the problem is more complex, and anyone who has studied addicts extensively is impressed by the fact that exposure to one drug is associated with experimentation with others.

One approach in treating addiction is to substitute for the addicting drug another drug which satisfies the craving of the individual, yet has less toxic properties. As we all know, this is currently exemplified by the Dole-Nyswander method of treating heroin addicts—that is, substitution of oral methadone for heroin.[12] Although quite widely accepted, this approach has been debated by some, since the chronic use of any drug is considered immoral.

I would like to stress that we should not rest on our laurels insofar as using drugs in treating addiction is concerned. Dr. Jaffe and his collaborators[13] have been experimenting with the acetyl methadols in treating heroin addicts. These compounds are effective orally for some seventy-two hours[14] and may be no more toxic than methadone; if so, our therapeutic approach may be simplified.

It may well be possible to develop new classes of drugs which induce a low-grade morphine-type euphoria, yet have no physical-dependence characteristics. In the case of alcohol abuse, current drugs such as chlordiazepoxide and diazepam may be improved so that there will be no significant urge to take the new drug in excess because of its euphorigenic capacity.

SUMMARY

1. Science has successfully developed pain-relieving agents, antitussives, antidiarrheal drugs and sedatives that are clinically effective, yet possess much less abuse liability than their former counterparts. Despite these medical discoveries, the problem of drug addiction has enormously expanded, particularly in the past several years.

2. Experiments in animals demonstrate that certain animals are addiction-prone. In self-injection studies, monkeys abused the same drugs as man—alcohol, barbiturates, amphetamines and narcotics. On the other hand, drugs which man does not abuse, such as chlorpromazine, nalorphine (a morphine antag-

onist) and mixtures of morphine and nalorphine, were not abused by monkeys. Studies in monkeys indicate that exposure to a given addictive agent renders the animal more susceptible to other types of addictive drugs.

3. Insofar as we can interpret, the studies in animals extend to man.

4. The pharmacological approach to problem of addiction— that is, the development of new drugs which separate the desired clinical effect from the abuse potential of the drug—has been incomplete and largely ineffective. Since we have a considerable percentage of our population which is drug-abuse–prone, obviously we need new approaches to this problem. One current method is to substitute for the addictive agent another drug which has less toxic properties and therefore permits the individual to conduct himself in society in a more responsible manner. Although this approach has been controversial, it is thought we should consider it seriously and attempt to discover new drugs without physical-dependence qualities that will substitute for alcohol, barbiturates and narcotics.

5. Our interest in new approaches for treating addiction should not distract us from the important preventive feature—this is, protecting individuals from an initial exposure to potentially addictive agents.

REFERENCES

1. Committee on Drug Addiction; National Research Council Reports and Collected Reprints, 1929-1941. Washington, D. C., National Research Council, 1941.
2. Pohland, A., and Sullivan, H. R.: *J Amer Chem Soc*, 75:4458, 1953.
3. Fraser, H. F. and Isbell, H.: *Bull Narcotics* 12(2):15, 1960.
4. Fraser, H. F., and Rosenberg, D. E.: *J Pharmacol Exp Ther*, 143: 149, 1964.
5. Fraser, H. F., and Isbell, H.: *Bull Narcotics*, 13:29, 1961.
6. Hill, H. E., Haertzen, C. A., and Glaser, R.: *J Gen Psychol*, 62: 127, 1960.
7. Hill, H. E., Haertzen, C. A., and Davis, H.: *Quart J Stud Alcohol*, 23:411, 1962.
8. Nichols, J. R.: *Amer J Psychol*, 17:398, 1962.
9. Weeks, J. R.: *Science*, 138:143, 1962.

10. Yanigita, T., Deneau, G. A., and Seevers, M. H.: *Proc Int Union Physiol Sci (23d Int Congr., Tokyo, Japan), 4*:453, 1965.
11. Yanigita, T.: Personal communication.
12. Dole, V. P., Nyswander, M. E., and Kreek, M. J.: *Arch Int Med, 118*:304, 1966.
13. Jaffe, J. H., Schuster, C. R., Smith, B. B., and Blachly, P. H.: *JAMA, 211*:1834, 1970.
14. Fraser, H. F., and Isbell, H.: *J Pharmacol Exp Ther, 105*:458, 1952.

17

A Current View of the Amphetamines

Jared Tinklenberg

T he amphetamines are synthetic chemicals which induce central nervous system stimulation and are pharmacologically classified as sympathomimetic amines. Dextroamphetamine (Dexedrine), dl-amphetamine (Benzedrine) and methamphetamine (Methedrine) are a few common examples of amphetamines. These drugs have a variety of colloquial terms: "uppers," "speed," "crystal," "crank," "bennies" and many others. There are also a group of chemicals which are not amphetamines but which have significant central nervous system stimulating effects and are commonly used in a fashion similar to the amphetamines. This nonamphetamine group of central nervous system stimulants includes methylphenidate (Ritalin), phenmetrazine (Preludin®), diethylpropion (Tenuate®, Apisate) and others. In this chapter, I will focus on the amphetamines, but the information is also generally applicable to the nonamphetamine stimulants.

MECHANISMS OF ACTION AND METABOLISM

The precise mechanisms of amphetamine action constitute an area of current investigation. There is considerable evidence that amphetamines exert their effects by influencing chemicals involved in the transmission of nerve impulses. These influences are quite complex; for example, they are mediated through somewhat different processes in the peripheral nervous system than in the central nervous system.[1] The chronicity of amphetamine intake adds further complexity in that the acute effects of amphetamines on the peripheral nervous system are different than the effects that ensue from the chronic administration of amphetamines.[2]

The amphetamines can be broken down into biologically active metabolites. Some of these metabolites may persist in the body and retain biological activity beyond the time period when amphetamines themselves are no longer present.[3]

The amphetamines are usually taken orally but may be injected intravenously or intramuscularly, sniffed through the nasal mucosa or absorbed through skin surfaces. The effects of the amphetamines begin within minutes after entering the bloodstream and are maximal one to four hours later. The duration of effects is quite variable, depending on dosage and chronicity of administration; the effects of short-term usage of low doses characteristically abate in six hours; the effects from chronic high-dose usage can persist for months. Although most of the amphetamines are degraded by the liver, up to 50 percent of the administered dose may be excreted unchanged in the urine.[3]

INITIAL EFFECTS OF THE AMPHETAMINES

The primary effects of the amphetamines, unlike many drugs in current usage, are well documented since they have been extensively investigated in a number of well-designed studies. These effects include a general increase in alertness, wakefulness, sensations of well-being and decreased feelings of fatigue or boredom. Amphetamines can significantly improve performance in activities requiring extreme physical effort and endurance such as strenuous athletic or prolonged military maneuvers.[4] The amphetamines can counteract the impairing effects of fatigue, boredom, depressant drugs and other factors on performance of a wide variety of tasks.

The pharmacological effects of amphetamines on other types of human performance are less definite and depend on the specific task and other factors. There are tendencies toward shortening of reaction time, occasional improvements in motor coordination and enhanced monitoring—that is, performing simple maneuvers such as flipping an appropriate switch in response to complex stimuli presented on a data display panel. These effects seem to represent actual improvement above baseline, normal performance. By contrast, and contrary to widespread belief, complex intellectual functioning involving comprehension, problem-solving and judgment is not appreciably modified by the amphetamines in normal subjects who are not fatigued.[4] Other well-documented effects of the amphetamines include suppression of the appetite, at least for short periods of time, and usually some increase in heart rate and blood pressure. The amphetamines can alter sleep patterns by suppressing the REM (rapid eye movement) component. There is some increased skeletal muscle tension, relaxation of smooth muscles, increased sweating and other indications of sympathetic nervous system activity.

CLINICAL USES OF THE AMPHETAMINES

Although the amphetamines are widely used in a variety of clinical situations, there is considerable controversy over which situations provide definite indications for amphetamines and which are better managed by other drugs or other forms of treatment. One clinical condition for which amphetamines are clearly indicated is hyperactivity in brain-damaged children. In these children, the amphetamines do not exert their usual stimulating effects; instead, there is usually a paradoxical calming effect. The mechanisms for this calming effect are unknown; however, the greater the evidence of brain damage, the more useful amphetamines seem to be.[5] The amphetamines have longstanding use in the treatment of narcolepsy—a rare condition which includes the tendency to fall asleep. However, this use has recently been challenged by the discovery that many narcoleptic patients are REM-deprived, and amphetamines may accentuate this pathological deprivation. The amphetamines are effective in transiently curbing appetite; but after a few weeks the user develops tolerance so that higher doses are necessary to maintain the anorexic effect. Furthermore, there is sometimes an appetite rebound after the cessation of amphetamine use so that the individual rapidly regains the weight he lost.

Amphetamines can help an individual function during short periods of depression or unusual stress. Unfortunately, such usage is too often the first step toward chronic amphetamine abuse; thus, clinicians must be extremely cautious and prescribe amphetamines only in situations which are not likely to be repeated and only for people who are unlikely to make drugs a permanent part

of their response to distress. Although in the past the amphetamines have been touted for a wide variety of other clinical conditions, including chronic depression, addiction to other drugs
and enuresis, subsequent experience and investigation have indicated that they are not effective in these situations and in some
instances are definitely harmful.

NONCLINICAL USES OF AMPHETAMINES

There are at least three distinct patterns of amphetamine use
in nonclinical settings. One pattern entails taking low oral doses
for limited time periods. This pattern is followed by students
cramming for examinations, overtired businessmen, military personnel on extended missions and long-distance truck drivers. Although this pattern is usually benign, untoward effects involving
bad judgment, impaired discrimination and postamphetamine
depression (unpleasant reactions for several hours after the stimulating effects has worn off) do occur. The greatest hazard of this
pattern of use is the propensity of a significant number of people
to escalate their use of amphetamines, not only by increasing the
dosage and duration of drug consumption in particular situations,
but also by using amphetamines or other drugs in an increasing
variety of situations.

The second pattern of amphetamine use in nonclinical settings
is the sustained use of oral doses which are initially in the therapeutic range, but which are gradually increased over prolonged
periods of time. This pattern is followed by people trying to
control their weight and by individuals self-medicating for chronic
depression or fatigue. With time, tolerance develops so that the
same amount of amphetamine no longer produce the desired
effect, and larger amounts are needed. As the cumulative amount
increases, there can be the insidious development of untoward
reactions, especially paranoid psychoses manifested by unfounded
suspiciousness, hostility and persecutory delusions.[6,7] To date,
these reactions provide the most useful "model psychosis," as they
are often indistinguishable from nondrug paranoid reactions,
except that they spontaneously remit after amphetamine use stops.[8]
Indeed, they more closely mimic the functional paranoid psy-

choses than do reactions induced by psychotomimetic drugs such as LSD.

A number of clinicians have suggested that these psychotic reactions can be attributed to the drug effects, per se, and are not merely the result of predisposing personality factors or sleep disturbance. These suggestions have recently been buttressed in carefully controlled studies involving six subjects who had none of the personality characteristics considered as predisposing to psychotic reactions.[9] In five of the six subjects, transient, florid paranoid psychoses developed after the oral administration of small, incremental amounts of amphetamines for variable periods of time up to five days (total cumulative dose 120 to 700 mg). These studies indicate that it is not difficult to induce paranoid reactions with cumulative amphetamine dosages in experimental subjects. Sleep deprivation did not seem to be essential to developing these transient paranoid reactions because two subjects went without sleep for only one night before developing the psychosis.

The third pattern of amphetamine use involves the intravenous injection of large doses. Although extensive data is not available, my impression is that intravenous users of amphetamines come from a more disturbed population than people who only take amphetamines orally. Initially, these intravenous users ingest oral amphetamines along with a great variety of other drugs; with time, they gravitate to intravenous amphetamines and frequently follow the pattern of a "run."[10] A run is a self-administered injection every few hours for a period of several days to occasionally more than a week. Immediately after each injection, there is a generalized pleasurable feeling termed a "flash" or "rush" and then a sense of invigoration and euphoria. These pleasant feelings which persist for a few hours are then gradually replaced by irritability, vague uneasiness and uncomfortable aching sensations. In this pattern, a setting for rapid operant conditioning is created as the user must periodically take an injection to recapture the pleasure of the initial "rush" and to avoid discomfort when the amphetamine effects are wearing off. Thus, a "speed binge" often develops during which the individual goes without adequate sleep, food or liquids and frequently develops the same kind of paranoid behavior that can result from the oral use of amphetamines. When this prolonged run is finally terminated, the so-called crash follows. There is a period of discomfort, a day or so of deep sleep and often an extended period of lethargy with considerable, sometimes severe, depression.

AMPHETAMINE USE AND OTHER PHENOMENA

A good deal of evidence links aggressive behavior with amphetamines, especially in the high-dose intravenous pattern of usage.[11] The pharmacological effects of the amphetamines which can contribute to assaultive behavior include greater propensity to impulsively take physical action, decreased inclinations for a mediating pause to consider future consequences, greater emotional lability and a high incidence of paranoid reactions with irritability, hostility and persecutory delusions. These tendencies interact in a complex way with certain psychosocial forces that are common among amphetamine users and that are likely to increase the probabilities of violence. These psychosocial forces include a high prevalence of concealed weapons, the tendencies for heavy users to lack close personal friends and, therefore, to have fewer opportunities to check out with others possible distortions, and a social milieu in which physical retaliation for any perceived wrongs is the expected norm of behavior.[12,13] Thus, responding to public concern about the connection between drugs and violence, one needs to carefully consider a variety of contributions to increased aggressiveness.

On the other hand, as previously described, there are well-recognized clinical situations in which amphetamines reduce destructive outbursts in certain hyperactive brain-damaged children. Although one pattern of amphetamine use is linked with violence, the same drug given in lower doses and with appropriate supervision can actually be helpful in reducing destructive behavior. This paradox illustrates the following recurrent theme of psychopharmacology: The behavior of drug users is multidetermined and is influenced not just by the pharmacology of the drug but also by the dosage, the modality and a variety of psychosocial factors.

Sexual behavior under the influence of amphetamines is variable and seems to be considerably influenced by the extent of amphetamine use. Most people who have used amphetamines for only short periods of time describe either no appreciable change in their sexual performance or some increase in subjective enjoyment and a delay of orgasm so that intercourse can be considerably prolonged. However, among chronic amphetamine users, particularly the high-dose intravenous variety, reports of reduced sexual drive and various degrees of impotency are common. These reports become more frequent as amphetamine use becomes more extensive and prolonged.

In discussing amphetamine use, one must keep in mind that drug use patterns are continually changing.[14] The popularity of amphetamines is quite faddish, varying over time and according to geographic area. Extensive amphetamine abuse was first noted in post–World-War II Japan. Vigorous restrictions by the government on the manufacture and distribution of amphetamines, plus extensive campaigns of education and treatment, effectively reduced the "epidemic."[15] In the 1950's, abuse of phenmetrazine (Preludin), an amphetamine-like stimulant, became widespread in Sweden and other Scandinavian countries.[16] Recently, there have been suggestions that this abuse is declining. Other reports indicate that in the last few years, amphetamine usage has dramatically increased among young people in England, and there are few indications of any downward trend.[17] The illicit drug use pattern in the Haight-Ashbury area of San Francisco evolved from one of heavy use of LSD and marijuana and light use of intravenous amphetamine before the summer of 1967, to a pattern of extensive high-dose intravenous amphetamine use in 1968.[18] However, by 1969, amphetamine use was declining as many users were switching to heroin as their drug of choice.[12] The reasons for these changing patterns are complex and poorly understood.

ADDICTION

Although the semantic problems raised by the term "addiction" are formidable, there is clear evidence for the following points. Amphetamine users can develop tolerance so that a given dose no longer produces the desired effect, and high doses are required. There is usually some discomfort and psychological distress upon abrupt cessation of high-dose amphetamine intake, although withdrawal symptoms are less pronounced than with the opiates. Amphetamine use can become compulsive, with individuals displaying marked drug-seeking behavior. Despite enforced abstinence of months or years beyond the time in which pharmacological factors are likely to be operative, many amphetamine users feel as strongly compelled as heroin users to return to their drug.[10] This illustrates that as in the case of "hard narcotics," the physical aspects of tolerance and withdrawal are not as important in perpetuating drug addiction as psychological factors such as conditioning and response generalization.[19] Getting a compulsive amphetamine (or heroin) user to temporarily "kick" his habit is relatively easy; preventing recidivism is extremely difficult.

Chronic amphetamine use definitely is associated with the most important aspect of addiction—harm to the individual and his society. Amphetamine use can gradually erode personal, occupational and social structures of the user's life to leave only an existence of procuring and using the drug. This progressive exclusion of formerly meaningful activities closely resembles the classical addiction syndrome of the opiate user. Difficulties occur despite the fact that the chronic abphetamine user is not so subject to financial pressures in supporting his drug consumption as the heroin addict. In California, for example, high amphetamine usage may cost $20 to $30 a day, whereas a comparable heroin habit would require $50 to $150 per day.

STEPPING STONE TO OTHER DRUGS

My clinical experience demonstrates that intravenous amphetamine use can be a direct stepping stone to the use of other intravenously administered drugs. This does not mean that the use of amphetamines creates a biological deficit which can only be satisfied with drugs; rather, the amphetamine-using individual is more likely to be exposed to a variety of other drugs and learns certain drug-using patterns of behavior which he can generalize to include other drugs. One sequence of progression to other drugs results from the pattern of a "run" which is previously described. People who follow this pattern of amphetamine use frequently try a variety of sedating agents to reduce the discomfort associated with the cessation of amphetamine intake. They discover that heroin is not only very effective in reducing the distress of coming down but can be a direct euphoriant, particularly if used repeatedly.

The modality of drug intake can also contribute to the progression from one drug to another. Thus, among intravenous amphetamine users, the act, per se, of using the needle to inject something into oneself can acquire pleasurable features; since a pleasurable sensation follows the injection, the injection process itself is rewarded. Other available injectable substances are tried, and transfer to other drugs, especially heroin and the barbiurates, does insidiously ensue in some individuals. In 1969, studies in San Francisco indicated that over half the people referred to a drug treatment program were former intravenous amphetamine users who had subsequently switched to intravenous heroin.[20] The tendency for drug-using behavior to generalize by the modality of drug intake is not limited to intravenous injection. For example, individuals who have had pleasurable experiences while smoking certain drugs are likely to try other psychoactive drugs by the smoking modality.[21]

In concluding the discussion about amphetamine effects, it is worth emphasizing that although many people are more concerned about consequences of marijuana use, the chronic use of amphetamines constitutes a far more serious problem. The amphetamine-associated consequences of paranoid reactions, increased aggressiveness, pronounced drug dependence are quite in contrast to marijuana where serious untoward reactions are unusual.

THE TREATMENT OF AMPHETAMINE USERS

The initial focus in treating amphetamine users is on reducing the toxic effects of the drug and managing any concomitant behavioral disturbances. A general physician can usually handle this stage by following certain guidelines.[22,23] The first involves assuring that the patient does not harm himself or others. Simple surveillance will often suffice, although chemical sedation may also be necessary. The amount of input impinging on the patient should be modulated to reduce unnecessary stimulations and yet avoid sensory deprivation and reduction of orienting cues. Thus, patients should be treated in quiet rooms with moderate lighting;

talking should be done in subdued but coherent tones, and rapid or sudden movements should be avoided. Because some impairment of brain function is the norm, the repetition of clarifying and orienting information is helpful. For example, I will repeatedly tell the patient the exact location and name of the hospital he is in; and that although he is suffering from the effects of drugs, his distress will gradually subside. Often such clarifying and supportive treatment is all that is required; however, if the patient remains distressed or becomes increasingly agitated, the administration of sedating drugs is indicated. My preference is for short-acting sedative-hypnotics such as diazepam (Valium) in an initial dose of 10 to 15 mg im or 15 to 20 mg po.[24] Subsequent dose levels are determined by the response of the patient and can be given at intervals of about one hour. If there is the possibility of mixed amphetamine-barbiturate or amphetamine-belladonna use, longer-acting anticonvulsants are initiated, for example, diphenylhydantoin (Dilantin®) 100 mg po tid. The use of ammonium chloride, 1 to 2 gm qd to acidify the urine, may help somewhat as the urinary excretion of amphetamines is accelerated in an acid pH.

Except in extreme situations such as the accidental ingestion of amphtamines by children[25] or where there is clear evidence of psychosis which antedated drug use, I do not see phenothiazines in the initial treatment of amphetamine users. My rationale stems largely from the fact that many amphetamine users either intentionally or unknowingly consume anticholinergic agents which act synergistically with phenothiazines to induce cardiovascular difficulties. Also, the immobilizing properties of the phenothiazines are extremely distressing for many young drug users and in some instances can markedly augment the untoward aspects of the drug experience.

The long-term management of amphetamine users is universally regarded as difficult and is fraught with high rates of recidivism regardless of the treatment regiment. In my experience, closely supervised brief hospitalization or at least physical separation of the drug user from his usual milieu is a necessary first step for treating the chronic amphetamine user. Tricyclic antidepressant medication such as imipramine (Tofranil®) is sometimes useful to reduce the symptoms of depression which so frequently accompany the cessation of prolonged amphetamine use. These depressions usually subside spontaneously, but individuals may require up to a year of abstinence for return to pre-drug use mood levels.

Almost invariably, there are marked deficiencies in the user's personal and social functioning; thus, during long-term management, treatment can appropriately be focused on these areas. A judicious blend of individual and group therapy can be helpful. In my experience, chronic amphetamine users respond best to therapies that directly emphasize the development of coping skills for situations which are likely to arise in the user's immediate future. The systematic application of behavioral modification techniques is helpful with some patients.[26] By contrast, these people do not seem to respond well to traditional insight-oriented techniques, despite valiant efforts by skilled therapists. Similarly, my experiences with groups that emphasize confrontive or Gestalt-sensitivity techniques have been disappointing. Not only are there very few leaders who are able to use these techniques skillfully, but the transfer of useful learning from these sessions into the real world is low. Long-term follow-up is essential; again, an emphasis on day-to-day difficulties and a development of social and vocational skills is most efficacious. Although the life history of amphetamine users is not well documented, my observations indicate that in addition to the high rate of return to amphetamines, there is a significant evolution toward abuse of other drugs, particularly alcohol, the barbiturates and, as mentioned previously, the opiates. The most common reason cited for these shifts in drug preferences is unwillingness to undergo the physical discomforts and paranoid reactions intrinsic to the continued use of amphetamines.

Certainly, the most effective methods of dealing with amphetamine use emphasize preventive education. Although the use of amphetamines is one phenomenon which easily crosses today's generation gap, the message to all age groups is the same: The use of amphetamines is definitely dangerous and frequently leads to serious consequences. They should not be used in any circumstances other than under the direct care of a physician. Physicians who prescribe amphetamines are obligated to familiarize themselves with the current information which clearly indicates the tremendous abuse potential of these drugs and the very limited clinical conditions for which amphetamines are more efficacious than other less dangerous drugs.[27]

In addition to education, other measures are worth pursuing. Although restrictive legislation should always be approached cautiously, the costs and extent of amphetamine abuse warrants the consideration of stringent controls on distribution of amphetamines and their chemical precursors. Further exploration is indicated of legislation which would make the vendor of the drug —whether legal vendor or illegal peddler— financially liable for any damages incurred by the user.[28]

Finally, we should retain a historical perspective and remember that drug use is cyclic. The abuse of amphetamines in certain parts of the country has clearly reached a crescendo and is now subsiding. Thus, our preventive and remedial efforts may be enhanced by a natural decrease in amphetamine use.

REFERENCES

1. Sulser, F., and Sanders-Bush, E.: Notes on biochemical and metabolic considerations concerning the mechanisms of action of amphetamines and related compounds. In *Psychotomimetic Drugs,* edited by D. H. Efron. New York, Raven Press, 1970.

2. Cavanaugh, H. H., Griffith, J. D., and Oates, J. A.: The effect of acute and chronic amphetamine administration on the adrenergic neuron in man. In *Amphetamines and Related Compounds,* edited by E. Costa, and S. Garattini, New York, Raven Press, 1970.

3. Smith, R. L., and Dring, L. G.: Patterns of metabolism of B-phenylisopropylamines in man and other species. In *Amphetamines and Related Compounds,* edited by E. Costa, and S. Garattini. New York, Raven Press, 1970.

4. Weiss, B., and Laties, V. G.: Enhancement of human performance by caffeine and amphetamines. *Pharmacol Rev, 14*:1-37, 1962.

5. Lasagna, L., and Epstein, L. C.: The use of amphetamines in the treatment of hyperkinetic children. In *Amphetamines and Related Compounds,* edited by E. Costa, and Garattini. New York, Raven Press, 1970.

6. Connell, P. H.: Amphetamine psychosis. *Maudsley Monograph 5,* London, Chapman and Hall, Ltd., 1958.

7. Ellinwood, E. H.: Amphetamine psychosis: Description of the individuals and process. *J Nerv Mental Dis, 144*:374-283, 1967.
8. Kety, S. S.: The hypothetical relationships between amines and mental illness; a critical synthesis. In *Amines and Schizophrenia*, edited by H. E. Himwich, S. S. Kety, and J. P. Smythies. New York Pergamon Press, 1967.
9. Griffith, J. D., Cavanaugh, J. H., Held, J., and Oates, J. A.: Experimental psychosis induced by the administration of d-amphetamine. In *Amphetamines and Related Compounds*, edited by E. Costa, and S. Garattini. New York, Raven Press, 1970.
10. Kramer, J. C., Fishman, V. S., and Littlefield, D. C.: Amphetamine abuse. *JAMA, 201*:305-309, 1967.
11. Tinklenberg, J. R., and Stillman, R. C.: Drug use and violence. In *Violence and the Struggle for Existence*, edited by D. N. Daniels, M. F. Gilula, and F. M. Ochberg. Boston, Little, Brown & Co., 1970.
12. Smith, R.: The Market Place of Speed: Violence and Compulsive Methedrine Abuse. Unpublished manuscript.
13. Ellinwood, E. H.: Assault and Homicide Associated with Amphetamine Abuse. Presentation at the American Psychiatric Association Meeting, San Francisco, California, May, 1970.
14. Cohen, S.: The cyclic psychedelic. *Amer J of Psychol, 125*:393-394, 1968.
15. Heyman, F.: Amphetamine abuse in Japan. *J Psychedelic Drugs, 2 (No. 2)*:217-233, 1969.
16. Berjerot, N.: An epidemic of phenmetrazine dependence in Sweden. *J Psychedelic Drugs, 2 (No. 2)*:209-216, 1969.
17. Connell, P. H.: The use and abuse of amphetamines. *Practitioner, 200*:234-243, 1968.
18. Schick, J. F., Smith, D. E., and Myers, F. H.: Use of amphetamines in the Haight-Ashbury subculture. *J Psychedelic Drugs, 2 (No. 2)*:150-185, 1969.
19. Wikler, A.: Interaction of physical dependence and classical and operant conditioning in the genesis of relapse. In *The Addictive States*, edited by A. Wikler. Baltimore, Williams & Wilkins Co., 1968.
20. Smith, R.: Personal communication, 1970.
21. Lipp, M., Tinklenberg, J. R., Taylor, Z., Benson, S., and Melges, F. T.: Drug use at four medical schools. *Int J Addictions*, in press.
22. Taylor, R. L., Maurer, J. I., and Tinklenberg, J. R.: Management of bad trips in an evolving drug scene. *JAMA, 213*:422-425, 1970.

23. Shoichet, R., and Solursh, L.: Treatment of the hallucinogenic drug crisis. *Appl Therapeutics, 11*:5, 1969.
24. Solursh, L. P., and Clement, W. R.: Use of diazepam in hallucinogenic drug crisis. *JAMA, 205*:644-645, 1968.
25. Espelin, D. E., and Done, A. K.: Amphetamine poisoning. *New Eng J Med, 278*:1361-1365, 1968.
26. Kraft, T.: Treatment of drinamyl addiction. *J Ner Ment Dis, 150*: 138-144, 1970.
27. Hamburg, D. A., Tinkenberg, J. R., and Melges, F. T.: Marijuana and amphetamines. Published by Salk Institute. (In press.)
28. Griffith, J. D.: Proposed Ban of Amphetamine Drugs. Statement before the Select Committee on Crime, U. S. House of Representatives, November 18, 1969. Unpublished manuscript, Department of Psychiatry, Vanderbilt University School of Medicine.

18

Marijuana and Adverse Psychotic Reactions
Evaluation of Different Factors Involved
Gurbakhash S. Chopra

O ver the past few years a new problem has arisen all over the world—that of the abuse of psychedelics such as LSD and marijuana. Most news and communication media have featured discussions and debates of the various aspects of these drugs, including their alleged use in art, music, and religious exercises and the hazards related to their abuse. This chapter will examine the controversy surrounding the role of cannabis in causing or precipitating psychotic reactions.

In order to better understand the effects and the psychological aspects of the use of cannabis on the human mind, it would be of interest to review briefly the historical background of the cannabis plant. This drug has been used as a psychedelic from ancient times. The various names and epithets in ancient literature suggest that the drug was commonly employed for its psychomimetic effects. It has exerted an influence upon human psychology and human thought.

Referring to ancient Aryan literature, cannabis is mentioned by various names in Atharva Veda, 200 BC, as "indracana," god's food, "bhanga" or "viyja," meaning victory and suggesting a mood of relaxation. In later works such as the Rajnirghantu, 1400 BC, hemp is called "ajaya," or unconquered, "vrapatra," hero-leaved, "ganja," "capta," light-hearted, "anads," joy, "harshani," the rejoicer. The psychedelic and psychomimetic effects of the drug were well known to the Indians of those days. Comparatively recent writings such as Bhavaparaka and Rajavallbha, 1600 AD, and Hindu Materia Medicas, described the drug as one producing infaturation, intoxication, creation of vital energy, correction of phlegmatic humor, and as an elixer/Vita.

In Arabic and Persian literature, there are frequent references to the plant and to its discovery. It is related that Sheikh Jafar, a monk of the order of Haider, lived alone on a mountain, where he had established a monastery. After having lived in seclusion, he returned one day after a stroll, with an air of joy and gaiety. On being questioned, he stated that in order to appease hunger and thirst, he had gathered and eaten leaves of a particular plant growing in the area and had experienced feelings of exhilaration. He then led his companions to the spot where all chewed the leaves and were similarly affected. The knowledge of the peculiar properties of the leaves gradually became known to the followers of Shirazi and a decoction prepared by soaking the leaves in wine became the favorite drink of the Haider sect. After that time, the Islamic world used the drug as a means of supposedly opening the gates of earthly paradise. The Arab's favorite was "hashish," a name which gave rise to the sect of Haschins or Hashnavis, from which we derive our word, "assassin." The founder of the sect was an astonishing character called "the old man of the mountain" and was a friend of Omar Khayam. The followers of Hassan committed heious crimes under the hallucinations of the drug, with the belief that if they died they would go to heaven.

Herodotus mentions the Scythians smoking cannabis in order to induce a state of excitement. Hemp was also used for mental disease. This use was brought to the attention of the Europeans by Sylvesto-de-lacy and Rouyer, who were attached to Napoleon's expeditionary forces in Egypt.

Cannabis preparations are obtained from the tops of the female plant, "cannabis indica," popularly known as hemp or marijuana. The potency varies widely, according to the climate, the mode of collection, prevention of pollination and the particular preparation used. "Bhang" is obtained from the dried mature leaves and the flowering tops of the wild or cultivated plant. It is cheap and low in potency and is usually drunk or eaten. "Ganja" is obtained by treading small top leaves and the resinous material into a homogeneous mass. It is three times as potent as "bhang" and is smoked. "Charas," "Chira" or "hashish" is pure resin, obtained directly from the plants' dried leaves or flowers. It is about four to five times as potent as "bhang."

Crude preparations like marijuana, "kif" or "dagga" are available in the rest of the world. They are roughly equivalent in potency to bhang, although they vary according to the country of origin. Roughly they are one-fifth to one-eighth as potent as hashish. Cannabis drugs are sometimes mixed with other drugs to potentiate its effects. A recent example found in Mexico and the United States is the boiling of marijuana with acetone in order to extract an oil which is mixed with hashish and rolled into pellets.

Hemp psychosis as observed by workers in India and Africa has not been reported by Western observers. The milder preparations of cannabis used in the West partially explains this comparative absence of such psychosis. In India there has always been a popular belief that prolonged and excessive use of these drugs leads to certain forms of mental disorder and crimes of violent nature. In previous studies I have discussed the relationship between hemp habituation and mental disease and crime. It became evident in these studies that excessive indulgence in these drugs by unstable and susceptible individuals was apt to produce states of confusion characterized by hallucinations, delusions and disorientation. Prolonged excessive use also appeared to lead to the possible development of toxic psychosis. This chapter is based upon the examination of two hundred cannabis dependents studied from 1963 to 1968. Taken into consideration were age of onset, education, socioeconomic status, dosage, motivation, psychological and general health, signs of malnutrition, type of personality, et cetera. An analysis of these observations will be presented at a later point in this presentation.

Motivation and environment have important roles in inducing psychotic states, Various individuals listed different reasons for using cannabis. First of all, it was used as a substitute for alcohol. Among the two hundred persons studied, 20 percent used the drug as a substitute for opium or alcohol. The low cost of hemp and the fact that there are practically no withdrawal symptoms made it an attractive substitute. In underdeveloped countries such as India, the use of cannabis drugs by certain sections of the population, can be compared to the use of alcohol in the West. A distinction should thus be drawn between occasional, regular and moderate users and those who indulge in excess. The latter category of users are obviously more prone to adverse psychotic reactions. The users in the United States belong mostly to the first two categories. This again partly explains the infrequency of psychotic reactions among users in this country. Like alcohol, excessive cannabis use can be attributed to preexisting personality problems. This is supported by a Moroccan saying which states that "You are a kif addict before you smoke your first pipe." The highest percentage of excessive hemp users are from the unemployed and low-income classes. For the most part, they are passive and nonproductive individuals and are more prone to psychosis than normal individuals who follow a regular, daily vocation.

Secondly, hemp was used for religious purposes. Cannabis has played a central role in the religions of Africa and South America, as well as in India. In Africa, there are instances when an entire village has exhibited spells of madness after indiscriminate indulgence in "dagga." In India the drug is commonly abused by religious mendicants in places of worship and in the "takyas" of Muslin fakirs.

Cannabis has also been used, and is used, by persons in the arts. Supposedly it enables one to expand creativity. It is likely that the drug enhances the emotional aspects of the art media. However, there is no proof that it helps in technical performance.

Hemp is also used for the relief of fatigue, monotony and boredom. Hemp is used among the laboring and working classes in urban areas, in order to relieve these states. The drug induces a feeling of restfulness and mild euphoria. Such use is not frequently excessive and is similar to the use of marijuana in Western Society.

There are, in addition, miscellaneous other uses for cannabis. It has been believed by some that hemp enhances sexual enjoyment. However, there is some evidence that it depresses sexual desire. Still others have used the drug as an inducement to homcidal violence. The followers of Hassan were such an example. These were persons who used cannabis expressly to achieve the courage needed to perform murder and violence. Among the two hundred individuals studied by me, three admitted using the drug for such purposes. There are recorded cases in India where persons intoxicated by cannabis drugs, ran amuck and attacked people without provocation, and even committed murder.

The design and execution of this study represents a compromise between the niceties of research methods and the limitations imposed by the realities of the situation. While considerable care was taken in the design, the standardization and the subsequent analysis of the following data, it was affected by factors over which there was no control. The patients were usually seen during acute and frequently agitated states. The amnesia and garrulousness in some cases made the examination difficult. Often, information could not be obtained until the patient had regained his memory. Some difficulties were imposed because the patients were examined in unconventional settings. Overall, the information about antisocial and criminal behavior are likely to be underestimates rather than overestimates.

The study was spread over a period of five years, from 1963 to 1968. These two hundred patients represented 11.1 percent of a total of 1,800 hemp abusers seen during this period. Of these, 95 percent were male. The median age was 31 years, and the range was from 18 to 60 years. As to the general condition of health, 65 percent were in good health, with no signs of anemia or malnutrition. The remaining 35 percent showed varying degrees of anemia. There were no other significant physical problems having bearing upon this study.

The majority (65 percent) were uneducated; 23.5 percent of the persons had received a primary school education. Adverse reactions were more common in the uneducated group. Again, a different situation exists in the United States where many marijuana users are educated youth from college campuses. With regard to occupation, persons in lower income groups were more susceptible to adverse reactions. This is again unlike marijuana users in the United States and other Western countries, where users are mostly from the middle class.

The subjects of the study were grouped into three main categories. Group I consisted of 78 (39 percent) individuals. They were healthy with little or no personality problems and had no history of mental disorder or neurosis. An invariable element was the history of their use of drugs. The patients' symptoms were so similar and uniform as to give a reasonable supposition of a definite effect following a definite cause. The symptoms were of a mental nature, stimulating acute toxic psychosis. There were no other concomitant elements, beyond the use of the drug. This eliminated the possibility of the toxic psychosis resulting from other causes.

Group II was comprised of 122 (61 percent) patients and formed the bulk of the study. Most of them were on the threshold of psychosis. They included psychopaths, delinquents, hypochondriacs and those suffering from varying degrees of personality problems. A large percentage of these persons also showed signs of schizophrenia and paranoia, and many were ambulatory psychotics. States of confusion were present in the early stages, thus making it sometimes difficult to separate persons in this group from those in group I. The duration of the reaction was fairly short. After the toxic reactions of the drug had disappeared, the symptoms of the preexisting psychosis became manifest in greater intensity. Schizophrenic and paranoid reactions predominated during the later stages. After withdrawal of the drug, the patients reverted to their preexisting psychotic tendencies and ambulatory psychosis.

Group III included 10 (5 percent) individuals with a history of psychosis. Most of them experienced acute intoxication. In the case of these individuals, the symptoms of cannabis psychosis were superimposed on preexisting psychotic states. Even after the drug was withdrawn, they ran a chronic course of their original psychosis. The use of the drug was either coincidental or a symtom of the preexisting psychosis.

It thus transpires that the most common reaction which could be solely attributed to cannabis, or associated with it, is the confusional state which often develops into toxic psychosis as seen in most of these patients. In order to be more specific, I will refer to one particular case:

J. M. was a 30-year-old brass worker with no history of hereditary mental disease and no addiction other than bhang. All inquiries failed to elicit any probable cause of psychosis.

He was under my treatment from October 1, 1967 to December 1, 1967. On admission he was found to be suffering from acute brain syndrome, seemingly due to the drinking of bhang. Upon withdrawal of the drug, he was completely cured and was discharged. He did well and secured a job until trouble of a trivial nature occurred, and he again reverted to the use of bhang. Immediately a fresh attack of a violent nature occurred, for which he again was brought to the clinic. He displayed the usual symptoms of garrulity, constant laughing, incoherent speech, restlessness, violence, insomnia, flushed face and congested conjunctiva. He recovered in about thirty days and remained under observation for a year. During this period he led a normal life working in an office. Like most of these patients, upon recovery he had no recollection of his condition until much later. He later told me that he had been in the habit of drinking 180 grains daily.

There were several others, including those who suffered relapses, who attributed their disease to the abuse of cannabis. On the other hand, persons who after being cured, abstained from the use of cannabis, remained sane, even after several years. There were, of course, other relevant factors such as preexisting psychosis, environment and personality. However, this study indicated that excessive use of cannabis was a definite agent responsible for inducing a psychotic state.

In 27 percent of the patients there was tentative or definite evidence of neurotic disturbances in early age. However, at the time of the psychotic episode, they appeared normal and stable. Nevertheless 30 percent exhibited various personality problems, while others were bordering on psychosis; 5 percent of the cases studied had been psychotic patients prior to cannabis abuse; 18 percent of the subjects had a history of criminal offenses and conviction; 13 percent admitted stealing; and 20 percent admitted committing acts of violence against their friends and associates on the slighetst provocation. They also admitted to sex offenses.

Those between 21 and 30 years of age were more involved with the drug, while the next most vulnerable age group was between 31 and 40 years of age. Beyond the age of 40, comparatively fewer individuals were involved.

Most of the subjects who were treated in the clinic presented themselves within forty-eight hours after experiencing the adverse psychotic reactions. Only a few (5 percent) presented themselves at a later time. These persons had previous psychotic problems and the use of cannabis drugs was a coincidental factor or a symptom of the preexisting psychosis. At the time of initial interview, both objective and subjective symptoms were recorded.

A diversity of reactions was noted in each case. It was thus not possible to attribute a particular symptom or categorize the episodes under specific diagnostic entities. However, the common and frequent symptoms which many of these individuals presented were confusional states, amounting to toxic psychosis (acute brain syndrome), hallucinations, delusions, schizophrenia, paranoia, amnesia and depersonalization. The significant physical changes observed were suffused face, bloodshot eyes and conjunctival congestion.

Schizophrenic and acute confusional reactions were more common in the case of acute disorders. This may be due to the fact that these persons had psychotic problems and had been leading lives of marginal existence. They seemed to react more intensely to the drug, probably because their balance between inner and outer reality was already very precarious. Individuals under stress were much more susceptible to a drug like cannabis and showed a tendency to become disorganized and fragmented under its influence.

Only 5 percent of the individuals suffered from chronic disorders. It is difficult to say whether these were due to chronic voluntary hemp intoxication or were symptomatic of preexisting psychotic disorders. Prolonged abuse of the drug may have led to progressive weakening of the higher control centers. This could eventually result in dementia, as was seen in two individuals. The remainder of this small group were schizophrenics who experienced relapses and ran a chronic course.

Mental derangement following the use of psychotoxic drugs like cannabis indica is nothing but an abnormal reaction on the part of cerebral cells whose physiological activities are either held in abeyance or partially or totally disorganized. This perverted activity releases the control by the higher centers, thus allowing the lower centers to be influenced by abnormal external stimuli. These reactions may occur in one or more parts of the central nervous system. Cannabis, when absorbed into the system, does not add any new element to the brain; it only removes this higher control and excites the preexisting trend of mental aberrations, if any.

All types of psychotic reactions resulting from cannabis intoxication are, therefore, characterized by certain common general symptoms. These are excitation of thought processes, a sense of intoxication and incoherent ideas and actions. However, these symptoms vary in each individual according to personality, mood, education, judgment and motivation. Persons with preexisting psychotic and neurotic tendencies appear to be more easily affected than normal healthy individuals. The same dose of cannabis does not produce similar effects in all individuals. The individual's psychotic threshold also plays a part in determining the effects.

Psychodysleptic drugs stimulate intellectual activity, but the positive reactions to which they give rise are really negative reactions resulting from the release of control by the higher centers. Cannabis, therefore, disturbs the physiological thinking process. This may give rise to delirium, distortion of reality and sense of judgment, and further confusional states may follow delusions and hallucinations caused by the drug. They may ultimately lead to depersonalization and a dream-like state of fantasy. This action is actually psychomimetic in nature.

This study indicates then that there is a relationship between marijuana and psychotic episodes which may be influenced by the basic personality of the individual using the drug. It seems that a particular symptom complex resulting from cannabis intoxication is dependent upon various factors, comprising personality, education, religion, socioeconomic status and motivation. The psychotic episodes are self-induced, exogenous in nature, which may at times be difficult to differentiate from endogenous psychosis, especially in the case of persons with preexisting psychotic disorders.

It also appears that among certain individuals, marijuana may be directly associated with various crimes. This may be as a primary cause or due to liberation of inhibitions. Some persons may have criminal tendencies prior to the use of cannabis drugs which are exaggerated by continuous abuse.

19

Implications and Direction

Paul H. Blachly

▶■◀●■◀

T he completion of school signals time for action. What are the implications of our efforts?

Like those parents who anxiously observe the growing sexuality of their children, our society has viewed the past decade of increasing drug abuse. At first secretive and unusual, varied drug use has become an open topic of conversation. Just a few years ago drug abuse was a romantic topic on college campuses; it now seems to excite less interest. It appears that on the campuses, marijuana is here to stay for awhile, while the other drugs are causing less pathology. This may be either because of decreased use or because users have learned how to avoid side effects, or both. The increasing use in high schools and grade schools I think simply reflects the usual way in which fads move, from the top—the colleges—down, and then out.

It is not surprising that in a technological society kids should learn and experiment with drugs, just as they do with rockets, electronics, astronomy and other new developments. Just as we are now benefiting from atomic power generators, I am sure we will benefit from the existing drug turmoil. I predict this early experimental interest will result in a tremendous growth in the next few years of a *constructive* interest in chemistry and pharmacology by students who will eliminate or control many of our present diseases.

As with a child, spanking may be very useful at some stages of development, but becomes ineffective or even detrimental at other stages. So it is with the influence of many of our laws controlling drugs. We must seriously consider whether in this area particularly, the greatest growth and responsibility occurs when laws are few, but respected and enforceable. Should we not take more seriously the observation of the Turkish farmers who, although they grow opium, do not use it in a way which constitutes a problem? Should we not consider the remarks of a high Bureau of Narcotics officer who, in reply to my inquiry regarding the marijuana problem in Mexico, said he was not aware of a marijuana problem there, although that is where it is grown and easily available. It is important to note here that in both cultures there are very strong family ties, and I probably need not repeat to this group that *people are drug substitutes.*

We have seen repeatedly that when laws against a crude form of a drug are enforced, people turn to a more concentrated and easily smuggled form. When opium smoking, a relatively mild addiction, was outlawed, it encouraged use of the more dangerous heroin. When alcohol was prohibited, persons shifted from large volume beer to concentrated whiskey. When marijuana laws are more seriously enforced, the move is to hashish or more dangerous heroin. Like the fisherman who tried to kill starfish by cutting off the legs, we are finding that each piece of drug abuse supposedly cut off through legislation simply grows to be another whole problem.

Alcohol prohibition was not ended because alcohol was found to be safter than some other substances. It was ended because of the criminality the prohibition laws caused. Prohibition like quarantine is good preventive treatment when it works. When it is ineffective, it is best abandoned. I suspect the time has come to get some tax revenues out of marijuana rather than spending our money trying to enforce the unenforceable. By relegalizing marijuana and treating it like tobacco we might just possibly be able to make some inroads into the use of truly dangerous drugs. But just as relegalizing alcohol has not eliminated moonshiners, we must be aware that when taxes on anything get extreme, illegal activity develops.

The new evidence presented at this meeting is highly significant. Dr. Smart, in showing that the use of drugs by students is more related to use of drugs by their parents than their peers, has taught us that we must decrease drug use generally in order to

decrease student use. Drug use is a learned way of solving problems. Dr. Fort reminded us that much of this learning occurs on
television. I urge you to write your congressmen to get them to
put pressure on the Federal Communications Commission to
eliminate the extremely destructive advertising of sleeping potions
and tranquilizers, and I urge physicians to ask their Board of
Medical Examiners to seek an injunction to stop such advertising,
which constitutes a form of illegal practice of medicine.

I would urge the National Institute of Mental Health and
mental health associations to demand equal time for countering
destructive commercials, even as the American Cancer Society has
done for cigarettes, and I would demand of the Federal Communications Commission that public service time be given to teaching
people problem-solving maneuvers other than drugs.

Dr. Deissler has expressed the opinion that the very moral
fiber of our society is rotten and that salvation is possible through
self-discipline and open confrontation with our peers. To my
knowledge every society has developed monasteries, even as every
society has developed drugs. Unquestionably, monasticism serves
a useful purpose, but always to a minority. Synanon certainly
deserves a trial by many.

Dr. Maurer in his humorous indirect fashion has shown how
passage of laws with noble intent pushed addiction into the underworld, via the poor Chinese laundryman. Neil Chayet described
the criminalization of 100,000 youth since passage of the marijuana laws in 1937. It is reassuring to find that even capable
attorneys and judges are perplexed by the spate of irrational laws
dealing with drugs. Mr. Sonnenreich, in describing the new federal drug statutes, is consistent with the desire of most law enforcement officers that if you have a law against everything, that
gives the officer and judge maximum opportunity to use discretion
(while creating the opportunity for graft).

Dr. Villareal's elegant model for analyzing drug use in monkeys
reminds us that we can not escape the significance of the chemistry
of the individual drug. Ideally people would not ever come in
contact with drugs of abuse, but how are we to manage that in
today's open society? Dr. Fraser, in showing how clinical evaluations are done in people, echoes Dr. Villareal's sentiments. Yet,

we must remember that both investigators did their work on imprisoned subjects from deprived ghetto backgrounds. They neglect to say that we all have had narcotics and sleeping pills at one time or another, did not get hooked, nor ever had the desire.

I cannot be pessimistic about drug abuse now. For the first time in decades, we are getting back to where drug abuse is viewed as an illness. When so viewed, it becomes a subject for systematic research. Drs. Mandell and Tinklenberg have presented some preliminary findings from such new scientific research. In the not too distant future I predict that there will be developed sustained action preparations of both methadone and narcotic antagonists, which may last several weeks.

Research will help us determine how we can most efficiently spend our therapeutic dollar and how to discriminate in matching the patient with treatment. However it will take courage and perseverance to apply these scientific findings to treatment on a large scale, when therapists so often seem creatures of habit and belief rather than operationally eclectic clinicians. I will only mention as an example that ten years ago evidence was published that group psychotherapy of addicts was without demonstrable value in changing their attitudes! Yet, ten years later, although there still remains no data refuting this, group psychotherapy of addicts remains in use. This phenomenon suggests a fundamental principle: *In the absence of definitive treatment of a condition, psychotherapy expands to relieve the demands of society, the guilt of the therapist and the time and fortunes of the patient.*

We see at the National Institute of Mental Health the development of greater interest in innovative programs in drug abuse, rather than the perpetuation of the basically sterile practices of the past. We can no longer afford the luxury of waiting thirty years to act on the finding that a particular treatment is worthless, as happened with the federal hospitals for the treatment of addiction.

The Food and Drug Administration (FDA) must become socially responsive. Much of the fundamental research on narcotics has been done by government researchers. Drugs so developed are not subject to commercial exploitation. Because of this, companies are unwilling to invest the vast sums needed to fulfill the often routine demands of the FDA. Somehow either government will have to financially support the efforts needed to satisfy the requirements of the FDA, or better yet, the FDA will set up a system whereby the social need for more effective drugs can be balanced against requirements of safety. That such a system should be able to withstand public scrutiny seems obvious, yet much of the FDA's decisions are made in private and are often arbitrary and capricious.

To you in law enforcement, I urge you to join us in treatment and prevention. We cannot yet do without you, and Judge Jones exemplifies how an enlightened judiciary can provide the conditions under which rehabilitation can occur.

Lastly, even if we found a cure for addiction tomorrow, it is unlikely that we would eliminate the problem. We have had penicillin to cure gonorrhea for two decades but gonorrhea is spreading. We could largely eliminate lung cancer, but cigarette smoking continues. That effective treatment or prevention exists does not necessarily mean that persons will avail themselves of it. Much depends on custom and fashion. Thus, it appears that 30 to 40 percent of heroin addicts may not avail themselves of methadone treatment, despite the risks of continued heroin use.

But the promise of the future is maturation in knowledge and emotion regarding drugs. Let's go to work in order to bring this about.

APPENDICES

A

Medical Progress with Marihuana

Richard Colestock Pillard

M arihuana is among man's oldest and most widely used drugs. It has been eaten and drunk, snuffed and smoked as long as medical history has been recorded and is currently used throughout the world by hundreds of millions of people.[1-4] The many published observations on marihuana users present a fairly consistent picture of its short-term effects. However, there are strongly contradictory opinions about whether the ultimate effects are harmful, harmless or beneficial to human functioning. This review will summarize present knowledge—clinical, pharmacologic and epidemiologic—describe the legal status of marihuana and comment on the problems of controlling nonmedical drug use.

Marihuana is obtained from the hemp plant that Linnaeus named *Cannabis sativa*. Hemp is an annual weed growing freely everywhere, including the entire United States. At one time it had commercial importance: the fiber was used for rope, the oil for paint, and seeds were a constituent of bird food. At present, however, other natural and synthetic fibers have gradually reduced the demand for hemp.

The intoxicating property of cannabis resides in several tetrahydrocannabinols, the concentration of which depends upon plant strain and to a lesser extent on soil and climate.[5] Table A-1 shows the tetrahydrocannabinol (THC) potency of plants grown in Mis-

Reprinted with permission from *The New England Journal of Medicine, 283 (No. 6)*, Aug. 1970.

Note: The study reported in this chapter was supported in part by a Research Scientist Development Award (K1-MH-32,896) from the National Institute of Mental Health.

TABLE A-1

Δ¹-THC POTENCY OF MARIJUANA PLANTS GROWN IN
MISSISSIPPI FROM VARIOUS SEED SOURCES

Seed Source	$\%\Delta^1$-THC
France	0.085
Italy	0.041–0.068
Mexico:	
Male plants	1.47
Female plants	1.31
Sweden	0.021
Turkey	0.05–0.40

Adopted from Waller.[5]

sissippi from seeds obtained in different locations. There is a difference of seventy times between the most and least potent plants in this sample.

Cannabis is dioecious: the leaves of both sexes contain similar amounts of THC, [5,6] but the female plant is bushier and its flowering tops secrete a clear, varnish-like resin that is the most potent material of all. Table A-2 defines various cannabis preparations. Most of these are traditional in India and the Middle East; the two of importance in the United States are marihuana leaf and hashish. The leaf is pulverized and rolled into a thin cigarette or

TABLE A-2

NAMES FOR COMMON CANNABIS PREPARATIONS*

Name	Composition
Hashish Charas (India)	Pure resin from tops of female hemp plants; most potent material.
Ganja (India)	Flowering tops of specially cultivated female plants; highly potent; used in smocking mixtures, beverages and sweets.
Bhang (India, Middle East)	Dried mature leaves.
Marijuana (America and Europe) Kif (North Africa) Dagga (South Africa) Macohna (Brazil)	Entire plant with variable proportions of leaves and flowering tops; used as smoking mixture, and occasionally as beverage; potency varies greatly; names such as "Panama red" and "Acapulco gold" describe highly potent preparations.

*See also Walton[1] (Ch. 11), *Report of the Indian Hemp Commission*[3] and Chopra[7] (pp. 220-221).

smoked in a pipe whereas hashish, the pure resin in the form of a hard, brown cake, is usually smoked in a pipe. Marihuana containing 1% THC is considered to be of good quality by users. One cigarette containing 250 to 500 mg of leaf will produce a moderate to intense intoxication within fifteen minutes. Hashish is up to ten times more potent and is used in proportionately smaller amounts.

Pharmacologically, marihuana is in a class by itself; it is neither a stimulant, sedative, tranquilizer, hallucinogen nor narcotic although it has properties in common with all those drugs. For example it potentiates both barbiturate sleeping time and amphetamine excitement in mice. Hallucinations occur with large doses but the true hallucinogens—lysergic acid diethylamide (LSD), 2,5-dimethoxy-4-methylamphetamine (STU), dimethyltryptamine (DMT), mescaline and peyote—show cross-tolerance to each other and not to cannabis.[8,9] Also, the stearic configuration of the cannabinol molecule does not suggest primary hallucinogenic activity.[10]

CHEMISTRY

The chemistry of cannabis has been reviewed most recently and extensively by Mechoulam and Gaoni.[11] A number of closely related compounds are natural constituents of cannabis resin. These include cannabinol, cannabinolic acid, cannabidiol, cannabiodolic acid, cannabigerol, cannabigerolic acid, cannabichromene, cannabicycol and several isomers of tetrahydrocannabinol. Their structural formulae are given in Figure A-1 along with that of synhexyl—a synthetic THC.[12] The major psychoactive compound is believed to be Δ^1-THC and to a lesser extent $\Delta^{1(6)}$-THC.* Both these substances have been extracted from crude marihuana, identified, synthesized and tested on animals.[13,14] Δ^1-THC has been administered to man and found to approximate the state of marihuana intoxication. Work is in progress on tritiation and on the C^{14} labeling of both compounds for metabolic studies.[5,15] Pure

---

*Four different numbering systems have been used for cannabinoids over the years. This article uses the monoterpene numbering system employed by Mechoulam. Some authors use the dibenzopyran system.

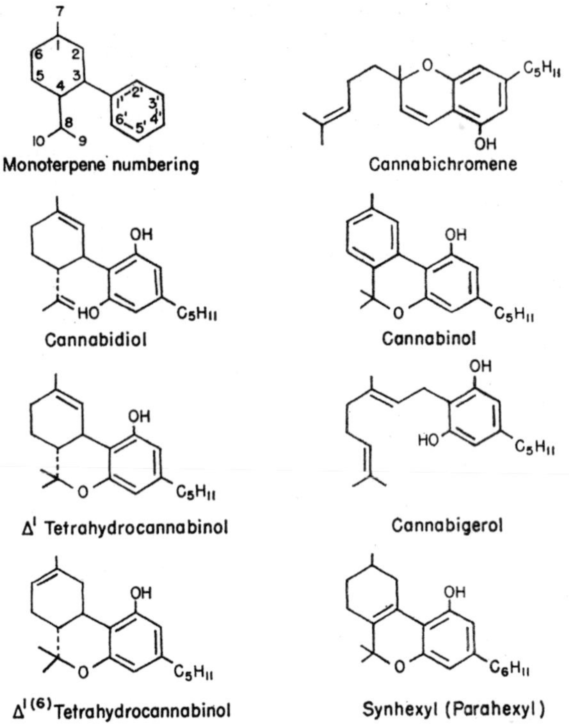

Figure A-1. Structural formulas of the major cannabinoids and a diagram of the monoterpene numbering system (after Mechoulam). Formulas of cannabinolic, cannabidiolic and cannabigerolic acids are obtained by addition of —COOH at position 3′.

Δ^1-THC and $\Delta^{1(6)}$-THC are being produced synthetically in quantities sufficient for research under contract by the National Institute of Mental Health.* Human experimentation with these compounds, however, will not be possible until animal toxicologic studies are complete.

Monoterpene		*Dibenzopyran*
Δ^1-THC	=	Δ^9-THC
$\Delta^{1(6)}$-THC	=	Δ^8-THC

---

*To H. Pars, Arthur D. Little, Inc., Cambridge, Mass.

ANIMAL PHARMACOLOGY

Most pharmacologic research has been done with extracts of cannabis such as "red oil,"† which, as pointed out above, contain a mixture of cannabinoids.[11] Furthermore, different strains of marihuana contain these compounds in different proportions. Thus, Loewe[16] showed that two major properties of cannabis—areflexia of the rabbit cornea and ataxia in the dog—were in part combined in the same molecule and in part embodied in different molecules. Santos *et al.*[17] found two strains from different parts of Brazil that were equipotent in producing corneal areflexia but different by fifteen times in reducing aggressiveness in the mouse. Current research will establish the effects of individual purified cannabinoids.

Gershon[18] has summarized the pharmacology of cannabis in laboratory animals. Two findings are of particular interest: tetrahydrocannabinol and marihuana extract have been shown to prolong barbiturate sleeping time and, paradoxically, amphetamine stimulation in a variety of animals.[19]

Garattini[20] and Carlini[21] and their co-workers have shown in several studies that marihuana extract decreases fighting behavior in mice and rats and does so in doses below those reducing total activity. More recently, Carlini and Masur[22] made the interesting observation that rats chronically starved and chronically injected with marihuana extract showed a striking *increase* in aggressive behavior though neither of those conditions alone could produce it.

There is no available assay for the presence of cannabis in body tissues or fluids.

EFFECTS ON HUMANS

Accounts of marijuana intoxication have been written by Baudelaire, Dumas, Rabelais and Allen Ginsberg[23] and among scientists by Ames,[24] Adams,[2] Bromberg,[23] Walton[1] and others.[23] Adequate description is difficult because the state of mind pro-

---

†First prepared by Wood[13] in 1896 by extraction of charas with an organic solvent and distillation under pressure. "Red oil" contains THC in high, but by no means pure, concentrations.

duced is not approximated in the usual states of consciousness or by other common drugs. (The hypnotic trance and the state of "transcendental meditation" may be the closest nonpharmacologic relatives.)

In an unpublished questionnaire study of drug use in medical students, Pillard, Meyer and Fisher asked subjects to describe briefly the effects they experienced from marijuana and from alcohol. With marijuana, the students overwhelmingly reported feeling relaxation and tranquillity. A great many also mentioned "increased awareness" of music, sex and food. Other responses were "a quietness of spirit"; "I was fascinated with ideas and objects"; "like the world around me was a new place"; "Sounds envelop me and become more distinct"; "more aware and compassionate of other people." Under the influence of alcohol they also felt relaxed and at ease but tended to report diminished awareness: "dulled senses," "muddled," "fuzzy" and "sleepy" were frequent descriptors.

Typically, the user feels a series of jittery "rushes" soon after inhaling. A sense of relaxation and well-being follows. There is awareness of being intoxicated not unlike that produced by alcohol. The user becomes acutely conscious of certain stimuli to the extent that his whole attention is focused, immersed and at times lost with the sensory experience. In this state, jokes are funnier, misfortunes more poignant and human relations more deeply perceived—and more seriously misperceived. The appreciation of food, sex and in particular music is intensified. The user may believe that his thoughts are unusually profound (an impression rarely shared by observers). Paranoid thoughts and feelings of depersonalization have been reported by subjects and observed in the laboratory. Visual imagery is increased,[26] and in larger doses, colors may shimmer and visual distortions occur, although this effect is not nearly so intense as with hallucinogens. There may be feelings of changed body proportion. Among the most striking perceptual changes is the subjective slowing of time.

As vivid as these effects are to the one who is experiencing them, the observer usually has little to observe. The subject may be laughing and gregarious or quiet and remote. His speech is often pecularily disconnected.[27] Mild states of intoxication, however, may be quite undetectable.

ACUTE ADVERSE REACTIONS

In addition to the typical effects of intoxication certain acute adverse psychologic reactions to marijuana have been described. These are of three general types:

Bromberg,[25] in 1934, was the first to report a state of reactive fright and panic associated with marijuana intoxication, and other reports have since appeared.[28,29] The smoker becomes appresensive, fearful or panic-stricken. The paranoid thoughts may get out of control, leading the smoker to fear he is going insane. The condition usually occurs in first-time users but has been reported after multiple use. Firm reassurance is effective treatment. The anxiety subsides as the drug effect wears off.

The cause of this reaction is not known. It is not limited to neurotic persons. Becker[30] views anxiety reactions as the result of a naïve user's fear that what he is experiencing is something more than the usual drug effect—an indication of impending psychosis. Without proper reassurance and "interpretation," anxiety escalates. Becker's view implies that fewer such reactions will occur among members of a drug-using subculture because they will have greater familiarity with idiosyncratic drug effects.

The incidence of these reactions can only be guessed at. An informal survey of the Boston University Student Health Service, which cares for a student population of 20,000, revealed that only five to seven marijuana-associated anxiety reactions are being seen yearly. Doubtless more occur but are not reported to physicians.

The second adverse effect, toxic psychosis precipitated by marijuana, has frequently been reported. In contrast to the anxiety reactions, toxic psychoses are marked by symptoms of thought disorganization, paranoia, depersonalization and hallucinations that last for days or weeks after the drug effects have stopped. In the LaGuardia study[31] seventy-seven persons were given various doses of cannabis extract, and nine had ill-effects. Three of these appear to have been coincidental schizophrenic reactions, but the other six were toxic delirium that followed directly after the cannabis administration. These six reactions were characterized by excitement, restless delirium and anxiety, which subsided in a few hours. These are similar to the panic reactions just described but more severe and long lasting, perhaps because the drug was given as an oral concentrate.

Talbott and Teague[32] reported twelve cases of acute psychosis in Vietnam servicemen characterized by excited, disorganized behavior, hallucinations and delusions. In all cases the illness occurred directly after the patient's first use of marijuana, and the symptoms remitted promptly. This syndrome was rare—twelve cases in a catchment population of 350,000 (of whom 32 percent were assumed to have tried marijuana)—but there are doubtless more cases than come for treatment. Weil[29] recently reported that marijuana may trigger psychotic-like states in persons with a history of psychosis or use of hallucinogenic drugs. It would be useful to study such patients further and to readminister a known dose of marijuana to determine psychodynamic or physiologic factors that may make persons vulnerable to decompensation.

Finally, Keeler[33] and Smith[34] have reported several cases of "flashback," a condition in which the subject suddenly feels the drug effect even though he has not used drugs for days or weeks. The cause is unknown, but it is more characteristic with LSD and more severe after use of that drug.

PREVALENCE

Reliable figures for the overall prevalence of marijuana use in the United States are not available, but news-media estimates suggest that about 10 percent of the population have smoked at least once. Observers agree that the frequency is highest in young adults and that it has been rapidly increasing during the past several years.

Unpublished surveys of high-school students show that 20 to 25 percent have smoked at least once. King[35] sent questionnaires to Dartmouth graduates from the Class of 1967. Of the 78.9 percent who responded 16.7 percent had used marijuana, and of the nonusers, 20 percent said that there was at least an even chance that they would do so sometime in the future. Hogan *et al.*[36] in a survey of 148 male undergraduates from two eastern universities, found 40.5 percent users and about 30 percent "adamant nonusers"—those who had not and never would use marijuana. In the winter of 1969 we surveyed first-year medical students: a 100 percent response was obtained, and of the responders, 45 percent had used marjuana at least once.

Nonstudents in the young adult group have a comparable frequency of use. Among American soldiers in Vietnam, marijuana smoking is estimated to occur in about 32 percent.[37] Manheimer et al.[38] carried out a census-tract survey on 1104 residents of San Francisco during 1967-1968. Among those 18 to 24 years old, half the men and a third of the women had smoked marijuana, but the percentage declined in the older age groups. Overall, 13 percent of their sample had smoked one or more times. Clearly, marijuana smoking is a common occurrence in this country.

Biographic and psychologic test data showed that users differed from nonusers in certain ways. Users tend to be more individualistic, politically liberal, not religious and somewhat impulsive and irresponsible. They are socially perceptive and sensitive to the needs and more commonly major in the humanities. Users of high-school age more often come from broken homes, engage more frequently in sexual intercourse and are more often in trouble with the law; however, their grades are as good as those of the nonusers. Nonusers are described as pleasant, responsible, considerate and dutiful but rather lacking in spontaneity and verve. A scale of social maturity rated both groups the same.[36]

In the San Francisco sample twice as many men as women had smoked marijuana.[38] The investigators found that within deviant subgroups, marijuana use was high, but overall the majority of users appeared to be reasonably conventional.

HUMAN PHARMACOLOGY

Our knowledge of the pharmacologic effects of marijuana in humans is based chiefly on the findings of five studies: the oldest and most comprehensive of these was the LaGuardia Report[31] done by the New York Academy of Science in 1939 at the request of New York's Mayor Fiorello LaGuardia. The scope and thoughtfulness of this investigation remain impressive after thirty years. Isbell et al.[39] in 1967, were the first to report the effects of pure synthetic Δ^1-THC in man. Hollister[40] and Waskow[41] and their colleagues also used pure Δ^1-THC. More recently Weil and his associates,[42] at Boston University Medical Center, studied "naïve" (inexperienced) subjects who smoked marijuana cigarettes. Observations have been added by Williams et al.[43] by Clark and Nakashima[44] and by Jones and Stone.[45]

Consistent physiologic changes were an increase in pulse rate and conjunctival injection. Dry mouth and increase of appetite were prominent. Pupil size and respirations were unchanged, and there were variable effects on blood pressure and body temperature.

The most general statement that can be made about psychomotor test performance is that simple tasks such as tapping speed, reaction time and continuous performance monitoring are not much affected whereas more complicated tasks—digit symbol substitution and complex reaction time—are obviously impaired.[31,44] Impairment is also reported in digit code memory, serial addition, figure closure and tasks that require physical coordination.[40,42] There is a good deal of variability between subjects, with inexperienced users doing less well.[31] As Clark[44] observes, the overall results are not much different from those often found in the study of the effects of many other drugs on complex behaviors.

If marijuana causes a specific and characteristic effect on perceptual processes, it has not yet been identified. Perhaps the phenomenon that comes closest is the striking distortion of subjective time estimation.[42,45] Subjects will *overestimate* an elapsed interval* and when shown a clock will express surprise that so little time has passed.

The ability to drive an automobile was tested by Crancer et al.[47] in a driving simulator. The authors had shown that a person's performance in the simulator was a good predictor of his actual driving record. Subjects familiar with marijuana were given alcohol, placebo or marijuana during three sessions. The alcohol condition caused a significant increase in accelerator, braking, speedometer and turn-signal errors, whereas on marijuana subjects did nearly as well as on placebo.

---

*Different psychophysical methods of measuring time estimation may lead to results that appear contradictory.[46]

Subjective effects in the studies referred to ranged from practically none in some of Weil's marijuana-naive subjects through the usual relaxation and euphoria to depersonalization, hallucinations and loss of reality testing with large doses of THC.

MEDICAL USES AND ADVERSE MEDICAL EFFECTS

Since the Marijuana Tax Act was passed in 1937 no medicinal preparation of cannabis has been available in the United States, and no clinical research using modern technics of drug evaluation has been done. Before 1937 a variety of therapeutic properties were recognized.[48] Tincture of cannabis was used as an analgesic, sedative and antispasmodic. Certain cannabis constituents possess antibacterial properties.[49]

Allentuck and Bowman[50] suggested that marijuana was useful in controlling symptoms of opiate withdrawal. Stockings,[51] in an uncontrolled study, gave synhexyl, a synthetic cannabinol, to fifty depressed patients and reported thirty-six "definitely improved"; however, later reports have contradicted this result.[52] Therapeutic uses will be more carefully explored as chemically pure cannabis constituents become available for clinical testing.

In 1969, Kew,[53] who performed liver-function tests on twelve regular marijuana smokers, suggested hepatotoxicity. Eight showed "mild liver dysfunction." Biopsy in three showed "striking parenchymatous degeneration." These patients had not taken intravenous drugs or used alcohol to excess.

After reports of chromosome damage from LSD,* cannabis was studied for its possible radiomimetic and teratogenic effects. Neu[55] added $\Delta^{1(6)}$-THC to human leukocyte cultures, and Martin[56] cultured cells from rat embryos exposed to cannabis extract. No increase of chromosomal aberrations was seen.

On the other hand, a teratogenic effect was observed by Persaud[57] and by Geber.[58] They produced fetal damage—litter resorption, stunting, encephalocele, phocomelia and syndactly—in rats, mice, rabbits and hamsters by injecting cannabis resin extracts early in pregnancy. The nature of the offending chemical and its mode of action are not known. Although the dose of resin used

---

*Contradicted by later studies.[54]

was larger than the amount humans would ordinarily ingest, and no case of human fetal damage has been attributed to marijuana alone, these results are ominous enough to suggest that women be specifically cautioned to avoid marijuana during pregnancy.

Finally, the physician should be skeptical about attributing adverse effects to marijuana alone. It is frequently adulterated with hallucinogens, opiates or scopolamine.[59] Reactions to "marijuana" may therefore involve a variety of other drugs that the patient may be unaware that he has ingested.

ADDICTION LIABILITY

The World Health Organization Expert Committee on Drug Dependence recommends that the term "drug dependence" replace "addiction" and "habituation" and offers the following definition of drug dependence, cannabis type:[60]

1. Desire (or need) for repeated administration of the drug on account of its subjective effects, including the feeling of enhanced capabilities.

2. Little or no tendency to increase the dose, since there is little or no development of tolerance.

3. A psychic dependence on the effects of the drug related to subjective and individual appreciation of those effects.

4. Absence of physical dependence so that there is no definite and characteristic abstinence syndrome when the drug is discontinued.

There is general agreement that cannabis tolerance and withdrawal syndrome do not develop in humans. Repeatedly injected mice performed better on a rope-climbing test than they did when first injected, but this was probably due more to practice than to true pharmacologic tolerance.[8,21] Observations on humans also suggest that users perform better as they gain experience with the drug.[31]

The problem with the WHO definition is that the meaning of "psychic dependence" is not made entirely clear.[61] Presumably, "psychic dependence" means something more than enjoyment or frequent use of a drug; it suggests that the user *needs* the drug to maintain his optimum level of psychologic function (for example, sexual potency or social relaxation) and would suffer impaired performance or dysphoric feelings without it. No one knows how many users conform to a definition of this sort. To find out would require psychiatric study and the psychodynamic understanding of a sample of users, both lacking so far. There is little doubt that marijuana is among a large number of substances that have the potential to serve as substitute gratifications and to produce psychic dependence as suggested in this definition.

PSYCHOLOGIC EFFECTS

The current issues of social interest have in general to do with possible influence of chronic marijuana use on psychologic functioning: Does it lead to crime, to narcotic addiction or to psychosis? Are there insidious effects on the personality that tend to diminish intelligence, motivation or effectiveness in work and study? There is a huge and opinionated literature on these subjects. Before some of it is reviewed, several guidelines might be considered and kept in mind.

In the first place, are the variables being studied clearly defined and accurately measured? For example, a presumable association between marijuana use and "motivation," "creativity" or "brain damage" would be difficult to investigate without a more valid measure of those variables than now exists. Even to determine the extent of marijuana use is not easy. Subjects may give an inaccurate report of how often they have smoked; also, samples of puported marijuana have turned out to contain other chemicals or to be inert.[59,62]

Secondly, is a relation truly demonstrated between the variables? If marijuana use is to be related to some outcome or dependent variable such as "psychosis," comparative rates are necessary. If, for example, five in one hundred smokers become psychotic, how does this differ from the number of psychoses occurring in a comparable one hundred nonsmokers? "Comparable" is stressed to suggest the importance of giving thought to the nonuser control sample, to how it matches the user sample and to extraneous variables that might distort the relation being examined.*

Thirdly, when a statistical relation has been shown, for example, between marijuana and heroin use, it cannot be assumed that a casual relation exists between them. Perhaps some unknown variable leads to the use of both drugs independently. In general, neither prospective, longitudinal nor any other purely observational studies will supply the needed data. The logical problems are similar to those encountered in studies of the effects of cigarette smoking. With present knowledge we are hardly able to say with certainty that habitual marijuana use does or does not cause anything.

As for the data, careful studies of the relation of cannabis to crime were made by Bromberg. Among sixty-seven criminals who had used marijuana there were none in whom the crime was attributable to drug use. In another sample of forty naval prisoners, Bromberg[64] found two with a history of more aggressiveness under the influence of marijuana. Forty nonusing prisoners chosen as controls had, if anything, a greater tendency to violent crimes. Chopra *et al.*[65] say, referring to the use of cannabis products in India, ". . . they not only do not lead to [violent crime] but actually act as deterrents. The action of the drug . . . is to quieten and stupefy so that there is no tendency to violence." Of Chopra's sample of users 8.24 percent had been convicted of crime, this rate being "higher than . . . usually met with among the general population."

On the other hand Marcovitz and Myers[66] and Charen and Perelman[67] describe groups of soldiers with psychopathic personalities in whom marijuana seemed to ". . . restore confidence which a criminal personality needs." Chopra *et al.*[65] also seem to contradict themselves in their statement that "in quite a number of cases, simple indulgence even in a single . . . smoke was responsible for a heinous crime." There are a number of opinions on all sides of this issue.[37,68,69]

---

*There are statistical technics to determine the relation between two or more variables with the influence of other specific variables removed.[63] The report by Manheimer *et al.*[38] illustrates one of these technics: the multiple-regression analysis.

When an assay for the presence of marijuana in body fluids is developed, it will be possible to assemble more evidence on its association with crime, automobile accidents and so forth. At present the most consistent summary of animal and human research indicates that intoxication usually decreases hostility and aggressiveness, but there may be circumstances (for example, Carlini's starved rats[22]) in which the reverse occurs.

Although marijuana is not itself physiologically addicting, various authors have been impressed by the frequency with which marijuana users seem also to be indiscriminate users of other drugs: LSD, methamphetamine (Methedrine), barbiturates and heroin. Is there a relation, and if there is, does marijuana specifically predispose to other drug use, or is there some general personality trait that leads independently to multiple drug use?

Leonard[70] cites a survey of 125 opiate addicts of whom 80 percent had used cannabis. Chapple's[71] British series of eighty opiate addicts had all used it. This probably represents greater marijuana use than would be expected in a matched group of nonaddicts. Silberman and Levy[72] report that marijuana users were more likely than a matched group of controls to be taking LSD and other drugs. Our survey of marijuana users shows a strong relation between LSD and marijunana use. In short, no one has failed to find a statistical relation between marijuana and the use of other drugs—legal and illegal.[73,74]

Some subjects have said that smoking marijuana was instrumental in their later use of LSD or heroin if only because they knew where illegal drugs could be obtained. On the other hand, current work at the Boston University Psychopharmacology Laboratory indicates that there are personality variables associated with the readiness of a person to try drugs[75] (both legal and illegal) and with response to the drugs when used.[76] The strength of this association and its mechanism is not known. Probably, both marijuana use and innate personality variables will turn out to be predictors of subsequent drug abuse.

Cannabis as a precipitant of schizophrenic reactions has received much attention. The acute toxic deliriums have already been described, but many authors believe that a more chronic schizophrenic reaction or a dementia lasting for months or years may also result. The condition is reported most frequently from India,[65,77] Morocco[78] and Africa,[79] where hundreds of cases have been reported. Few have occurred in England[80] or the United States.[29,31] I have difficulty evaluating these reports, but they appear to describe schizophrenic reactions in persons who also happen to be using cannabis. Some authors say specifically that cannabis psychosis is difficult or impossible to distinguish uniquely on clinical grounds.[65,77] Good epidemiologic studies have not been done, but there is nothing to indicate that psychosis or mental deterioration is more prevalent among populations prone to the use of cannabis products nor that within such populations users have a higher incidence of psychosis than nonusers.

Bromberg comments: "The . . . relationship between cannabis and the onset of a functional psychosis is not always clear . . . what role did the drug play? Could the psychosis have begun without the drug? Was the use of cannabis the patient's attempt to cure his developing psychosis?[81] These questions are as pertinent now as when Bromberg asked them in 1939.

Physicians have been concerned about less specific effects of cannabis, especially on young people.[82] These concerns are well expressed by McGlothlin and West.[83]

> . . . it appears that regular use of marijuana may very well contribute to some characteristic personality changes . . . Such individuals exhibit greater introversion, become totally involved with the present at the expense of future goals, and demonstrate a strong tendency toward regressive thinking. They report a greater subjective creativity but less objective productivity; and, while seeming to suffer less from vicissitudes and frustrations of life, at the same time they seem to be subtly withdrawing from the challenge of it.

It would be hard to make a definitive test of these impressions.

In a survey of drug use among medical students, we correlated the extent of marijuana use with class rank. We reasoned that successful participation in the medical-school curriculum involved just the sort of effectiveness and the capacity to carry out complex plans, to endure frustration, follow routines and to master new material that marijuana use seemed to impair. We used each student's score on the science section of the Medical College Aptitude Test as a covariate to control for the possibility that users had initially greater or less aptitude for school work.[1]* We found no relation between use of marijuana and class standing. However, we emphasize the fact that most of our "users" were infrequent users. Our sample did not contain enough heavy users (those who smoked more frequently than once a week) to extend our conclusions to that group.

The information summarized above has been collected over seventy-five years, and no one is able to make a judgment about the "safety" of marijuana. Goode[84] points out that "many of the issues . . . [go] beyond the test of scientific instruments . . . they sum up styles of life . . . cultural perspectives . . . outlooks on the world, which shape the individual's behavior . . ." Future research must be concerned with more than pharmacology if it is to resolve these issues.

LEGAL STATUS OF MARIJUANA

Legal regulation of marijuana was attempted by the Marijuana Tax Act of 1937. This act permits physicians, researchers and commercial users of marijuana to register and to obtain marijuana by paying a transfer tax of $1 per ounce . Nonregistered citizens may also possess marijuana, but the tax is prohibitive— $100 per ounce. Failure to comply with these tax provisions is punishable by $2,000 fine and up to five years in prison. In 1969 certain provisions of this act were declared unconstitutional by the United States Supreme Court. In the case of Timothy F. Leary vs. United States, the Court reversed Dr. Leary's conviction for possessing marijuana on the grounds that to obtain an order form and pay a transfer tax would tend to place him in a "select group inherently suspect of criminal activities," and would thus be self-incriminating. Legislation is now pending in Congress to prohibit possession of marijuana directly rather than by means of a tax act. Possession is also illegal in all fifty states and is a felony in twenty-eight. There is, however, a tendency toward reduced penalties for first-offense possession. In the past three years,

---

*As it turned out, they did not.

twenty-four states have reduced their penalty structures—most of them substantially.[85]

The legal status of marijuana in our society is the subject of fierce debate.[86,87] However, the various scientific and medical committees that have studied the matter have come to a surprisingly unanimous conclusion: marijuana should not be legalized for general consumption but that harsh legal penalties are unwise.

The following quotations are representative:

> There . . . appears to be good reason to moderate present punitive legislation so that penalties are more in keeping with what is now known about risks; that is, they are not great.[88]
> . . . the possession of small amounts . . . should not normally be grounds for imprisonment . . . but only for a fine. . . .[89]
> Legalization of marijuana would create a serious abuse problem in the United States [but] penalties for violations of the . . . laws are often harsh and unrealistic. . . . The lives of many young people are being needlessly damaged.[90]

The scientific study of legal penalties deserves more attention. In addition to their useful deterrent effect, we must recognize that such penalties carry a social cost[91,92]—chiefly that they may further diminish the capacity of the person to deal maturely with authority and to identify with constructive social goals.

Dissatisfaction with the law-enforcement approach to control of drug use has given impetus to educational programs. The National Institute of Mental Health sponsors television commercials and leaflets that briefly describe adverse drug reactions. Many communities are also taking steps to inform themselves and in particular their high school and college students about contemporary drug use. Some are recognizing the importance of providing young people with life opportunities that will serve as attractive alternatives to drug use.

To obtain marijuana for research complicated regulations* must be complied with. Administrative controls are needed to protect both the researcher and his subjects, but these should not be so burdensome as to discourage or to delay needed research greatly. Nor should there be any suspicion that an investigator's

---

*Copies are obtainable from the Center for Studies of Narcotic and Drug Abuse, National Institute of Mental Health, Chevy Chase, Maryland 20203.

work is being obstructed because his results did not support prevailing administrative views.

Drugs are making dramatic changes in our psychologic environment. Educational, research, treatment and law-enforcement programs all have a place in helping us to deal as rationally as possible with these changes. When this is done, however, we must remember that recreational drug use has always been a part of human society. It is not possible, and it may not be desirable to bring it to a stop. As physicians we must be ready to deal with the casualties of youthful pharmacologic experimentation, recognizing that by no means all users will be harmed. The ultimate place of marijuana in our culture will reflect social as well as medical pressures.

REFERENCES

1. Walton, R. P.: *Marijuana: America's New Drug Problem*. Philadelphia. J. B. Lippincott Company, 1938.
2. Adams, R.: Marijuana. *Bull NY Acad Med, 18*:705-730, 1942.
3. *Marijuana: Report of the Indian Hemp Drugs Commission 1893-1894*. Silver Spring (Maryland), Thomas Jefferson Publishing Company, 1969.
4. Grinspoon, L.: Marijuana. *Sci Amer, 221*:17-25, December, 1969.
5. Waller, C. W.: *The National Marijuana Program: First Annual Report, 1969*. Pamphlet published by National Institute of Mental Health.
6. Valle, J. R., Lapa, A. J., Barros, G. G.: Pharmacological activity of cannabis according to the sex of the plant. *J Pharm Pharmacol, 20*:798-799, 1968.
7. Chopra, G. S.: Man and marijuana. *Int J Addict, 4*:215-247, 1969.
8. Silva, M. T. A., Carlini, E. A., Claussen, U. *et al:* Lack of cross-tolerance in rats among (—) Δ^9-*trans*-tetrahydrocannabinol (Δ^9-THC), cannabis extract, mescaline and lysergic acid diethylamide (LSD-25). *Psychopharmacologia (Berlin), 13*:332-340, 1968.
9. Isbell, H., Jasinski, D. R.: A comparison of LSD-25 with (—) Δ^9-trans-tetrahydrocannabinol (THC) and attempted cross tolerance between LSD and THC. *Psychopharmacologia (Berlin), 14*:115-123, 1969.
10. Snyder, S. H. and Richelson, E.: Relationships between the conformation of psychedelic drugs and their psychotropic potency. In *Psychopharmacology: A Review of Progress, 1957-1967*,

edited by D. H. Efron. Washington, D. C., Government Printing Office, 1968 (PHS Publication No. 1836), pp. 1199-1222.

11. Mechoulam, R. and Gaoni, Y.: Recent advances in the chemistry of hashish. *Fortschr Chem Organ Naturst, 25*:175-213, 1967.

12. Adams, R., Baker, B. R. and Wearn, R. B.: Structure of cannabinol. III. Synthesis of cannabinol, 1-hydroxy-3-*n*-amyl-6,6,9-trimethyl-6-dibenzopyran. *J Amer Chem Soc, 62*:2204-2207, 1940.

13. Wood, T. B., Spivey, W. T. N. and Easterfield, T. H.: Charas: the resin of Indian hemp. *J Chem Soc [Org], 69*:539-546, 1896.

14. Mechoulam, R., Braun, P. and Gaoni, Y.: A stereospecific synthesis of (—)-Δ^1- and (—)-$\Delta^{1(6)}$-tetrahydrocannabinols. *J Amer Chem Soc, 89*:4552-4554, 1967.

15. Burstein, S. H., Menezes, F., Williamson, E. *et al:* Metabolism of $\Delta^{1(6)}$-tetrahydrocannabinol, an active marijuana constituent. *Nature (London), 225*:87-88, 1970.

16. Loewe, S.: The chemical basis of marijuana activity. *J Pharmacol Exp Ther, 84*:78-81, 1945.

17. Santos, M., Sampaio, M. R. P., Fernandes, N. S. *et al.*: Effects of cannabis sativa marijuana) on the fighting behavior of mice. *Psychopharmacologia (Berlin), 8*:437-444, 1966.

18. Gershon, S.: On the pharmacology of marijuana. *Behav Neuropsychiat, 1(10)*:9-18, 1970.

19. Garriott, J. C., King, L. J., Forney, R. B. *et al.:* Effects of some tetrahydrocannabinols on hexobarbital sleeping time and amphetamine induced hyperactivity in mice. *Life Sci, 6*:2119-2128, 1967.

20. Garattini, S.: Effects of a cannabis extract on gross behavior. In *Hashish: Its Chemistry and Pharmacology* (Ciba Foundation Study Group No. 21), edited by G. E. W. Wolstenholme, J. Knight. Boston, Little, Brown & Company, 1965, pp. 70-82.

21. Carlini, E. A.: Tolerance to chronic administration of Cannabis sativa (marijuania) in rats. *Pharmacology (Basel), 1*:135-142, 1968.

22. Carlini, E. A. and Masur, J.: Development of aggressive behavior in rats by chronic administration of cannabis sativa (marijuana). *Life Sci, 8*:607-620, 1969.

23. *The Marijuana Papers,* edited by D. Solomon. Indianapolis, Bobbs-Merrill Company, Inc., 1966.

24. Ames, F.: A clinical and metabolic study of acute intoxication with *cannabis sativa* and its role in the model psychoses. *J Ment Sci, 104*:972-999, 1958.

25. Bromberg, W.: Marijuana intoxication: A clinical study of cannabis sativa intoxication. *Amer J Psychiat, 91*:303-330, 1934.

26. Keeler, M. H.: Marijuana induced hallucinations. *Dis Nerv Syst,* 29:314-315, 1968.
27. Weil, A. T. and Zinberg, N.: Acute effects of marijuana on speech. *Nature (London),* 222:434-437, 1969.
28. Keeler, M. H.: Motivation for marijuana use: a correlate of adverse reaction. *Amer J Psychiat,* 125:386-390, 1968.
29. Weil, A. T.: Adverse reactions to marijuana: classification and suggested treatment. *New Eng J Med,* 282:997-1000, 1970.
30. Becker, H. S.: History, culture and subjective experience: an exploration of the social bases of drug-induced experiences. *J Health Soc Behav,* 8:163-176, 1967.
31. Mayor's Committee on Marijuana: *The Marijuana Problem in the City of New York: Sociological, Medical, Psychological and Pharmacological Studies.* Lancaster, Jacques Cattell Press, 1944.
32. Talbott, J. A. and Teague, J. W.: Marijuana psychosis: acute toxic psychosis associated with the use of *Cannabis* derivatives. *JAMA,* 210:299-302, 1969.
33. Keeler, M. H., Reifler, C. B. and Liptzin, M. M.: Sponstaneous recurrence of marijuana effect. *Amer J Psychiat,* 125:384-386, 1968.
34. Smith, D. E.: Acute and chronic toxicity of marijuana. *J Psychedelic Drugs,* 2:37-47, 1968.
35. King, F. W.: Marijuana and LSD usage among male college students: prevalence rate, frequency, and self-estimates of future use. *Psychiatry,* 32:265-176, 1969.
36. Hogan, R., Mankin, D. and Conway, J. E.: Personality correlates of undergraduate marijuana use. *J Consult Clin Psychol.*
37. Sapol, E. and Roffman, R. A.: Marijuana in Vietnam. *J Amer Pharm Ass,* 9:615-618, 1969.
38. Manheimer, D. I., Mellinger, G. D. and Balter, M. B.: Marijuana use among urban adults. *Science,* 166:1544-1545, 1969.
39. Isbell, H., Gorodetzsky, C. W., Jasinski D. *et al.:* Effects of (—) Δ⁹-trans-tetrahydrocannabinol in man. *Psychopharmacologia (Berlin),* 11:184-188, 1967.
40. Hollister, L. E., Richards, R. K. and Gillespie, H. K.: Comparison of tetrahydrocannabinol and synhexyl in man. *Clin Pharmacol Ther,* 9:783-791, 1968.
41. Waskow, I. E., Olsson, J. E., Salzman, C. *et al.:* Psychological effects of tetrahydrocannabinol. *Arch Gen Psychiat (Chicago),* 22:97-107, 1970.
42. Weil, A. T., Zinberg, N. E. and Nelson, J. M.: Clinical and psychological effects of marijuana in man. *Science,* 162:1234-1242, 1968.
43. Williams, E. G., Himmelsbach, C. K., Wikler, A. *et al.:* Studies on

marijuana and pyrahexyl compound. *Public Health Rep, 61*: 1059-1083, 1946.
44. Clark, L. D. and Nakashima, E. N.: Experimental studies of marijuana. *Amer J Psychiat, 125*:379-384, 1968.
45. Jones, R. T. and Stone, G. C.: Psychological studies of marijuana in man. Presented at the 125th Annual Meeting of the American Psychiatric Association, Bal Harbour, Florida, May 5-9, 1969.
46. Carlson, V. R. and Feinberg, I.: Individual variations in time judgment and the concept of an internal clock. *J Exp Psychol, 77*:631-640, 1968.
47. Crancer, A., Jr., Dille, J. M., Delay, J. C. *et al.*: Comparison of the effects of marijuana and alcohol on simulated driving performance. *Science, 164*:851-854, 1969.
48. Mikuriya, T. H.: Historical aspects of cannabis sativa in western medicine. *New Physician, 18*:902-908, 1969.
49. Radosevic, A., Kupinic, M. and Grlic, L.: Antibiotic activity of various types of cannabis resin. *Nature (London), 195*:1007-1009, 1962.
50. Allentuck, S. and Bowman, K. M.: The psychiatric aspects of marijuana intoxication. *Amer J Psychiat, 99*:248-251, 1942.
51. Stockings, G. T.: A new euphoriant for depressive mental states. *Brit Med J, 1*:918-922, 1947.
52. Parker, C. S. and Wrigley, F.: Synthetic cannabis preparations in psychiatry: (1) synhexyl. *J Ment Sci, 96*:276-279, 1950.
53. Kew, M. C., Bersohn, I. and Siew, S.: Possible hepatoxicity of cannabis. *Lancet, 1*:578-579, 1969.
54. Judd, L. L., Brandkamp, W. W. and McGlothlin, W. H.: Comparison of the chromosomal patterns obtained from groups of continued users, former users, and nonusers of LSD-25. *Amer J Psychiat, 126*:626-635, 1969.
55. Neu, R. L., Powers, H. O., King, S. *et al.*: Cannabis and chromosomes. *Lancet, 1*:675, 1969.
56. Martin, P. A.: Cannabis and chromosomes. *Lancet, 1*:370, 1969.
57. Persaud, T. V. N. and Ellington, A. C.: Teratogenic activity of cannabis resin. *Lancet, 2*:406, 1968.
58. Geber, W. F. and Schramm, L. C.: Effect of marijuana extract on fetal hamsters and rabbits. *Toxic Appl Pharmacol, 14*:276-282, 1969.
59. Graff, H.: Marijuana and scopolamine "high." *Amer J Psychiat, 125*:1258-1259, 1969.
60. WHO Expert Committee on Drug Dependence: Sixteenth report. *Who Techn Rep Ser, 407*:5-28, 1969.

61. Eddy, N. B., Halbach, H., Isbell, H. *et al.:* Drug dependence: its significance and characteristics. *Bull WHO, 32:*721-733, 1965.
62. Shulgin, A. T.: Recent developments in cannabis chemistry. *J Psychedelic Drugs, 2:*15-29, 1968.
63. Linn, R. L. and Werts, C. E.: Assumptions on making causal inferences from part correlations, partial correlations, and partial regression coefficients. *Psychol Bull, 72:*307-310, 1969.
64. Bromberg, W. and Rodgers, T. C.: Marijuana and aggressive crime. *Amer J Psychiat, 102:*825-827, 1946.
65. Chopra, R. N., Chopra, G. S. and Chopra, I. C.: *Cannabis sativa* in relation to mental diseases and crime in India. *Indian J Med Res, 30:*155-171, 1942.
66. Marcovitz, E. and Myers, H. J.: The marijuana addict in the army. *War Med, 6:*382-391, 1944.
67. Charen, S. and Perelman, L.: Personality studies of marijuana addicts. *Amer J Psychiat, 102:*674-682, 1946.
68. Moraes, Andrade, D.: The criminogenic action of cannabis (marijuana) and narcotics. *Bull Narcot, 16:*4, 23-28, 1964.
69. Murphy, H. B. M.: The cannabis habit: A review of recent psychiatric literature. *Bull Narcot, 15:*1, 15-23, 1963.
70. Leonard, B. E.: Cannabis: A short review of its effects and the possible dangers of its use. *Brit J Addict, 64:*121-130, 1969.
71. Chapple, P. A. L.: Cannabis: A toxic and dangerous substance: A study of eighty takers. *Brit J Addict, 61:*269-282, 1966.
72. Silberman, D. and Levy, J.: A preliminary survey of 24 Victorian marijuana users. *Med J Aust, 2:*286-289, 1969.
73. McGlothlin, W. H., Arnold, D. O. and Rowan, P. K.: Marijuana use among adults. *Psychiatry.*
74. Robins, L. N., Darvish, H. S. and Murphy, G. E.: The long-term outcome for adolescent drug users: A follow-up study of 76 users and 146 non-users. In *Psychopathology and Adolescence,* edited by J. Zubin, A. Freedman. New York, Grune & Stratton.
75. Fisher, S., McNair, D. M. and Pillard, R. C.: Acquiescence, somatic awareness, and volunteering. Presented at American Psychosomatic Society, Washington, D. C., March 22, 1970.
76. McNair, D. M., Kahn, R. J., Droppleman, L. F. *et al.:* Compatibility, acquiescence and drug effects. International Congress Series No. 129. *Neuro-psycho-pharmacology: Proceedings of the Fifth International Congress of the Collegium Internatione Neuro-Psycho-Pharmacologicum.* Washington, D. C., March 28-31, 1966. Edited by H. Brill, J. O. Cole, P. Deniker *et al.* Amsterdam. *Excerpta Medica,* 1967, pp. 536-542.
77. Grossman, W.: Adverse reactions associated with cannabis products in India. *Ann Intern Med, 70:*529-533, 1969.

78. Benabud, A.: Psycho-pathological aspects of the cannabis situation in Morocco: Statistical data for 1956. *Bull Narcot, 9*:4, 1-15, 1957.
79. Boroffka, A.: Mental illness and Indian hemp in Lagos. *E Afr Med J, 43*:377-384, 1966.
80. Baker, A. A. and Lucas, E. G.: Some hospital admissions associated with cannabis. *Lancet, 1*:148, 1969.
81. Bromberg, W.: Marijuana: A psychiatric study. *JAMA, 113*:4-12, 1939.
82. Wurmser, L., Levin, L. and Lewis, A.: Chronic paranoid symptoms and thought disorders in users of marijuana and LSD as observed in psychotherapy, Problems of Drug Dependence. National Academy of Science—National Research Council, Washington, D. C., 1969, pp. 6154-6177.
83. McGlothlin, W. H. and West, L. J.: The marijuana problem: An overview. *Amer J Psychiat, 125*:370-378, 1968.
84. Goode, E.: Marijuana and the politics of reality. *J Health Soc Behav, 10*:83-94, 1969.
85. Mathias, C. M.: Analysis of state laws concerning marijuana. *Congressional Record, 116*:S240-S245, No. 2, 1970.
86. Keup, W.: The legal status of marijuana: A psychiatric opinion poll. *Dis Nerv Syst, 30*:517-523, 1969.
87. Mead, M.: Hearings, Subcommittee on Monopoly, United States Senate. Competitive problems in the drug industry, *13*:5455-5477, 1969.
88. Blum, R. H.: Mind-altering drugs and dangerous behavior: Dangerous drugs. President's Commission on Law Enforcement and Administration of Justice. Task Force Report: *Narcotics and Drug Abuse: Annotations and Consultants' Papers.* Washington, D. C., Government Printing Office, 1967, pp. 21-39.
89. Lister, J.: Cannabis controversy and other sundry troubles. *New Eng J Med, 280*:712-714, 1969.
90. Council on Mental Health: Marijuana and society. *JAMA, 204*: 1181-1182, 1968.
91. Advisory Committee on Drug Dependence: *Cannabis.* London, Her Majesty's Stationery Office, 1968.
92. Greenberg, D. S.: "Pot" and politics: How they "busted" Stony Brook. *Science, 159*:607-611, 1968.

B

Management of "Bad Trips" in an Evolving Drug Scene

Robert L. Taylor, John I. Maurer and Jared R. Tinklenberg

"Bad trips" arise out of an increasingly complex drug scene. Rational therapy must consider completely, social psychological and physiological factors. Complexity results from the development of new drugs, indiscriminate ingestion, contamination, and adulteration. Drug-induced psychological changes occasionally lead to fatal behavior. Bad trips from anticholinergic compounds may be seriously worsened by phenothiazine treatment. Protection of the patient from dangerous behavior is fundamental to treatment. A clear history is invaluable but should be augmented by physical and mental examinations. Treatment begins with establishment of verbal contact without the use of tranquilizers, if possible. Reassurance and reality defining are often sufficient. With severe ego disruption, medication in combination with verbal interaction may be required. Administration of phenothiazines or sedatives helps to reestablish the observing ego with rapid dissolution of perceptual distortion and reestablishment of the premorbid ego functioning in most cases. Optimal treatment includes a follow-up visit.

*   *   *

Psychedelic drugs produce perceptual and cognitive distortions which, in the majority of instances, are experienced by an individual as strange but tolerable, if not pleasant or even exhilarating. Although the exact reasons for a person's feeling threatened by these changes are unknown, periodically, the necessary mix of factors occurs, and a state of anxiety varying from mild apprehension to panic evolves. The crisis created in an individual when he perceives himself in a threatening situation following psychedelic drug usage is commonly known as a "bad trip." It arises out of an extremely complex drug scene, making effective management an increasingly difficult problem. Attempts at therapeutic intervention should take into account such complicating factors as the increase in the number of drugs available, impulsive use of unknown compounds, adulteration and contamination of drugs, and the lethal potential of psychedelic agents.

COMPLICATIONS OF THE DRUG SCENE

The rising incidence of psychedelic drug usage is paralleled by the evolution of new drugs. The ever-increasing list of "mind expansion" drugs now includes lysergic acid diethylamide (LSD) ("acid"), Peyote, mescaline ("cactus"), psilocybin ("magic mushroom"), marijuana ("pot"), 2, 5-dimethoxy-4-methyl-amphetamine (STP), dimethyltryptamine (DMT), methylenedioxyamphetamine (MDA), N, N-dimethylthyptamine (DMA), trimethoxyamphetamine (TMA), methoxymethylene + dioxyamphetamine (MMDA), thiocarbanidin (THC), the amphetamines ("speed"), phenylcyclidine (Serny) [PCP], and various solvents.[1] Recently, reports have appeared describing the use of cough syrup, cold tablets, sleeping pills, heart stimulants, nasal inhalants, insecticide aerosols, asthma remedies, throat disks and aerosol refrigerants to create the mind-expanding kick (*Medical World News*, 9:24-26, 1968). The rapid expansion of this psychedelic pharmacopoeia is accounted for by several factors: (a) the ease with which derivative compounds can be synthesized; (b) the availability of numerous proprietary agents containing potential psychedelics, such as atropine, scopolamine, and various solvents; (c) the desire of an increasing number of people for the psychedelic experience; (d) the prevalence of naturally occurring psychedelic agents, such as mescaline, belladonna and marijuana; and (e) the large profit that can be realized through the sale of these drugs.

The growing number of psychedelic agents results in changing drug fads as the popularity of one drug gives way to more recent arrivals on the drug scene. The medical director of the Haight-Ashbury Clinic has recently commented on this evolution in psychedelic drug usage:

"For better or for worse, San Francisco was the "acid" capital of the world for a long time, and now it has become the "speed" capital of the world."[2]

The tendency of drug users to ingest indiscriminately adds further complexity to an already complicated drug problem and creates a significant danger. Research in the hippie community shows that almost one half of the persons interviewed had taken unknown drugs. At a San Jose, Calif. rock festival, 4,000 unidentified pills were taken! In addition, mixing of various drugs is common, resulting in combinations such as LSD and methamphetamine hydrochloride (Methedrine) and marijuana "cut" with a variety of substances including amphetamines, heroins, mescaline, cocaine and opium. Contamination of marijuana with tincture of camphor containing 2.2 gm of opium per ounce has been reported in California.[3]

The mixing of cheap psychoactive agents with more expensive psychedelic drugs can greatly increase profits and thus has become common practice. Unfortunately, such adulteration can create serious treatment problems. For example, the central anticholinergics, particularly the belladonna alkaloids, are frequently used for "spiking," thus making treatment of bad trips with phenothiazines potentially hazardous. The anticholinergic effects of these alkaloids are enhanced by the addition of a phenothiazine, and this combination may lead to coma and cardiorespiratory failure. The undesirable consequences resulting from the interaction between anticholinergic agents and phenothiazines have been adequately demonstrated in clinical studies. Patients receiving an anticholinergic agent treated with a representative phenothiazine showed marked central nervous system (CNS) depression.[4]

The psychedelic drugs have established their lethal potential. Although deaths have been reported following the ingestion of STP (probably adulterated with belladonna alkaloids)[5] as a result of cardiovascular and respiratory effects,[6] death from the physiological effects of these drugs is rare. The psychological changes and their behavioral manifestations represent a greater threat to life. Feelings of omnipotence or panic, with an associated increase in irrational risk-taking, have led to deaths resulting from such things as leaping from high places with the intention of flying, or standing in front of oncoming vehicles in an attempt to push them back. Heavy usage of methamphetamine has been associated with an increase in paranoia and violent behavior.[7]

EVALUATION OF THE "BAD TRIPPER"

Protection of the individual from dangerous behavior either to himself or others should be a fundamental concern in treating the bad trip. For this reason, the patient should not be left unattended while he is awaiting medical attention. An attempt should be made to provide a quiet place, away from unnecessary stimulation, since the patient is already overwhelmed by external and internal input. His main task is to reassemble and control this input overload, and extraneous data can only aggravate the situation. After initial safety is established, treatment of the bad trip should include an attempt to clarify the situation. Frequently, bad trippers are brought in by friends who have already unsuccessfully attempted to alleviate the condition. Usually some knowledge of what has happened can be elicited from them. Most importantly, the physician should try to determine what drug was taken, the amount involved, and the approximate time the patient took the drug. Knowledge of the amount of drug and when it was taken will determine to some degree the course of the trip and may give the treating physician a rough idea of the amount of intervention that will be required, assuming he possesses a certain familiarity with the dosage, range and duration of the common psychedelic agents. This area has been thoroughly covered in a recent review.[8] The experience of other drug-taking participants should be determined. This information may allow the examiner to determine whether he is dealing with an effect that is primarily the result of the unusual susceptibility of one person. Any attempts to treat the bad trip prior to the patient's being brought for help should be explored, particularly in terms of medication that might have been administered. Accompanying friends often cannot give reliable information, either because of the drug effects they are experiencing or because they simply do not know what has happened. A clear history is the exception—not the rule. Fear concerning the possible legal implications of drug ingestion may block history taking. Emphasizing the confidentiality of this information may be helpful. A history of the patient, obtained in order to facilitate medical treatment, comes under the rule of privileged communication and should not be shared with authorities.

Sometimes bad trippers are brought in alone by the police without any history. In such situations, a physical examination may yield some clues as to what drug was taken. Because of the ever-increasing problem of drug contamination, even a straightforward history which identifies the drugs should be substantiated, if possible, by physical findings.

The hallucinogens, such as LSD and mescaline, generally produce dilated pupils and reflex hyperactivity. Accompanying anxiety may mimic moderate sympathomimetic signs such as mild increase in pulse rate and blood pressure, sweaty palms and tremor.[9] Anticholinergic agents produce somewhat similar physical findings which usually cannot be distinguished from those of other psychedelic agents. Excessive dryness of the mouth and absence of sweating, however, may be useful clues in establishing that an anticholinergic drug was involved. Amphetamines such as speed produce marked sympathomimetic effects such as rapid pulse rate, moderately elevated blood pressure and excessive sweating, as well as increased motor activity. Miosis is a symptom of opiate usage. Marijuana causes dilatation of conjunctival blood vessels, creating a reddened appearance similar to that seen in conjunctivitis. There is no dilatation of pupils[10] (use Table B-1).

A wide variation of mental states ranging in severity from

TABLE B-1

PHYSICAL FINDINGS

Agent	Effects
Hallucinogens (LSD, mescaline)	Dilated pupils, Reflex hyperactivity Anxiety symptoms
Anticholinergics	Dilated pupils (with cycloplegia), Reflex hyperactivity, Anxiety symptoms, Dry mouth, Absence of sweating
Amphetamines	Rapid pulse, Increase in blood pressure, Increased sweating, Increased motor activity (variable)
Opiates	Miosis
Marijuana	Dilation of conjunctival blood vessels, Rapid pulse No pupillary dilation

mild apprehension to severe panic may be seen in persons undergoing bad trips. With high doses, a picture, best described as a toxic acute brain syndrome with disorientation and clouded consciousness, is present. Perceptual changes, such as illusions and hallucinations, are usually present and can be terrifying. A person may feel that he is going to "lose control" or "never come back." Sever feelings of depersonalization or even total loss of one's sense of identity may appear. Gross distortions of body image may be present such as the sensation that one's "brain is melting." But these same sensations that are experienced by one individual as extremely frightened and threatening may be experienced by another as mystical or beautiful.

An important indicator of the severity of psychological disruption is the amount of observing ego present. The degree to which an individual is able to "get outside" this experience, seeing it as apart from himself and the result of taking a drug, can be of important prognostic significance. The individual who develops the awareness that what he is experiencing is drug-induced and time-limited generally reintegrates successfully at the end of the experience. The absence of observing ego, however, indicates severe disruption; if it fails to reappear as treatment proceeds, the possibility of functional psychosis triggered by the drug experience should be considered.

TREATMENT OF THE "BAD TRIPPER"

Establishment of verbal contact with the minimum use of tranquilizers should be a fundamental rule in the management of "bad trips." In cases of apprehension or even panic where contact with reality is maintained as evidenced by the presence of observing ego, reassurance and repetitive defining of reality often prove to be adequate treatment. In defining reality, the physician should emphasize statements which attribute the distortions and frightening feelings of the experience to the drug. It is often useful to get the individual to put into words the experience he is having. Patients who are able to grasp and verbalize these experiences may thus be able to bring them under control rather than feel overwhelmed by them. One therapist found it helpful to pick up simple concrete objects such as a book and say to the patient, "This is a book; feel the book." Simple repetitive concrete statements about person and place are useful. The temporary nature of what the patient is experiencing should be repeatedly emphasized. For a panicked "bad tripper," it can be very reassuring to be repeatedly told his name, that he is in a hospital bed, and in such and such a city. Concrete labeling helps the patient reassemble his reality, allowing him to firmly establish that he is indeed a real person experiencing a drug-induced "bad trip" that is time-limited.

While a person "comes down," he experiences a phasic "in and out" alternation of mental clarity and confusion. This should be expected and predicted by the therapist. Reassurance should include making explicit this waxing and waning of awareness. Caution should cause the physician to make certain that a patient who evidently has come down is truly "all the way down," not just in a temporary or transient clear spell.

The verbal "talkdown" with continuing reassurance and reality-defining is usually effective when given an adequate period of time. The treating physician, however, may not have sufficient time or staff. In these instances, medication should be used and in the majority of cases will result in rapid dissolution of perceptual distortion and reestablishment of premorbid ego functioning. If medication is used, initially, it should be administered in a dose related to the size of the individual, not to the extent of the toxic effects. Subsequent doses, however, will depend to some degree on severity of symptoms and response to initial medication. Most experience has been with chlorpromazine (Thorazine). A 70-kg (154.3-lb) person could be given a first dose of 50 mg of chlorpromazine (intramuscularly) (100 mg of chlorpromazine should be given initially if the oral route of administration is used). The intramuscular route is preferable for its rapid onset of action and because bad trips are frequently accompanied by gastrointestinal disturbances such as nausea and vomiting. If, after forty-five minutes, no symptom improvement has occurred and blood pressure has been adequately maintained, the initial dose can be repeated. This treatment can be continued every forty-five minutes until a favorable response is achieved, but usually after the second dose, oral medication can be substituted. The physician should exercise caution in administering repeated injections of phenothiazines. Orthostatic hypotensive episodes can occur. If this happens, the medication should be discontinued and the patient placed in a reclining position. Levarterenol may be given, but is usually not indicated.

The main contraindications for phenothiazine medication are previous allergic reactions to phenothiazines, the presence of significant hypotension, and the suggestion of an anticholinergic drug etiology.

Treatment of the bad trip should include caution concerning the possible development of excessive anticholinergic effects. A large dose of a centrally acting anticholinergic agent such as scopalamine (commonly found in proprietary sleeping medication) or the combination of a centrally acting anticholinergic compound and phenothiazine may result in an "anticholinergic crisis." This medical emergency can be effectively handled with quick reversal of symptoms by the oral or intramuscular administration of 2 to 4 mg physostigmine salicylate. Since physostigmine has a short duration of action, the patient must be closely observed for recurrence of symptoms. Additional doses in one to two hours may be necessary. This treatment regimen must be undertaken with considerable caution, however, so as to avoid overtreatment and a resultant cholinergic crisis.[11] Although extensive experience with chlorpromazine supports its efficacy, it should be used only when support and reassurance are ineffective or time is a primary consideration, such as might be the case in a busy city-county hospital emergency room.

Clinical experience has suggested to the authors that the therapeutic affect of the phenothiazines in the treatment of bad trips may not be related to their antipsychotic properties, but rather to their sedative qualities. This observation has led to the use of such sedating drugs as paraldehyde, diazepam and the short-acting barbiturates, thus avoiding the possible complication of anticholinergic potentiation. Results of initial clinical trials have been promising.

Most patients with adverse drug reactions respond favorably to supportive psychotherapy with or without medication to the extent that hospitalization is not needed. If the perceptual distortions have subsided and the patient feels comfortable in returning home, this is a reasonable disposition. The patient should be with a responsible person for the next twenty-four hours. Thus, if he lives alone, he should only be released if he is able to stay with a friend or relative.

Certain exceptions to this disposition should be considered. Prolonged use of speed often results in severe depression with increased suicidal risk when the person is "brought down." Hospitalization may be required. In addition, complicating medical problems such as abscesses and hepatitis are present in some patients treated for adverse drug reactions, particularly where the intravenous route has been used. Patients should be carefully screened for medical problems and hospitalized if indicated. Overnight hospitalization is advisable in those cases where observing ego fails to return or contact with reality is tenuous so that the individual does not appear in control of his thoughts or impulses. If these deficits persist beyond twenty-four hours, the diagnosis of functional psychosis is strongly suggested. It is good practice to avoid the use of phenothiazines as a sleeping medication when the patient is hospitalized overnight. They may mask a psychosis and falsely reassure the physician that the individual is reintegrated the following morning.

Once the acute reaction is over, the physician may be tempted to investigate the reasons for drug use. He should be cautious about this, however. Patients just recovering from a bad trip are unlikely to be able to discuss more general issues such as continued drug use or underlying emotional problems at this time. Decisions about future use of drugs are likely to be in reaction to the bad trip rather than based on rational thought and therefore easily reversible. The physician should confine his treatment to the immediate situation that prompted the request for medical help. He should encourage the patient to return for a follow-up, and at that time, when the patient is far more likely to be receptive and open, a discussion of drug use and possible underlying emotional problems could be started. Questions about drugs and the possible need for continued counseling can be explored. If there are no signs of continuing ego disruption and the person feels no need for counseling, further follow-up is not indicated.

REFERENCES

1. Smith, D. E., Fort, J. and Craton, D. L.: Psychoactive drugs. In *Drug Abuse Papers 1969*. Berkeley, Calif. Continuing Education in Criminology, University Extension, University of California, 1969, p. 10.
2. Smith, D. E.: Changing drug patterns on the Haight-Ashbury. *Calif Med, 110*:151-157, 1969.
3. Unwin, J. R.: Illicit drug use among Canadian youth. *Canad Med Assoc J, 98 (pt 2)*:449-454, 1968.
4. Gershon, S., Neubauer, H. and Sundland, D. M.: Interaction between some anticholinergic agents and phenothiazines. *Clin Pharmacol Ther, 6*:749-756, 1965.
5. Snyder, S. H., Faillace, L. and Hollister, L.: 2,5-dimethoxy-4-methyl-amphetamine (STP): A new hallucinogenic drug. *Science, 158*:669-670, 1967.
6. Solursh, L. P. and Clement, W. R.: Hallucinogenic drug abuse: Manifestations and management. *Canad Med Assoc J, 98*:407-410, 1968.
7. Unwin, J. R.: Illicit drug use among Canadian youth. *Canad Med Assoc J, 98 (pt 1)*:402-413, 1968.
8. Smith, D. E. (Ed.): *Drug Abuse Papers 1969*. Berkeley, Calif. Continuing Education in Criminology, University Extension, University of California, 1969.
9. Hollister, L. E.: *Chemical Psychoses*. Springfield, Illinois, Charles C Thomas Publisher, 1968.
10. Weil, A. T., Zinberg, N. E. and Nelson, J. M.: Chemical and psychological effects of marijuana in man. *Science, 162*:1234-1242, 1968.
11. Crowell, E. B. and Ketchum, J. S.: The treatment of scopolamine-induced delirium with physostigmine. *Clin Pharmacol Ther, 8*:409-414, 1967.

C

Table of Contents from DRUG ABUSE: Data and Debate

Note: These Proceedings of the Second Annual Western Institute of Drug problems Summer School, 1969, were also published by Charles C Thomas, Publisher, Springfield, Illinois, 1970.

Name Index

Subject Index